THE
HUMAN PROVINCE

ALSO BY ELIAS CANETTI

THE
HUMAN PROVINCE

ELIAS CANETTI

Translated from the German by
JOACHIM NEUGROSCHEL

FARRAR STRAUS GIROUX
New York

FOR VEZA CANETTI

Library of Congress Cataloging in Publication Data
Canetti, Elias.
The human province.
Translation of: Die Provinz des Menschen.
Reprint. Originally published: New York:
Seabury Press, 1978.
I. Title.
PT2605.A58P713   1986   838'.91203 [B]   84-25934

Preface

This volume contains my jottings from 1942 to 1972. Thirty years of a conscious life are a long time. My aim was to make my own choice and presentation of this entire period. Whatever these years may have been like (and I have never concealed their terror, which I perceived as my own), I have to be grateful for experiencing them with an *alert* mind. If such a summing-up appears rather erratic, it is close to each moment in every sentence and it does contain the truth of *one* man.

I would like to describe the background of these jottings with the same words that prefaced one of my earlier volumes. Since their contents, from the years 1942 to 1960, have largely been included here, I may be permitted a briefer repetition of these words.

I realized that *Crowds and Power* might absorb me for several more decades. And the concentration on a single work, as well as a sort of prohibition that I placed on any other and especially a purely literary work, exerted a pressure that eventually took on dangerous dimensions. A safety valve was indispensable, and I found it, at the start of 1942, in my jottings. Their freedom and spontaneity, the conviction that they existed only for their own sake and served no purpose, my irresponsibility in never reading them again or changing them in any way, saved me from a fatal paralysis.

Gradually, they became an indispensable daily exercise. I felt that a special part of my life went into them. They ultimately grew into many volumes, and this presentation is merely a meager selection.

In late 1948, after lengthy preliminary work, I began to write *Crowds and Power*. This stretched over many years. There were qualms and doubts, and when the delays became perilous, I permitted myself, very rarely, to do some literary writing. It was only in 1959 that I could get myself to finish the manuscript that I regarded as my life's work. It is not surprising that a great deal of that opus flowed into the jottings that I regularly committed to paper during those years.

The reader should not be denied the adventure of encountering a few little known but enormously consequential source works. In such cases it would be wrong to think of "reading" in the normal sense of the word. Such vehement excitement, keeping a man in suspense for weeks and months and not releasing him afterwards, has an effect like that of explorations among unknown tribes. The power is sometimes that of, I cannot put it any more tamely or calmly, Revelations. Likewise, a few examples of encounters with "enemies," namely thinkers whom one respects even though they offer a topsy-turvy picture of the world, strike me as sufficiently noteworthy to figure here. I have always particularly sought those who kept my sense of protest on the alert.

In one issue, which is the most important to me—the question of death—I have found only adversaries among all thinkers. That may explain why my own opinion appears here with the strength of a faith, never being declared without zeal and vehemence. Not even the jottings of 1961–1972, of which a selection is presented here for the first time, could remain free of that.

However, they had long since lost their safety valve character. They no longer emerged under the pressure of a task that had weighed heavily upon me. Whereas in the past, I had often felt that I would have to suffocate without the jottings, they now had their own inviolable right. The idea that I might publish some of them later on did not interfere with their freedom, for the selection was uncertain and could include only a very tiny portion.

Many men have tried to grasp their lives in the full spiritual and intellectual context, and those who have succeeded will never grow old. I wish that some men would also record the leaps in their lives. It seems that the leaps belong to *all* people; anyone can easily take whatever pertains to oneself. The loss of a superficial unity, inevitable in such an enterprise, cannot be regretted, for the true unity of a life is secret, and it is most effective when it unintentionally conceals itself.

1942

As of a certain age it would be nice to grow smaller again from year to year and go backwards over the same steps that we once so proudly climbed. The ranks and honors of old age would still have to be the same as today; so that very small people, the size of six- or eight-year-old boys, would be considered the wisest and most experienced. The oldest kings would be the shortest; there would only be very tiny popes; the bishops would look down on cardinals, the cardinals on the pope. No child could wish to become something great. History, because of its age, would lose significance; we would feel as if the events of three hundred years ago had taken place among insect-like creatures, and the past would have the good fortune to be overlooked.

The word *freedom* serves to express an important, perhaps *the* most important tension. People always want to get *away,* and if the place they want to get to has no name, if it is uncertain and they can't see any borders in it, they call it freedom.

The spatial expression of this tension is the vehement wish to cross a frontier as if it didn't exist. Freedom in flying—for the old, the mythical feeling, reaches as high as the sun. Freedom in time is the triumph over death, and people are quite content just to shove it further and further away. Freedom among *objects* is the liquidation of prices; and the ideal spendthrift, a very free man, desires nothing so much as an incessant changing of prices, undetermined by any rules, an aimless up and down, as though caused by the weather, beyond influence and not even really predictable. There is no freedom "to something," its blessing and its fortune are the tension of the man who wants to disregard barriers, and he always seeks the worst barriers to fulfill this wish. The man who wants to kill has to deal with the dreadful threats accompanying the shalt-not of killing, and if these threats hadn't so deeply tormented him, he would have certainly charged himself with happier tensions. The origin of freedom, however, lies in

1

breathing. Anyone can draw breath from any air, and the freedom to breathe is the only one that has not really been destroyed to this day.

Only an image can please you *totally*, but never a human being. The origin of angels.

How quickly flying, that ancient, precious dream, has lost all charm, all sense, its soul. Dreams come true, one after another, fulfilling themselves to death. Can you have a *new* dream?

How inconceivably modest are human beings who bind themselves to only one religion! I have very many religions, and the one overriding them is only forming throughout my life.

One sees thoughts stretching their hands out of the water, one believes they are calling for help. A mistake: They live below, intimate and very familiar with one another, just try and pull a single one out alone!

The balance between knowledge and ignorance determines how wise we get. Ignorance must not be impoverished by knowledge. Every answer must make a question (remote and seemingly unconnected) spring forth from its crouching slumber. The man with many answers has to have even more questions. The wise man remains a child all his life, and answers alone make his soil and his breath arid. Knowledge is a weapon only for the powerful, the wise man despises nothing so much as weapons. He is not ashamed of his wish to love more people than he knows; and he will never arrogantly isolate himself from all those he knows nothing about.

In the best times of my life I always think I am making room, even more room in me. Here I shovel away snow, there I raise aloft a piece of fallen sky; there are superfluous lakes, I let them run out (I save the fish), overgrown forests, I drive crowds of apes into them, everything is astir, but there's never enough room, I never ask why, I never feel why, I just have to keep making room, on and on, and as long as I can do so, I merit my life.

To think that this face has managed to bring on this war, and we didn't wipe it out! And we are millions strong, and the earth teems with weapons, there is enough ammunition for three thousand years, and this face is still here, stretching wide above us, the gargoyle of the Gorgon, and we have all turned to stone in murdering.

More than anything we resemble bowling pins. They set us up in families, approximately nine. Squat and wooden, we stand there, not knowing what to do with our fellow pins. The way has long been paved for the stroke that is to bring us down; foolishly we wait; in falling we take along as many fellow pins as we can, it is the stroke that we pass on to them, the only contact we grant them in a hasty existence. Supposedly, we are set up again. But if that is so, then we are exactly the same in a new life, only we have changed places among the nine, in the family, and not even always; and wooden and foolish we wait again for the old stroke.

My greatest wish is to see a mouse devour a cat alive. But first she has to play with it long enough.

The days are distinct, but the night has only one name.

He has the heartless eyes of a man loved more than anything else in the world.

On Praying. Praying is the most effective and most dangerous form of repetition. The only protection against it is that it becomes mechanical, as in priests and prayer-mills. I fail to understand how people can undertake to work up the necessary fervor in each of their countless prayers. The total energy of all mankind would not be great enough for the praying babble of a single man who has fallen prey to this vice.

The infantilism of praying: people pray for what they get anyway instead of for the unattainable.

If we couldn't get along without prayers, we would be better off addressing many and very different gods. We would benefit from practicing transformations, which would be indispensable for praying.

The man who meant it earnestly would have to spend weeks and weeks screwing up his courage for a single prayer.

They can take their God into their mouths like bread. They can name him, call him, explain him as often as they like. They chew up his name, they swallow his body. Then they say there's nothing higher for them than God. I suspect that many praying people contrive to get hold of all sorts of things from God, things they wouldn't give to anyone else and which they swipe before anyone else can get at them. The funny thing is that they all want the same thing, to wit, the most common necessities of life, and that they do pray together after all. They are like a gang of beggars who, an impudent, bothersome swarm, pounce together on a lone stranger.

Even if I could believe, I couldn't possibly pray. Praying has always struck me as the most insolent pestering of God, as the really most disgusting sin, and I would insert a long period of repentance for every prayer.

Sometimes I think the sentences I hear were negotiated by other people three thousand years before my lifetime. If I listen closely, they get older and older.

The inklings of poets are the forgotten adventures of God.

You lofty words, you gazes to the sun, you kisses from star to stars, you vain storms, you swaggering, hopping lightning—birds will sing tenderly when people have completely wiped one another out. And the birds will yearn for us, and the mocking birds among them will preserve our conversations for a long time.

We would have to have a yearly festival for training people to endure being robbed. There could not be anything that the mystes of this festival could not put their hands upon, no valuable, no object of the most sacred memory. Nothing could ever be given back. Protective measures before the outbreak of the festival would have to be strictly forbidden. Nor would it be permitted to track down the further destinies and uses of the missing objects. Only human beings, the oldest and the youngest, would be exempt from the fate of being stolen. Perhaps they would thereby regain some of the value that things have taken from them. One can imagine the woe of some unfortunates after these saturnalia; but it could almost be made up for if they themselves made thorough use of the time of the festival. Property would lose much that was divine and eternal about it. During the remaining, honest time of the year, a man would have to put up with stolen goods in his house along with things that are bought or given; and only those stolen goods would be sacrosanct, that is, safe against further robbery at the next festival.

Man has all the wisdom of his forebears put together, and just look at what a lunkhead he is!

Proof is the hereditary misfortune of thinking.

Knowledge has a tendency to show itself. If kept secret, it has to wreak vengeance.

It is not in God's power to save *even one single* person from death. That is what makes God one and only.

The outer bearing of people is so ambiguous that you only have to present yourself as you are to live fully unrecognized and concealed.

A war always proceeds as if humanity had never hit upon the notion of justice.

History preserves something different from any earlier forms of transmitting the past. It is hard to determine what. More than anything, history strikes one as a fixated vendetta of the masses, of *all* masses, and that is exactly what condemns history. It provides for the perpetuation of all religions, nations, classes. For even the most peaceful among them have at some point drawn blood from someone, and history faithfully screams it to high heaven. Much has been attempted against it, but we never escape. History is the giant serpent that imprisons the world. An age-old vampire, it sucks blood from the brain of every young person. It is not to be borne the way it commands exactly the same thing in many different languages. The most disgraceful forms of belief, which everyone ought to be ashamed of, are kept alive by history as it proves their age. No one has ever felt obligated to it except for a few thin priests, and they would have had an easier time without history. One can object that history has brought the earth very close to unification, but at what price, and *is* the world already at one with itself? It seems to me as if history used to be better or at least more innocuous in the days when it got lost from time to time. Today it is shackled to itself with the chains of writing. It offers to the future centuries the falsest, basest, and most untruthful documents. No one can sign a contract today without people knowing it a thousand years hence. No one can come into the world unnoticed; he is at least included in some statistic. No one can think, no one can breathe, history corrupts his pure breath and twists the words around in his brain. How powerful the Heracles who could strangle it! Even death will be overcome more easily than history, and the first and only exploiter of a triumph over death will once again be history.

Humanity as a whole will never again be able to *resign* itself.

It takes years to destroy a person's love; but no life is long enough to lament this murder, nothing is more of a murder.

The law of correspondences in psychological life: we cannot do anything to another person, no matter how secretly, without something corresponding happening to us. It may be possible that retribution is already contained in the form of our actions.

The thought of a future religion, of which we as yet know nothing, has something unspeakably agonizing about it.

People are downright innocent in the use of their pet words and sayings. They fail to sense what they betray when prattling innocuously. They believe they are concealing a secret by talking about other things, but lo and behold, their most frequent expressions suddenly make their secret loom out, threatening and somber.

The lowest man: he whose wishes have all come true.

God himself loosed the serpent on Adam and Eve, and everything depended on its not betraying Him. This venomous creature has stayed loyal to God even to this day.

Molière's death: He cannot give up acting, the great parts he performs and the applause they evoke from the crowd mean too much to him. His friends keep asking him to leave off acting, but he rejects their well-meaning advice. On the very day of his death he explains he cannot deprive the actors of their earnings. In reality, however, he only cares for the applause of the crowd, it seems as if he can't live without it. How strange then that on the day of his funeral a hostile crowd gathers before his home, the negative to that crowd in the theater. The hostile crowd consists of church-followers; but, as though realizing it has a mysterious connection to that clapping crowd, the new crowd disperses when money is thrown to it: it is the admission price refunded.

The various languages you ought to have: one for your mother, which you will subsequently never speak again; one which you only read but never dare to write; one in which you pray but without understanding a single word; one in which you do arithmetic and to which all money matters belong; one in which you write (but no letters); one in which you travel, and in this one you can also write your letters.

The fact that there are *different* languages is the most sinister fact in the world. It means that there are different names for the same things; and one would have to doubt that they are the same things. All linguistics hides the striving to reduce all languages back to *one*. The tale of the Tower of Babel is the tale of the second Fall of Man. After losing their innocence and eternal life, human beings wanted to grow artificially to the heavens. First they had tasted of the wrong tree, not they mastered its ways and grew straight up. In return, they lost what they had managed to retain after the first Fall: the unity of names. God's deed was the most diabolical ever committed. The confusion of names was the confusion of his own Creation, and it is impossible to tell why he bothered to save anything from the Flood.

If people had even the faintest and most non-committal idea of the life and living that go on in them, they would shrink back from many words and phrases as from poison.

Whenever you observe an animal closely, you feel as if a human being sitting inside were making fun of you.

On drama. It is gradually becoming clear to me that in drama I was trying to realize something derived from music. I treated constellations of figures like themes. My chief resistance against the "development" of characters (as though they were real live people) recalls the fact that in music the instruments are givens. As soon as you have opted for a certain instrument, you hold fast to it, you cannot rebuild it into another instrument as the work progresses. Something of the beautiful severity of music is based on this specificity of the instruments.

Reducing a dramatic figure to an animal is quite compatible with this notion. Every instrument is a specific animal or at least a particular and delimited creature that can only be played with on its own terms. Drama has the divine possibility, beyond all other arts, of inventing new animals, that is to say, new instruments, and always a different form according to the thematic structure. Thus there exists an inexhaustible variety of dramas as long as there are new "animals." Creation, whether exhausted or else outstripped by rapid Man, is thus literally shifted into drama.

It remains to be proven how greatly opera has confused drama. Musical drama is the untidiest and most nonsensical kitsch that was ever devised. Drama is a very specific kind of music and endures the addition of music only seldom and sparingly. In no event are instruments to be attuned to dramatic figures, otherwise the figures turn allegorical and dramatically quite insignificant; these are merely fable animals acting here; with the music becoming everything, drama becomes nothing.

It's no use, you can sing choruses, goggle at cannibals, climb two hundred years back up the tree trunk, you can lock up the month for lunacy, go on a pilgrimage to Palestine in harmless hosts of crusaders, with a whole hardware store on your body, listen to Buddha, propitiate Mohammed, believe Christ, keep watch over a bud, paint a blossom, prevent a fruit; and you can follow the sun as soon as it doubles, train dogs to meow, cats to bark, give a hundred-year-old man all his teeth back, pick forests, water bald pates, castrate cows, milk bulls; you can, if everything is too easy (we deal with everything so quickly) master the language of the Neanderthals, clip Shiva's arms, empty Brahma's heads of the antiquated Vedas, dress the naked Veddahs, hinder the chanting of the angelic choruses in God's heavens, spur on Lao-tse, incite Confucius to partricide, knock the cup of hemlock from Socrates' hand and immortality from his lips—but it's no use, it's no use, there is no deed, there is no thought but one: *When will the murdering stop?*

Oh, for a stethoscope, a fine stethoscope to identify the generals in their wombs!

Never have people known less about themselves than in this "Age of Psychology." They are not able to stand still. They rush away from their own metamorphoses. They don't wait for them, they forestall them, they would rather be anything but what they could be. They drive cars through the landscapes of their own psyches, and since they only halt at gas stations, they think they're made of gasoline. Their engineers build nothing else: whatever they eat smells of gasoline. They dream in black pools.

There is no uncannier notion than that of the abandoned earth, abandoned by human beings. People tend to think that they emigrate, if for no other reason than to take along their memory of the earth. They could never be as well-off as here. Far-reaching instruments would have to enable them to observe the world but without recognizing what is really happening on it. They would understand what they have lost, an inexhaustible homeland, and the false religion to which they have to ascribe this loss would already have been traded in, far too late, for another. One can assume that this new religion would be the right one; had it come in time, it would have saved the earth for mankind.

It is advisable to tempt the gods, the more often, the better; and do not give them a moment's peace. They sleep too much and leave man alone on the raft of his dying brothers.

The dead are nourished by judgments, the living by love.

No fool and no fanatic will ever take from me the love for all those whose dreams were overshadowed and curtailed. Man will still become all and whole. The slaves will redeem the masters.

The "slain"—how grand that sounded, how open, how broad and courageous: the "choked," the "crushed," the "charred," the "burst," how penny-pinching that sounds, as though it had cost nothing!

We have no standard any more for anything, ever since human life is no longer the standard.

A man undertakes to count all the *leaves* in the world. The essence of statistics.

He stole my left ear. I took his right eye. He concealed fourteen of my teeth. I sewed up his lips. He stewed my behind. I turned his heart inside-out. He ate my liver. I drank his blood. *War.*

A fight that is not fought with intellectual weapons alone disgusts me. The dead opponent attests only to his own death.

I do not want to inspire fear, there is nothing in the world I am so ashamed of. Better to be despised than feared.

He joins the army: he no longer wants to know what happens; he no longer wants to know what he does.

The Peace Conference resolved to give Europe the fair shake it had earned in a long and hard war. Everything is to start on the same level. To make this possible, an interterritorial fleet of bombers is formed for destroying any cities that still happen to be standing.

God is the greatest arrogance of mankind; and when they have atoned him, they will never find a greater arrogance.

Honorary posts are for the feeble-minded; it is better to live in disgrace than in honor: anything but honors; freedom at any price, to *think*. Honors are hung around your eyes and ears like tapestries; who can still see; who can still hear; dreams choke to death in honors, and the good years wither.

He keeps his money in his heart, the beats count it.

He will return to the full and wonderful world if no one dies anymore and people carry out their wars by means of ants, who are very human.

The poet is probably the man who senses what has been in order to predict what will be. Thus he doesn't really suffer, he merely remembers; and he doesn't *do* anything because he first has to predict it.

There is always something shady about subscribing to a faith that very many people have shared beforehand. There is more resignation in that act than could be framed in human words. Faith is a human faculty that can be *expanded,* and anyone who can do so ought to contribute to this expansion.

Men's voices are God's bread.

It is strange to see an Oriental come to the fore in an Englishman. Recently, upon encountering such an astonishing Englishman, I thought it must be a mistake, the Oriental would vanish again. But then I saw him increasing, and he became very weighty, almost a Buddha. For such a man there is nothing left to do but believe in reincarnation; how else could he get his bearings in his English situation.

He shows himself to be an Oriental as follows: He likes to sit calmly in his spot, and he will not permit this calm to be railed against as laziness; for through it one can attain great wisdom. He likes to be worshipped by women; he is impressed with a new woman he meets even though he knows many others; one doesn't exclude the other; and he doesn't hesitate to show he likes her. As soon as he senses that he is not hurting any feelings, he utters peculiar and destructive thoughts about God, products of his sitting which strike him as original even though he heard them in India; for England they are still original.

He is imprecise; he easily confuses names, dates, and places. He knows it and he doesn't care. Relationships are empty and meaningless; all he cares about is the deeper meaning of his sentence. Now the English are ill with precision; unpunctuality is the second greatest sin, ranking just below murder; in shaving, no hair must be overlooked; the minutes of a visit are counted before it begins; the fence around a property is sacred; a book consists of a number of letters; no one lies. It is easy to imagine how this Oriental in his emphatic phlegmatism towards all precision stands out from his fellow Englishmen.

Even his friendliness has a different tinge. He praises every single person in question, not as loudly, to be sure, but certainly as extravagantly as a Southerner. The most ludicrous person is marvelous, exemplary, and sublime. He addresses people with titles that they might wish for. But with no real irony (he lacks all sharpness), he hints at how unimportant titles are. His yearning for everlasting peace is full of regret that he will soon no longer be here, he has a weak heart; and he is not ashamed of speaking about his illness; his thorough way of doing it particularly reveals that regret. He would like people to admire his ill heart, and they ought to be amazed that he still works "creatively," he writes. Of all human activities, writing is certainly the calmest, hence proper for the Oriental, who with his legs crossed, his bearing dignified, can let it proceed on a small table, with small round motions. If he were really still an Englishman, he would take care not to mention that he possesses a heart, let alone a sick one, and as for his writing, he would have demurely locked it away.

If you have seen a person sleeping, you can never hate him again.

Man is in love with his weapons. What can we do against that? Weapons should be constructed in such a way that they frequently and unexpectedly turn against the man using them. Their terror is too one-sided. It is not enough that the enemy operate with the same means. The weapon itself ought to have a capricious and unpredictable life, and people ought to be more afraid of the dangerous thing in their hands than of the enemy.

Of all human religions, war is the most tenacious; but it too can be disbanded.

If you all had to face one another naked, you would have a hard time slaughtering. The murderous uniforms.

Belief in God has something crucial in its favor: People believe in the existence of a being that cannot be killed, not even with the worst efforts.

In the dark, words weigh double.

Today it is no longer true that apes are closer to man than other animals. For a long time we may not have been very different from them; back then, we were closely related; today, countless changes have brought us so far away from them that we have no less of the birds in us than of the apes.

To understand how we have become human beings, the most important thing would surely be to examine the imitative faculties of apes. Such experiments would have a very specific meaning of their own. We would have to keep the apes for a long time with animals previously unknown to them and carefully register the extent to which their behavior is influenced by these animals. We would have to change the animals of their environment in a changing succession. Sometimes, after such powerful impressions, we would have to leave them to their own devices. With many experiments of this kind, the empty concept of imitation could fill up somewhat, and we might realize that it always involved a change, not merely for the sake of "adjustment," and that adjustment is merely the result of semi-successful awkward changes.

In regard to human beings, these processes can best be studied in myth and drama. Dreams, in which they were always present, offer much less precision and allow arbitrary interpretations. Myth is not only more beautiful, it is also more useful for the purposes of such an investigation, for it remains constant. Its fluidity is internal, it does not dwindle away before your very eyes. Wherever it is played, it always returns in the same way. It is the most constant thing that people are capable of bringing forth; no instrument has been as consistent through the millennia as some myths. Their holiness protects them, their depiction eternalizes them, and whoever can imbue mankind with a myth has accomplished more than the most daring inventor.

Drama is, of all human possibilities of summing-up, the least untruthful.

Whenever the English go through bad times, I am wonder-struck by their Parliament. It is like a soul that has been made radiant and sonorous, a representative model offering to all eyes something that would otherwise remain secret. In addition to the freedom they are always talking about, the people here have acquired an unknown freedom: the freedom of openly confessing political misdeeds and receiving an absolution that depends on an earthly body. There is a possibility here of attacking the rulers, a possibility that has no equal anywhere in the world. And they are no less rulers for it; everything truly depends on their decisions; they probably have the strong consciousness necessary for that, but not the bumptiousness, for the latter is thoroughly marred for them by Parliament. Six hundred ambitious men watch one another with hawks' eyes; weaknesses cannot remain concealed; strengths make a difference as long as they are strengths. Everything takes place out in the open; they are incessantly quoted. But one can also stand aloof and warn, in the middle of the daily hustle and bustle.

The prophet, if only he has enough patience, can wait here. He learns to express himself in such a way that the world understands him. In general, the clarity of all utterances brought forth here is the primary condition for effectiveness. As complicated as the real play for power may be—on the outside, it proceeds along carefully established demands and stakes.

There is nothing more remarkable than this nation doing its most important business in a ritual, sporting way, and not deviating even when the water is up to its neck.

The novel should not be in any hurry. Once, hurry belonged to its sphere, now the film has taken that over; measured by the film, the hasty novel must always remain inadequate. The novel, as a creature of calmer times, may carry something of that old calm into our new hastiness. It could serve many people as a slow-motion; it could induce them to tarry; it could replace the empty meditations of their cults.

He has the wit of his wickedness, the forgetfulness of his age, the narrow-mindedness of his ancestry, and the brutality of his profession: a great general.

I hate the eternal willingness for truth, truth out of habit, truth out of duty. Truth is supposedly a storm, and when it has cleared the air, it passes on. Truth should strike like lightning, otherwise it will have no effect. Whoever knows truth should be afraid of it. Truth should never become the dog of mankind; woe to him who whistles for it. We should not take it on a leach, we should not take it in our mouths. We should not feed it, not measure it; one should let it grow in its dreadful peace. Even God got too familiar with truth, and *that's* what he choked on.

Man is as eternal as he cares about the eternal—so long as he doesn't drown in it.

Animals do not realize that we name them. Or else they do realize it, and that may be why they fear us.

Dying is too easy. It ought to be much harder to die.

14

A land of unlimited eternity: You have to walk for days before bumping into anyone who lifts his little finger slightly; all the others sit around, mute and Egyptian.

The English never wrote down their laws, they carry them about with them on their person.

In England, words waste away.

Jews will still have to exist even when the last Jew is wiped out.

The greatest danger a man with increasing consciousness has to watch out for is the quick change of the light in which things and convictions appear to him more and more. Everything fluctuates; the most fluid things become visible; one cannot get to the end of anything; every wall has its gate, there is always something else behind it; the same flowers present themselves in new colors; the granite-hard street softens into clay. One may have wanted something very definite for twenty years, and then, in a greater consciousness, one no longer wants it. What one regarded as ugly turns into manifold beautiful forms: they dwindle after an airy and shimmering dance. Everything becomes possible, disapproval weak, judgment bends like a blade of grass in the wind; the bones expand to any length, a thought has as much blood as one likes; and man, who has become everything, is capable of anything.

How many objects did mankind have to produce to bring about a philosophy of materialism.

Swift's central experience is power. He is a frustrated ruler. His satirical assaults stand for death verdicts. They were denied him in his life, they slipped into his satire. So the latter is, in the truest sense of the word, the most dreadful thing a writer ever had at his disposal.

He imitates kingdoms, he refashions them, the courts won't leave his mind. He always scornfully depicts the way courts regulate their realms; and he always lets us feel (it is the only thing he lets us feel) how much better he could regulate them.

Journal to Stella is unique because it shows, naked and unvarnished, and with very few false pretensions, the intellectual who, amid the ruthless two-party system of his time, is after power but cannot have it because he has seen through this system all too accurately.

These worm-souls, how are they to understand that one has to despise money even while needing it.

People are delighted over wishes that come true for others, especially if they haven't had anything to do with it: as if there were, invisibly, such things as well-wishing and heeding, who knows where.

Act as you could never act again.

The successful man hears only clapping hands. Otherwise he is deaf.

All the past dominion of the world, all scorn, oppression, subjugation, has concentrated in the sick heart of a single man; the earth has fallen to him, the reverse scapegoat, and he is punishing it for *its entire history.*

I have never heard of a person attacking power without wanting it, and the religious moralists are the worst in this respect.

The monstrous life of dogs with each other: the smallest can get to the biggest, and on occasion the result is puppies. Much more so than we, dogs live among giants and dwarves, who, however, are their equals and speak the same language. The things that can happen to them! What grotesque antipodes try to mate! How afraid they can be, how greatly they feel drawn to the wickedest things! And always their gods at hand, always a whistle and a retreat into the more rigorous world of symbolic burdens. If often seems as though the entire religious existence that we have pictured for ourselves, with devils, dwarves, spirits, angels, and gods, is taken from the real existence of dogs. Whether we have represented our manifold beliefs in them, whether we have become human beings only by keeping dogs—in any event we can tell from them what we ourselves are doing, and presumably most masters are more thankful for this semi-conscious knowledge than for the gods whose names are on their lips.

Music is the best solace if for no other reason than because it doesn't make new words. Even when it is set to words, its own magic prevails and snuffs out the danger of the words. It is purest, however, when playing for itself. One believes it absolutely, for its assurance is one of the feelings. Its course is freer than anything else that seems humanly possible, and this freedom contains its redemption. The more densely populated the world and the more machine-like the formation of life, the more indispensable music has to become. There will come a time when music alone will provide a way of slipping through the tight meshes of functions; leaving music as a powerful and uninfluenced reservoir of freedom must be accounted the most important task of intellectual life in the future. Music is the truly living history of humanity, of which otherwise we only have dead parts. One does not need to draw from music for it is always within us; all we have to do is listen simply, otherwise we would learn in vain.

I really know what a tiger is only since Blake's poem.

Miracles as wretched vestiges of the ancient, vigor-filled metamorphoses.

Any idiot can befuddle the most complicated mind whenever he feels like it.

The promise of immortality is enough to put a religion on its feet. The mere command to kill is enough to wipe out three quarters of humanity. What do people want? Life or death? They want to live and kill, and as long as they want that, they will have to make do with the various promises of immortality.

Some sentences release their poison only after years.

What hope is for the poor man, an heir is for the rich man.

Believe no one who always speaks the truth.

Success, the rat poison of mankind; very few people escape.

Doubt deludes itself more than faith.

17

Every language has its own silence.

In all events, those men have triumphed who forced the world back into the psychological structure of war. They can all perish to the very last man: they leave behind the war and the following wars.

The Jews are in Egypt again, but they have been divided into three groups: some have been allowed to leave; the others have been forced to do hard labor; the rest are being killed. Thus all their old destinies are to be repeated at once.

One can't do a thing. One can lament. One can become better.

Cursed be revenge, and if they murder my most beloved brother, I want no revenge, I want other people.

Wars are fought for their own sake. As long as people refuse to admit this, they cannot really fight against war.

1943

Since the war began, thoughts and sentences have gotten terse, conforming to the tone of commands. People want anything, except prolonging and continuing what has come about in this time. They would like to leave it all behind like machine-gun fire. No one knows who is coming home, and no one knows where he will be at home. So no one settles too broadly in any sentence, and we brush many sentences away like leaves on a road. The newspapers, "running something different every day," and radio reports are the apes of the moment; by the time you notice them on one tree, they have already leapt to the next. The Methuselah of war is one day old, normal existences count by hours. Supposedly, some people don't even know what they were fighting for an instant earlier; and some say that hundreds of thousands of corpses are obstructing the clearest goal. The corpses are not floating off on willing rivers everywhere; the traveling cremation kitchens are often late. The well-cemented skull towers of the Tartars were more advisable; they offered a rich view. However, the experiments on utilizing dead hearts and bowels have made progress; it is not out of the question that each side will resurrect its own corpses with those of the enemy, and then wars would have a deeper meaning, of which only its prophets have had any foreboding until now. The interpretations of such colossal processes have not gone very far; but the figures are already stating that these must be eminently vital processes, for would millions of people be dying for nothing? And going to a willing death and feeling pride and fighting to be first? It is always figures that shame the skeptic. People do not *like* to die. In war, millions of them do die. So wars must have some special meaning, and perhaps no one knew how to exploit the enemy corpses properly. Head-hunting was ridiculed, and the cannibals were made fun of. But there's a healthy core in these children of nature, and just as they know about healing herbs and venoms, they must certainly know, and in any case better than we, why they have to eat their enemies of all people. One thing cannot be denied: they *are* consistent, and the ludicrous sentimentality of our pseudo-culture has not made them reject a heart merely because it is human—on the contrary, they prefer it to animal hearts.

History talks too little about animals.

The Neanderthal thinks: there will always be wars, even in three million years; he can already count to a million.

Disown anyone who accepts death. Who will be left for you?

God's legacy is poisoned.

The future, which changes every instant.

A host of pregnant women near their time; towards them come trucks, tanks, trucks, tanks, filled with precisely armed soldiers. The vehicles are past; the women, in the middle of the road, start singing.

War is so orderly that people begin feeling at home in it.

Since they started sitting on chairs and eating at tables, they have been waging longer wars.

The dead are afraid of the living. The living, however, who do not realize it, are afraid of the dead.

All the old borders on earth, since men have existed, and a commission making sure that this is what they are: the Border Commission. A lexicon of borders, improved from one edition to the next. An estimate of the costs of these borders. The heroes who died for them, and their posterity, who pull the borders away from under their graves. Walls in the wrong places, and where they actually ought to be put up if they didn't have to stand in other places long since. The uniforms of dead border officials, and the mischief in difficult passes, eternal transgressions, dislocations, and unreliable detritus. The arrogant ocean; uncontrollable worms; birds from country to country, a proposal for exterminating them.

20

Science betrayed itself by becoming an end in itself. It has turned into a religion, the religion of killing, and it wants to make us believe that the step from the traditional religions of dying to this religion of killing is progress. We will soon have to put science under the control of a higher drive, that demotes it to a servant without destroying it. There is not much time left for this subjugation. Science likes being a religion and is hurrying to wipe out mankind before anyone gets up the courage to dethrone it. Hence, knowledge is truly power, but a crazed and shamelessly worshiped power; its worshipers are content with its hairs or flakes, and, if they can't manage to get hold of anything else, with the imprints of science's heavy, artificial feet.

The ancient travel accounts will some day be as precious as the greatest works of art; for the earth was holy when *unknown,* and it will never be that again.

The devil was very noxious, because he was so harmless and lulled people into a false sense of security.

Before the collapse in Germany, peddlers offered pictures of the Führer that went up in flames when you looked into the eyes.

Many simple people ask you: "Do you think the war will be over soon?" And if you innocently answer: "Yes, very soon," you suddenly notice—and at first, you refuse to believe it—fear and dismay spreading over their faces. They are slightly embarrassed at this and at least know that they ought to be glad for humane reasons. But the war has brought them bread and a good income, for some the first time in their lives, for others the first time in years, and so one single feeling torments them: If only it goes on for a while, if only it doesn't end that soon! Whole nations, down to the lowest strata, have become war-profiteers, with all the concomitant reactions to the world. If I were to express the thing that has filled me with the most despair during this war, it would be this daily experience: the war as a bread-winner and as security.

Passionate flatterers are the unhappiest of men. From time to time they are seized with a wild and unpredictable hatred of the creature they have been flattering for so long. This hatred is out of their control;

they cannot tame it for anything in the world; they give in to it the way a tiger gives in to his blood lust. It is an astonishing moment: the man who earlier had only words of utterly blind adoration for his victim is now taking back every last one of those words in an equally exaggerated tongue-lashing. He forgets nothing that might ever have gladdened the other. In the midst of his insane fury, he runs through the list of his old blandishments, translating them accurately into the language of hate.

What should give us heart among all the things we observe if not observation itself?

We should not even hush up the worst deeds of the dead, for they are so intent on surviving in *any* way.

It is a time that distinguishes itself with new things but no new thoughts.

The boldest thing about life is that it hates death, and the religions erasing this hatred are despicable and desperate.

If a piece of advice that I had to give, technological advice, were to cause the death of even a single human being, I could not grant myself any right to my own life.

"Culture" is concocted from the vanities of its promoters. It is a dangerous love potion, distracting us from death. The purest expression of culture is an Egyptian tomb, where everything lies about futilely, utensils, adornments, food, pictures, sculpture, prayers, and yet the dead man is not alive.

One cannot read the Bible without indignation and without temptation. It makes just about anything of men—rascals, hypocrites, despots—and does just about anything against this! It is the dignified image and model of humanity, a grand creature, lucid and mysterious at once, it is the true Tower of Babel, and God knows it.

The real trick would be to love without storing up the appurtenant hatred.

Humanism took things too easily; people knew almost nothing as yet; serious endeavors were basically for *one* single tradition. But even if nothing of this movement except for the name were to survive, it would still be holy; and the discipline carrying it on today far more widely and knowledgeably, its true heir, anthropology, bears a name that's related, yet so much less confident.

There are books that one has for twenty years without reading them, that one always keeps at hand, that one takes along from city to city, from country to country, carefully packed, even when there is very little room, and perhaps one leafs through them when removing them from a trunk; yet one carefully refrains from reading even a complete sentence. Then, after twenty years, there comes a moment when suddenly, as though under a very high compulsion, one cannot help taking in such a book from beginning to end, at one sitting: It is like a revelation. Now one knows why one made such a fuss about it. It had to be with one for a long time; it had to travel; it had to occupy space; it had to be a burden; and now it has reached the goal of its voyage, now it reveals itself, now it illuminates the twenty bygone years it mutely lived with one. It could not say so much if it had not been there mutely the whole time, and what idiot would dare to assert that the same things had always been in it.

Perhaps I despise *actions* so much because I wish that every action had its general meaning, cast its shadow in a very specific way, covering both heaven and earth at once. However, man's real actions have been atomized, and they have to collide violently to notice that each of them is doing something. What a void between them! What a violent humiliation! What a senseless universal raging! For they are heated from the outside and keep raging faster and faster! Their first commandment is: Act. And it almost doesn't matter how. One might think it's the hand, turned furious, that drives them from one action to the next; and indeed, their feet are less and less meaningful. One could chop off their hands all around; but it is to be feared that they would then press buttons with their noses, buttons that are no less dangerous. They act, and what they do is idle; and being idle, it is bad. They reckon with short lives, but not even the moment is holy for them. For an action, they would sacrifice any other man's life, and often their own. They are the parrots of the gods and confer with them about deeds; any deed is always pleasing to the gods, most of all: killing. The ritual of sacrifice, it is said, has brought forth a whole wise literature; and thus wisdom itself must be a daughter of action. Many of them believe that; and for even more, war has taken the place of sacrifice: the butchery is more precious and takes longer. It is quite possible that doing and killing can no longer be separated; and unless the earth does not care to go under in splendor, human beings would have to wean themselves of action. Oh, if only they would finally sit in front of their dilapidated houses, with legs crossed, nourished mysteriously by breathing and dreaming; and moving a finger only to shoo away a fly whose bustle disturbs them because it recalls the old, the overcome, the embarrassing time, the time of atoms and actions.

History despises the man who loves it.

Impossible to imagine how dangerous the world will be without animals.

There have been millennia unlike the thousand-year Reich: Plato's, Aristotle's, Confucius'.

How much weight can the mind shake off. How much can it forget, and can it forget something so utterly as though it had never known it?

For historians, wars are almost holy; as wholesome or inevitable storms, they break from the sphere of the supernatural into the course of the world, a course that is explained and taken for granted.

I hate the respect of historians for Anything merely because it happened, their falsified, retrospective standards, their impotence, their kowtowing to any form of power. These courtiers, these toadies, these ever-partial jurists! It would be nice to cut up history into little bits that couldn't be found anymore, even by a whole beehive of historians. Written history, with its impertinent manner of defending everything, makes the desperate situation of mankind even more desperate with all the lying records. Each man finds his weapons in this arsenal, it is open and inexhaustible. Using the rusty old plunder that lay there peacefully, men start hitting away at one another outside. Then the dead parties shake hands as a sign of reconciliation and go down in history.

The rusty stuff, which had the honor, is culled in the field by the historians, those Samaritans, and carried back to the armory. They are meticulous about not wiping away even one bloodstain. Since the death of the people in whose veins the blood flowed, every dried drop of blood is holy.

Every historian has an old weapon on which he dotes, and which he makes the center of his history. There it stands now, erect, proud, as though it were a symbol of fertility, and in reality it is a cold murderer turned to stone.

For a while now, and not all that long, the historians have chiefly aimed at paper. They have turned from bees into termites and digest only cellulose. They ignore all the colors of their days as bees; blind, in covered channels—for they hate the light—they tackle their old paper. They do not read, they eat it, and what they put out is re-eaten by other termites. In their blindness, the historians have naturally become seers. No past can be repulsive and hateful enough for some historian not to imagine some kind of future in its terms. Their sermons, as they believe, consist of old facts; their prophecies, long before they can come true, are already proven. Aside from paper, they also love stones, which, however, they cannot enjoy or digest. They merely keep rearranging them as different ruins, filling any lack by means of wooden words.

To judge men by whether they accept history or are ashamed of it.

Men will not find any more unknown objects. They will have to make them. How dismal!

To be so alone that you don't overlook anyone—anyone or anything.

The study of power, if one aims at accuracy, has utmost dangers. One accepts false goals because they have long since been attained and outstripped. Magnanimity and dignity move one to forgive at points where one should be least willing to forgive. The powerful, and those who want to become powerful, in all their disguises, utilize the world, and the world, for them, is whatever they find. They have no time to seriously question anything. Whatever once created masses has to help them to their own masses. So they scour history for any pasture, and if they find one that seems to offer rich grazing again, that is where they hastily settle. Old kingdoms or God, war or peace, either one or anything offers itself to them, and they choose whatever they can handle more deftly. There is no real difference between the powerful; if wars have lasted for a time, and the adversaries have to adjust to one another for the sake of their victory, then that lack of difference becomes obvious. Everything is success, and success is the same everywhere. Only one thing has changed: the growing number of people has led to growing masses. If something breaks out anywhere in the world, then it breaks out everywhere; no annihilation can be delimited anymore. The powerful, however, with their old aims, still live in their old limited world. They are the real provincials and villagers of this age; there is nothing more unsophisticated than the realism of cabinets and ministers, except for that of the dictators, who regard themselves as even more realistic. In the struggle against frozen forms of faith, the Enlighteners have left one religion intact, the most preposterous of all: the religion of power. There were two ways of confronting it. One way, in the long run the more dangerous of the two, chose not to speak about it, to silently keep practicing it in a traditional manner, strengthened by the inexhaustible and, alas, immortal models in history. The other way, far more aggressive, first glorified itself before commencing; it publicly declared itself to be a religion, in the place of the dying religion of love, which it mocked with strength and wit. It announced: God is power, and whoever has it is his prophet.

Power even goes to the head of those people who have no power, but here it blows over faster.

I cannot become modest; too many things burn me; the old solutions are falling apart; nothing has been done yet with the new ones. So I begin, everywhere at once, as if I had a century ahead of me. But, when my few real years are up, will others be able to do anything with these rough premonitions? I cannot be satisfied with little: the limitation to a particular, as though it were everything, is too despicable. I want to feel everything in me before I think it. I need a long history so that things can come to feel at home in me before I may look at them with justice. They ought to marry in me and have children and grandchildren, and I will test them by the latter. A century? A hundred measly years! Is that too much for an earnest intention?

Earlier men laugh at me. They are satisfied if their thoughts move in a circle. They believe they have really understood something, and yet it's only their own single thought going in circles! The faster it moves, the more correct it is, they think, and if it starts feeding on its own body, they go wild with delight. But I live in one fear: that my thoughts may be right too early, and that is another reason why I give them time to unmask their entire falsehood or at least slough off their skins.

It would be nice to take each man apart into his animals and then come to a thorough and soothing agreement with them.

People are deceiving themselves if they have any hope for the postwar period. There are private hopes, and they are legitimate: a man will see his brother again, ask his forgiveness even if he didn't do anything to him, merely because he could have done something to him, and because after such separations people are firmly resolved to be as emotional as possible. A man will pass through the grave of a city to visit his mother's grave, and he will bless her for having died before this war. That is how greatly people will act against their innermost natures. They will visit familiar towns and find a few familiar people still alive there, and the strangest stories will be circulating about the others. They will be able to settle down in a hundred enticing memories, there will be much love between people, individual people. But the real, the pure hopes, the ones people don't have for themselves, whose fulfillment can be of no personal benefit, these hopes, which people keep ready for everyone else, for the grandchildren who will not be their grandchildren, for the unborn, of bad and good parents, of warriors and gentle apostles, as though we were the secret forebear of all grandchildren—these hopes, from the innate goodness of human nature, for even goodness is innate, especially after such wars—these sunny, yellow hopes must be fostered, must be nourished, admired, caressed, and cradled even though they are futile, even though people deceive themselves with their hopes, even though they will never come true for even an instant, for no deception is as holy as this one, and on no deception are we as dependent for not choking.

My distaste for the Romans, as I am astonished to note, has to do with their costume. I always imagine Romans as one sees them in pictures during boyhood. The statuary quality of their togas, the very fact that one thinks of them only as standing, reclining, or fighting—all these things are grating. Marble and wreaths in solemn paintings have added their bit. These Romans love what lasts, and they make sure that their name will survive in stone; but what sort of life wants to last!? Our cheerful ways would strike them as slavish, and they would promptly consider themselves, were they suddenly to turn up in our midst, as our natural masters. Their clothing has the sureness of commands. It expresses absolute dignity, but no humanity. It is quite stone-like: and there is no costume more remote from the living animal hide; that's exactly what strikes me as inhuman about it. The dead folds are, as ever, a punctilious ceremony, and each one is like the others, and each is casually brought to its place. How my heart laughs when I see a bunch of Eskimoes coming ashore from their kayaks! How I love all of them at first sight, and how ashamed I am that so much separates me from them and that I will never feel completely at home with them. The Roman, however, approaches you cold and alien and is about to order you around. He has numberless slaves, who do everything for him, not so that he can do something better or more difficult, but so that, whenever he desires, he can issue an order. And the things he orders! Nothing ridiculous was ever concocted under the sun that some Roman, craving to give orders, did not appropriate and, by having it carried out, make even more ridiculous. But the costume! The costume! The costume is also to blame. The purple stripe indicating the rank! The way a toga falls down to the feet, with no special entwinings to excuse that bluntness. Everything is covered with folds and orders, and everything becomes so untouchable. That space that a Roman takes for stumbling! That self-confidence of being above it all! Those rights, that power! What for?

The history of the Romans is the greatest single reason for perpetuating wars. Their wars simply became the paragon of all success. For civilizations, they are the example of imperiums; for barbarians, the example of booty. But since all of us have both—civilization and barbarity—the earth may be destroyed by the heritage of the Romans.

What bad luck that the city of Rome survived when its empire was smashed! That the Pope kept it going! That vain emperors could capture her empty ruins and the name of Rome within them! Rome conquered Christianity by becoming Christendom. Every apostasy from

Rome was merely a new great war. Every conversion to Rome, in the farthest corners of the world, was a continuance of the classical plunderings. America was discovered to reanimate slavery! Spain, as a Roman province, was the new lord of the world. Then the renewal of the Germanic plundering forays in the twentieth century. Only the measure gigantically magnified, the entire earth instead of the Mediterranean, and a hundred times as many people meeting with destruction, participating in it. Thus twenty Christian centuries were necessary to give the ancient and naked Roman idea a garment for its nakedness and a conscience for weak moments. And now that idea is here, perfect and equipped with all the forces of the soul. Who will destroy it? Is it indestructible? Has mankind, with thousandfold efforts, carefully conquered its own annihilation?

People are thankful to their forebears because they never knew them.

With every thought, the important thing is what it leaves unsaid, how much it loves this unsaid, and how close it comes to it without touching it.

Some things are said so that they never can be said again. These include the *bold* thoughts; in repetition, their boldness is dead. Lightning shouldn't strike twice in the same place. Its tension is its boon, but its light is only fleeting. If a fire is kindled, it is no longer lightning.

Thoughts fitting together into a system are irreverent. They gradually exclude the unsaid and then leave it behind, until it dies of thirst.

One wishes that of all people the Italians should be the last to be preoccupied with ancient Rome. *They* survived it.

The wind: the only *free* thing in civilization.

Now that they must know more, the poets have become angry.

It is only in exile that one realizes to what an important degree the world has always been a world of exiles.

What guiles, what excuses, what pretexts and deceptions would we not use just to bring back a dead man.

The Englishman tries to reach a *single* judgment, as demanded by the circumstances, and he refuses to string together abstract judgments. Thinking, for him, is an immediate exercise of power. Thinking for its own sake strikes him as suspicious and repulsive; the thinking man is always an alien to him, especially in his own language. He likes to seek out a small area where his own knowledge is superior, and here he really doesn't have to yield to anyone. A man aiming at many such areas is not an Englishman's cup of tea; he senses the land-hungry conqueror in him, and he is not mistaken. Enigmatic to him are people who have no goal for their knowledge. Such people, if they don't care to be ridiculous here, would do better to conceal their light.

The essence of English life is distribution of authority and ineluctable repetition. Precisely because authority is so important, it has to disguise its omnipresence and retreat to modest sentences. Others detect the slightest encroachment, for the sake of their own authority, and they reject it coolly and resolutely, though politely. Borders, as an expression of what is permitted, are more certain here than in any other country, and what is an island but a more clearly bordered country? Then again, repetition gives life here its endless security; the years have been ramified into the tiniest details of existence, and, not only in time, everything will again be as it has been a thousand times already.

Sadness does not inspire him with any more warm words; it has become as cold and hard as the war. Who can lament now? Tanks and bombers are tenanted by calculated creatures, who press their fingers on buttons and know exactly why. They do everything correctly. Each of them knows more than the entire Roman senate. Each of them knows nothing. Some of them overcame this, and in some inconceivably remote time known as peace, they will be recalculated for other jobs.

An anxious feeling of strangeness while reading Aristotle. During the first book of the *Politics,* which defends slavery in every way, one feels as though one were reading the *Witches' Hammer*. A different air, a different climate, and an entirely different order. The dependency of science on Aristotle's systems, even now, becomes a nightmare when getting to know the "antiquated" part of his opinions, which carry those others, the ones still valid today. It could very well be that the same Aristotle, whose authority was to blame for the stagnation of the medieval knowledge of nature, had an equally disastrous effect as soon as his authority was broken. The coexistence in modern scientific activity, the cold technology, the specialization of disciplines are quite Aristotelian. The special manner of his ambition has determined the structure of our universities; a whole modern university corresponds to that one Aristotle. Research as an end in itself, à la Aristotle, is not really objective. It merely tells the researcher not to let himself be carried away by anything he undertakes. It excludes human enthusiasm and metamorphosis. It wants to keep the body from noticing what the fingertips are doing. Whatever you are, you are aside from how you pursue science. The only truly legitimate thing is curiosity, and a strange kind of commodiousness that makes room for everything raked in by curiosity. The ingenious system of boxes that the researcher has set up in himself is filled with everything that curiosity points out. A thing need only be found to enter here, and it has to remain dead and still in its box. Aristotle is an omnivore, he proves to man that nothing is inedible once you know how to fit it in. The things in his collections, whether alive or not, are always objects and useful for something, at the very least for showing how harmful they are.

His thinking is first and foremost a partitioning. He has a developed sense of ranks, places, and kinship terms, and he carries something like a system of ranks into everything he investigates. His partitions aim at neatness and evenness and not so much at accuracy. He is a dreamless thinker (quite the opposite of Plato); he flaunts his scorn for myths; even poets are something useful to him, otherwise he has no regard for them. Today, still, there are people who cannot approach an object without applying his classifications to them; and some people even think that in Aristotle's boxes and drawers things have a clearer appearance, since in reality they are only more lifeless there.

A nation has truly disappeared only when its very enemies too have a different name.

To live long enough to know all the mores and events of man; to recover all past life since further life is refused; to pull yourself together before you dissolve; to earn your birth; to think about the sacrifices that every breath costs other people; not to glorify suffering although you live from it; to keep for yourself only what cannot be handed on, until it becomes ripe for others and hands itself on; to hate every man's death like your own, conclude peace with everything, but never with death.

There is something insane about the demand that everyone must gather by himself the articles of his thinking and believing; as though everyone had to build by himself the town he lives in.

And what is the original sin of animals? Why do animals suffer death?

One loves a country as soon as one gets to know many ridiculous people in it.

In war, people act as though each had to avenge the death of all his ancestors and as though none of them had died a natural death.

The blind man asks God for forgiveness.

A mysterious system of prejudices. The rate at which a man grows old is dependent on their consistence, their number, their structure. One has a prejudice wherever one fears a transformation. But one doesn't escape that change; it is retrieved with great strength, and only then are you free. It is not true that you can put due transformations off forever. They hurl you in the opposite direction, but man has an elastic soul, and sooner or later, with sureness and weight, he falls right back down on them. Many transformations are merely designated by the anathemas of the parents; these are the most dangerous. Others bear the hatred of all humanity; only very few and select minds come into them.
   The man who transforms himself a great deal needs many prejudices. They should not bother us in a very lively man; we should measure him by his vibrations and not what holds him down.

The theory of metamorphosis bids fair to become a panacea before it is fully thought out. It is something like a theory of transmigration or a Darwinism (but with no—in a narrower sense—religious or strictly scientific focus) applied to psychology and sociology, so that both become one, and dramatically heightened in that everything is possible side by side and at the same time, there doled out over generations of life or even geological periods.

You can talk to Englishmen only about what you have really seen. The present is what counts; everything takes place as in a court of law. One passes judgment, but not without having seen the defendant, a city, a whole countryside. You are called to testify, and you must adhere strictly to the truth, to what is meant by that in a courtroom. There is no pleading. Influences are left to a professional, who has been expressly summoned for that purpose. The judge is you yourself, or else you are at least a witness; one takes direct part if not in the verdict then in the event. You do not dilate on wishes to strangers; as mere dreams, they are despicable. As resolutions, they have been carried out, goals are all that counts. A wish that doesn't lead to an action is no one else's concern, you keep it to yourself. Actions, however, are public; since they are open and obvious to all eyes, you only impair them by talking about them. Others have to judge them, one does not influence the verdict. The Englishman judges a great deal, but he also puts himself under judgment. He does not have the feeling that a mysterious and despotic power suddenly overwhelms him, no matter what, no matter how his case may stand, even God is just to him.

Experiencing and judging are as distinct as breathing and biting.

It is not good that animals are so cheap.

People can only redeem *one another*. That is why God takes a human disguise.

A more accurate study of fairy tales would teach us what we can still expect of the world.

People who cannot find their way out of history are lost, and so are their nations.

What is man without reverence, and what has reverence made out of man!

The war divides people into two parties: one is absolutely warlike, the other absolutely peaceful. The former continues the war in plans of revenge; the latter celebrates reconciliation long before winning.

My whole life is nothing but a desperate attempt to overcome the division of labor and think about everything myself, so that it comes together in a head and thus becomes one again. I do not want to know everything, I merely want to unify splintered things. It is almost certain that such an undertaking cannot succeed. But the very faint prospect that it *might* succeed makes any effort worthwhile.

It is good to think of the gods as forerunners of our own human immortality. It is less good to watch the One God appropriating everything.

With growing knowledge, animals will come closer and closer to human beings. When they are once more as close as in the most ancient myths, there will be no animals.

To study curses, all the oldest, all the most farfetched curses, so that we know what lies in store for us.

To sing? About what? About old, mighty things that are dead. War too will die.

When intoxicated, nations act as if they were one and the same nation.

The great writers of aphorisms read as if they had all known each other very well.

If, despite everything, I should survive, then I owe it to Goethe, such as one owes it only to a god. It is not one work, it is the mood and care of a full existence that suddenly overwhelmed me. I can open up to any page I like, I can read poems here, and letters, or a few pages of an account there, and after a few lines it grabs me, and I am full of hope, such as no religion can inspire me with. I know quite well what has the biggest impact on me. It was always my superstition that the potential of a vast and rich mind has to be manifest at each of its moments. Nothing should be insipid or indifferent—it shouldn't even be relaxing. I despised salvation and joy. The revolution was a kind of model, and something like an incessant, insatiable revolution, brightened by abrupt and unpredictable moments, was the life of the individual himself. I was ashamed of owning anything, I even invented elaborate excuses and rationales for having books. I was ashamed of the chair I sat on to work if it wasn't hard enough; and under no circumstances could it belong to me. But this chaotic, fervid existence only looked like that in theory. In reality, there were always more and more areas of knowledge and thought to arouse my interest without my immediately devouring them, to take shape quietly and increase annually, as with reasonable people, whom I did not throw out as alien if they didn't begin making noise at once, who promised fruits only for much later, and then actually did bear some at times. And thus, almost imperceptibly, something like a mind grew; but it was ruled by a moody despot, who valued restlessness and vehemence above everything else, who practiced such wrong, lazy, erratic foreign politics that everything always went amiss, and who was also receptive to flattery from any worm.

I believe that Goethe is about to free me from this despotism. Before rereading him, I was always slightly ashamed—just to mention this one thing—of my interst in animals and the knowledge I gradually acquired about them. I didn't dare tell anyone that now, in the middle of this war, flower buds can excite and fascinate me as much as any human being. I used to prefer reading myths to any complicated psychological creation of the modern age; and in order to justify to myself this hunger for myths, I turned it into scholarly matter, paying careful heed to the nations they came from and connecting them with the life of those nations. But all I really cared about was the myths themselves. Since I've been reading Goethe, everything I undertake strikes me as legitimate and natural; not that these are *his* undertakings, they are different, and it is very questionable whether they can lead to any results. But he gives me the right: Do what you have to, he says, even if it is nothing tumultuous; breathe, observe, reflect!

We need simple, sober news from the lives of similar people, if only to take the deadly sting from the disappointment at our own failure.

Oh, animals, beloved, cruel, dying animals; writhing, swallowed, digested, and appropriated; predatory and bloodily rotten; fleeing, united, lonesome, seen, hunted, smashed; uncreated robbed by God, exposed in a deceptive life like foundlings!

The curse of *having* to die should be changed into a boon: to *be able* to die when living is unendurable.

35

One should not let oneself be terrified by melancholics. What they suffer from is a sort of hereditary indigestion. They complain as though they'd been devoured and were lying in some stomach. Jonah would be better off as Jeremiah. Thus they really express what's in their own stomachs; the voice of the assassinated prey enticingly paints death. "Come to me," it says. "Where I am, there's decay. Don't you see how much I love decay." But even decay dies, and the melancholic, suddenly recovered, easily and abruptly goes hunting.

Of all words in all languages I know, the greatest concentration is in the English word *I*.

Might you perhaps overestimate the transformations of others? There are so many people who always wear the same mask, and when you try to pull it off, you realize it's their *face*.

Most philosophers have too little sense of the variability of human customs and potentials.

The hardest thing will be not to hate oneself, not to give in to hatred, even though everything is full of it; not to hate oneself without reason, to be fair towards oneself, as towards others.

You live as a beggar on the crumbs of the Greeks. How does your pride feel about that? If you find in them what you yourself have thought, then never forget that it found its way to you by some route or other. You have it from them, after all. Your mind is their toy. You are a reed in their wind. You can conjure up the storms of the barbarians as long as you like: but you must think in the clear, the invigorating, the healthy wind of the Greeks.

For many years now, nothing has so deeply moved and filled me as the thought of death. The highly concrete and serious, the admitted goal of my life is to achieve immortality for men. There were times I wanted to give this goal to the main character in a novel, calling that man the "mortal enemy." During this war, it became clear to me that one should express convictions of such moment, actually a religion, immediately and undisguisedly. So now I record everything connected to death as I wish to impart it to others, and I have pushed the "mortal enemy" off into the background. I do not mean to say that this is how it will remain; he may be resurrected in future years, though different from how I pictured him. In the novel, he was to be thwarted by an immoderate undertaking; an honorable death was planned for him; he was to be slain by a meteor. Perhaps the thing bothering me most today is his failure. He must not fail. Yet I can't let him win either while people keep dying by the millions. In both cases, something that is quite earnest is turned to sheer irony. I would have to make a fool of myself. The cowardly use of a character as a front is to no avail. I have to perish on this field of honor, even if they bury me like a nameless cur, decry me as a lunatic, avoid me as a bitter, an obstinate, an incurable torment.

How many people will find it worthwhile living once they don't have to die.

I cannot look at any more maps. The names of cities reek of burnt flesh.

Six uniformed people around a table, no gods, determine which cities will vanish within the hour.

A piece of every bomb leaps back into the six days of creation.

The Bible is in keeping with human unhappiness.

We are never sad enough to improve the world. We are hungry again too soon.

It is bizarre that the Russian revolution is flowing back to the war from whence it came.

It becomes ever clearer to me that Francis Bacon is one of those rare and central figures from whom we can learn everything we wish to learn from other human beings. Not only does he know whatever men could know in his era; he constantly discusses it; and he thereby pursues distinct goals. There are two sorts of great minds; the open and the closed. His is one of the latter: he likes purposes; his intentions are limited; he always wants something; and he knows what he wants. Instinct and consciousness fully overlap in such men. What is known as his enigma is his total lack of enigma. He has much in common with Aristotle, by whom he always measures himself; he wants to supplant Aristotle's dominion. Essex is his Alexander. Through him, he hopes to conquer the world; he spent many of his best years on this plan. When he saw it was doomed, he dropped him cold. Power in any form is what interests Bacon. He is a systematic lover of power; he leaves none of its lairs unexamined. Crowns alone do not suffice for him, as splendidly as they may shine. He knows how secret a rule may be. Especially fascinating, for him, is a man's post-mortem rule, as a law-giver and philosopher. He despises interference from the outside, miracles, except as intentional devices to govern believers. In order to vitiate traditional miracles, he has to strive to *work* them himself; his philosophy of experiment is a method of edging up and *stealing* them.

The transience of scientific theories makes them despicable, but how transient are the great religions of the world, measured by what preceded them?

What *can* we tell without great impudence?

It is cheering to see how every man works out his tradition for himself. We need a lot of old counterweights for the new things tugging at us everywhere. We pounce upon bygone people and times as though we could grab them by the horns, and when they express a joyous fury, we run off in terror. India, we say, earnestly and knowingly, after absconding from Buddha. Egypt, we say, after closing Plutarch's *Isis and Osiris* in the middle of chapter three. It's wonderful being certain now that people once actually lived under these names, and no sooner do we utter those names than they race towards us furiously. How much they want to live again! How they beg and glare and threaten! How deeply they believe we mean them when we call their names; how forgetful they are of what they themselves did to more ancient peoples! Didn't Thales and Solon travel to Egypt? Wasn't the wise Chinese pilgrim at the court of Harsha in India? Didn't Cortez cheat Montezuma of his empire and his life? They found the cross there, yet they brought it themselves. The ancients are to breathe so that we see them in the flesh, yet they are to remain over there, among the shades. They are to doze while being at our beck and call. They are to think nothing of themselves; after all, they have no blood. They are to flutter, not stamp; leave their horns among the shades; never bare effective teeth; be fearful and compose a petition for indulgence. For there is no empty space for them, their air was used up long since. They may sneak into dreams like burglars and be caught red-handed.

There is an old security in language, which dares to give itself names. The writer in exile, and especially the playwright, is seriously weakened in more ways than one. Remote from his linguistic air, he misses the familiar nourishment of names. Earlier, he may not have noticed the names he heard daily; but they noticed him and called him fully and surely. When he sketched his characters, he drew from the certainty of a huge tempest of names; and though he may have then employed one that was meaningless in the clarity of remembering, that name had existed at some point and had heard itself being called. Now the emigré has not lost the memory of his names, but there is no living wind here to bring them to him; he watches over them as a dead treasure, and the longer he must stay away from his old climate, the more avaricious the fingers through which the old names slip.

Thus, for the poet in exile, there is only one choice if he won't surrender totally: he has to breathe the new air until it too calls him. It takes a long time, the air begins and goes dumb. He feels it and he is offended; he may even close his ears, and then no name can reach him. The foreign atmosphere grows, and when he awakes, it is the old dried heap that lies next to him, and he allays his hunger with grain that comes from his youth.

Happiness is: peacefully losing your unity, and every emotion comes and is silent and goes, and every part of the body listens on its own.

On metamorphosis. When I stepped out to eat today, a car came driving at my right, the kind used to deliver packages for shops. The driver was a woman, of whom not much more than her head could be seen. A car like that normally brings me the oil for heating my stove; a very ugly girl with a mangled face drives the car and pours the oil into my canister. I was always interested in the girl's background, but I know next to nothing about her. I wondered whether it was she driving by in the car, and I peered as hard as possible. I couldn't make up my mind, but I did sense that her eyes rested on me very definitely. Perhaps for another second or two after she passed, I still wondered whether it wasn't really she. Then I looked to the left and suddenly I felt as if I were speeding along the houses. They glided past me as though I were in a car. This feeling was so powerful and inescapable that I began thinking about it. I cannot doubt that this was a concrete and simple case of what I call metamorphosis. Through my gaze at her and hers at me, I had changed into the girl at the wheel; and was now driving along in the car.

To depict death as though it didn't exist. A community in which everything proceeds in such a way that no one takes note of death. The language of these people has no word for death; nor is there any conscious euphemism. Even if one of them wanted to break the law, especially this prime unwritten and unspoken commandment, and speak of death, he would be unable to do so, for he could not find a word for it that the others understood. No one is buried and no one cremated. No one has ever seen a corpse. People vanish, no one knows where; a feeling of shame suddenly drives them away; since it is regarded as sinful to be alone, an absent person is never mentioned. Often they return, people are glad to have them back. That period of being away and alone is considered a bad dream, which no one is obligated to recount. Pregnant women bring children back from such trips, they give birth alone; at home, they could die during a delivery. Even very young children are suddenly up and away.

It will some day turn out that people grow meaner with each death.

Will death, if life is greatly extended, vanish as a way out?

This wincing delicacy towards people when we know they might soon die; this scorn for everything we felt earlier that was good or bad about them, this irresponsible love for their life, for their body, their eye, their breath! And if they happen to recover, how much more do we love them, how we beg them never to die again!

Sometimes I believe that as soon as I acknowledge death, the world will dissolve in nothingness.

Even the rational consequences of a world without death have never been thoroughly pondered.

There is no telling what people will manage to believe once they have abolished death from the world.

All dying people are martyrs of a future world religion.

The difficulties in noting things down—if they are to be conscientious and accurate—consist in their being personal. It is precisely the personal that one wishes to escape; one shrinks from setting it down, as though it might then no longer change. In reality, everything keeps changing in many ways if one only leaves it alone once it is written down. It is rereading which traces the avenues of the mind. One remains free by having the strength to seldom reread oneself. However, the dread of personal notes can be overcome. It suffices to speak about oneself in the third person: "he" is less troublesome or voracious than "I"; and as soon as one has the courage to range "him" among other third persons, then "he" is subject to confusion with anyone else and can only be recognized by the writer. One runs the risk that such notes might fall into the hands of people unable to distinguish between the various third persons, so that misinterpretations could put one in an undeserved bad light. The man who cares about the truth and immediacy of his notes, who loves thinking or observing for their own sake—that man will take that danger upon himself and save the first person for solemn occasions in which one cannot be anything but "I."

How odd. Only the Bible is strong enough for what is happening today, and its dreadfulness is what comforts us.

Refugees call themselves everything that they would have eventually become at home.

The prophet is obviously a man who does not allow his discontent with everything around him to shatter. His discontent keeps him together and gives him his wild direction. Life always comes later for him; it can never just happen to be there. He predicts things in order to debase them. If a thing comes true, it is despicable *because* it really happens. One must always think of the true prophet as inimical to his own predictions. Dreadful things to come express his torment at the things already here. His exaggerations are the future. He can endure the pressure he lives under only by picturing the splendors that shall supplant evil. But the splendors always come, only much later. And

41

there is something malevolent about him. He never likes anyone, not even himself, to have the splendor *now*. Now everything is bad because everyone is bad. In the future, there will be sheer happiness and glory, a remote future which malevolence places very far away. In between, however, there are huge and deserved darknesses. It is the baseness of human beings that nails the prophet down to his petty and concrete predictions. He wants to show men that they are bad. *They* want to go by his prophecies and have a better time of it in their badness.

There are no powerful words left. People sometimes say "God" merely to speak a word that used to be powerful.

History restores our false confidence.

The more accurate the accounts by travelers on "simple" peoples, the stronger our need to ignore all the prevailing or controversial ethnological theories and to start thinking from scratch. The most important thing, the thing appealing first to oneself, is always omitted from theories. We have to make our selection ourselves. How can we bank on the thoughts of people whose forte was not thinking; whose imagination was paralyzed by their precision; who cared far more for completeness than clarity; who lived primarily for collections and only secondarily for knowledge; who were narrow to the point of despising or exclusively loving what they saw. The old-time traveler was merely curious when he didn't care for just souls—or other quarry. The modern ethnologist is methodical; his training makes him an able observer, but incapable of creative thinking; he is equipped with the finest nets, and becomes their first prisoner himself. People cannot thank him enough for his material; he deserves the monuments once put up for kings and presidents. However, we should guard the accounts of old-time travelers more carefully than the most precious artworks. On the other hand, we have to provide the thinking ourselves. We should not let ourselves be talked into believing anything, and we should allow time and vital air for the conclusions we come to through extensive reading. Little is accomplished by repeating old theories. There is truly no lack of rich accounts, and we must use them to achieve a full and calm view of men as they live everywhere and always differently. We must not gather individual traits and things; their adjacency is random and artificial. If something can be grasped as a whole, we have to preserve it within ourselves until it can hold out against the next totality. The more things touch one another in us, the richer and more accurate our notions will be of mankind altogether.

Detachment is the English national virtue. Its historical influence on the character of modern science.

I fear history, its uninfluenced course, because of the new false models it creates daily.

The struggle for the earth is being waged today between four national groups: Anglo-Saxons, Germans, Russians, and Japanese. The others are satellites. France and Italy, considering themselves too old to be satellites, take part only half-heartedly. The Anglo-Saxons have a head start that the others won't be able to catch up with. They have made themselves invincible and indispensable in two ways. For one thing, they have colonized the entire earth with people of their own stock. There are Englishmen everywhere; and not only as masters of other nations. For another thing, they have set up the best part of a continent as an asylum, and there, in America, they have welded the most enterprising members of all nations into something like Anglo-Saxons. That's how they have secured territories and people. Thus they now exist in two quite different forms: as the old master race and as a modern race brimming with life, a mixed race. The Russians, in contrast, have their real continent, a new social faith, and revolutionary followers throughout the world. It is quite possible that their earnest conquerings are only just commencing. The Germans and the Japanese, in incomprehensible blindness, have begun like very ancient conquerors, relying only on modern technology, which is equally accessible to their enemies. Like the Romans, they started out from a single point—measured by today's huge number of people—and wanted to achieve in years what the Romans took centuries to accomplish. They did not reckon seriously with the totally different condition of the world around them. All they thought they needed was a purely subjective feeling of superiority, which they tried to stoke in every way. It was enough for them that they knew little about others. It was particularly fatal for the Germans that they measured themselves against the unwarlike Jews. They so thoroughly conscripted them as their enemies that gradually all their other enemies took on something of a Jewish tinge for them. Thus their faith in the uncombativeness of Englishmen and Russians became their catastrophic dogma.

There is *one* legitimate tension in the writer: the nearness of the present and the energy he repulses it with; the yearning for it and the energy he pulls it back with. The present can never be close enough to him. He can never repulse it far enough.

Every man needs a legitimate sphere of suppression in which he is permitted to despise and to carry his pride higher than the moon. The choice of this sphere, usually made early, is just about the most important event in one's life. Here, a teacher can truly accomplish something; he has to wait a long time, practice cautious empathy, and, upon finding the right thing, energetically draw the boundaries of that sphere. These boundaries are what counts; they have to be strong and resistant to any assault; they have to protect the rest of the man against the rapacious lusts of pride. It's not enough for someone to say: I am a great painter. He has to feel that he is otherwise little, and less than many others. The sphere of pride itself has to be spacious and airy. The underlings are best widely scattered on the outside. One lets them sense that they are underlings only on rare and special occasions. The important thing is actually that someone carry the glass sphere in himself and protect its thin air. One can breathe more purely and more calmly inside that sphere, and one is all alone. Only fools and knaves would want it to grow until it becomes a prison for all. The experienced man keeps it in such a way that he can take it in his hand; and when he playfully lets it grow, he never forgets that it has to shrink back into his hand before he turns to grosser things.

To exist one needs a store of unquestioned names. The thinking man takes one name after another from his hoard, bites into it, and holds it against the light; and when he sees how counterfeit this name is for the thing he wants to designate, he scornfully scraps it. Thus the store of unquestioned names keeps shrinking; the man gets poorer day by day. He can remain in total emptiness and meagerness unless he secures help. Help is not hard to find, the world is rich; how many animals, how many plants, how many rocks has he never known. If he now concerns himself with them, he takes their names with the first impression of the way they look—names that are still unquestioned, that are fresh and lovely as for the child learning how to speak.

The *missing* animals: the species that the rise of man has prevented from evolving.

The philosopher is characterized by the tiny number of his chief ideas, and the stubborn and irksome way he reiterates them.

To think that someone still has to defend death, as though it didn't have the overpowering upper hand! The "deepest" minds treat death like a card trick.

Knowledge can lose its deadliness only through a new religion that does not acknowledge death.

Christianity is a step backwards from the faith of the ancient Egyptians. It permits the decay of the body and makes it despicable by picturing its decay. Embalming is the true glory of the dead man, so long as he can't be resurrected.

For the man of forty, the lures of power are irresistible. He cannot delude himself about them, or else he will all the more readily fall prey to them. He has to see his responsibilities in their true gradation, and then opt for the highest one. If it is higher and further than his own life, he must avoid power like the plague, because it binds him to present conditions.

Truth is a sea of grass tossed by the wind; it wants to be felt as motion, drawn in as breath. It is a rock only for the man who neither feels nor breathes it; he can bang his head bloody against it.

It is better for me to *read* about primitive peoples than to see them. A single pygmy in Africa would bring me to more confusing questions than science can ask in the next hundred years. I am scornful about reality only because it has such a tremendous impact on me. It is then no longer what others call reality, neither hard nor consistent, neither deed nor object; it is like a jungle growing before my eyes, and while it grows, everything belonging to the life of a jungle takes place within it. Thus I have to guard against too much reality, otherwise my forests will burst in me. In a milder and just barely endurable form, one secures reality through images and depictions. They too come alive in you, but they have a slower way of growing. They are calmer and more scattered, and they grope for one another gingerly. It takes a good long time for them to find each other. What they particularly lack is the dreadful weight of reality plunging upon you, a lovely glistening predator that devours man.

I would like to remain simple so as not to confuse the many characters I consist of.

Anything you don't accomplish yourself seems overwhelmingly big and important.

Nature has grown narrower through the theory of evolution. It would be nice to find the spiritual moment when it was both vastest and richest. Even as a strictly genealogical effort, the theory of origins is dull and petty, for it refers everything to man, who has achieved dominion over the earth anyway. It legitimates his claim by putting him at the end. It frees him from any tutelage by higher beings. Nothing and no one, says that doctrine, can deal with him the way he deals with the animals. The dreadful error lies in the term "man"; he is no unity; everything he has violated is contained within him. All men contain it, though not to the same degree; and thus they can do the worst things to one another. They have the spite and the strength to go as far as total extermination. They may succeed, and perhaps enslaved animals will be left when there are no more people.

Not even the scientific utility of the theory of origins strikes me as particularly great. We might have made greater discoveries if we had started with the more generous view that any animal can potentially be transformed into any other animal.

The most dangerous thing about technology is that it distracts us from what really makes up man, from what he really needs.

Anthropology, the study of the "simple" peoples, is the most melancholy of all disciplines. How painstakingly and precisely, how strictly, how strenuously did peoples hold on to their ancient institutions—and withal they died out.

My friend, the regional writer. I have once again come close to that strange creature calling itself a regional writer, and I believe I have finally tracked down his secret.

For *my* regional writer what's nearest is dearest. But it is wrong to think that cows or sloughs are nearest. There are even nearer things, and these are the organs of his body. A process that fascinates him, that fills him with new excitement every hour, that thrills and chills and moves him, is his own digestion. Not even the heartbeat means so much to him; it neither devours nor leaves traces. Digestion is his central experience; in his dismal world, it has the position given to the sun in brighter worlds. When visiting someone else's home, he will first find the toilet and then certainly the kitchen. His stomach permitting, he wanders through the country, from kitchen to kitchen, toilet to toilet. He would rather hike than ride, for it cuts him to the quick when unfamiliar houses whiz past before he can nose out their digestive processes.

He loves peasants because they sit together around a huge bowl, and he arranges it so that he can visit several in a row. Among workers, he is a Socialist. He belongs to their party and loudly advocates an improvement in their living conditions. He abhors factories; but the canteens appeal to him; to make what they serve enjoyable, the workers ought to take over the factories themselves. A revolution is objectionable because it could imperil the food supply for a time. On the other hand, he doesn't resent the wealth of the burghers when they invite him to eat and tolerate him at their tables. In exchange, he entertains them with the digestive stories of all his past years. On such occasions, he emphasizes that he is a beggar. They can send him money by all means, for on less festive days he has to buy his meat himself. During a repast, no one can insult him, if the food tastes good and he keeps getting more. He has thus a highly developed sense of the individual classes. He is familiar with the guts of a peasant, a worker, a burgher. From food to stool, he values tangible reality over anything else. He despises images and dreams; and he cares for knowledge only when it turns into food. One can assume that in earlier ages, when whole oxen were roasted on spits for royalty, he would have become a loyal and upright singer for his prince, but these grand occasions are long gone, and the hungry aristocrats of his country today are quite an unspeakable horror to him.

Friendships, for him, are expressed in invitations. He himself never invites anyone. He judges people solely by how much food they serve him and how good it is. The word "create" has an inimitable sound in his mouth. It doesn't sound quite as decisive as "defecate," although it does recall it. It has something almost chaste about it, for not every poem of his can be about the things that actually are always on his mind, and so he has to forgo a great deal when writing. Yet it sounds matter-of-fact, for this is the coin he pays with.

His exaggerations have a visible boundary. They go as far as he could overeat, but no further.

All opinions exist morally; that is, nothing is so immoral that it might not be valid and binding somewhere. Thus, after finding out everything about the mores of all people, we know nothing and we have the right to begin all over again in ourselves. But no pains were futile. We have become more honest and less proud. We know our forebears better and feel how dissatisfied they would be with us. And they are no longer holy, except in *one* way: they are not alive; and in this holiness we will soon have nothing over them.

The most dreadful of all statements: someone died "at the right time."

At the Last Judgment, a single creature will rise from every mass grave. And let God dare to judge it!

The joyous tears of the dead over the first man not to die.

Is everyone too good to die? One can't say that. First everyone would have to live longer.

A shattering thought: there may be nothing to know, and error comes only because we try to know it.

Sometimes we sense that a war is about to end, and we are as happy as children that people are left, and before it's over we start calling them, and they reply that they sensed the same thing.

In the plethora of contradictory events, philosophers make room for one another.

Nothing among all human emotions is more beautiful and more hopeless than the wish to be loved for oneself alone. Who are you anyway, next to countless others, to deserve such preference? We do not want to be interchangeable; let no one be able to pinch-hit for us. A figurative unmistakability claiming to be spatial and spiritual. As though the earth had only one heaven, and heaven only one earth, we lay claim to the validity of both and, if we have one, we want to be the other. In reality, however, we are filled with planets, and countless heavens open their doors to us.

The system of rewards and penalties jeeringly comes to a head, until, in heaven and hell, we have to be ashamed of it.

It must have been 120 or more generations ago that I dwelt among the Egyptians. Did I admire them as much back then?

How much one has to say in order to be heard when silent.

One would like to write just so much that the words give life to another, and just so little that one can still take them seriously oneself.

With growing maturity, we perceive a distaste for the individual voices of the writers. We seek the nameless, the great tales of the nations, tales that were for everyone, such as the Bible and Homer and the myths of the still primitive tribes. Beyond this ocean, however, we are interested in the most private foibles and inadequacies of those who can talk about them; and thus we are back with the individual writers. Yet they can spellbind us not as writers, but merely as gatekeepers to the most private realm; and the porcelain that they paint and exhibit as their own products is something we'd like to smash.

When speaking, he composes his words too calmly, he always has control of his words, they never chase him, they never jeer at him, they never make a fool of him—how can I trust this man?

I'm fed up with seeing through people; it's so easy, and it gets you nowhere.

It is just about unbearable to think how much knowledge we will never take in during our lifetime. Yet it is quite impossible even to set about excluding this knowledge.

One can touch the unhappiness of the whole world in one single man, and as long as we don't give him up then nothing is given up, and so long as he breathes, the whole world breathes.

You talk and enthuse about animals constantly; but then you don't even notice when you're closest to animal life: among deceivers, and when deceived.

Once again, this is the second or third time, I have thought of Death as my salvation. I fear I might still greatly change. Perhaps I may even become one of his eulogizers, the people who pray to him through their old age. I therefore wish to record once and for all that that second future period of my life, in case it comes, shall be invalid. I do not want to have lived merely to cancel out what I have lived for. Let people treat me as two men, a strong and a weak one; and let them listen to the voice of the strong one, for the weak one will never help anybody. I do not want the senile words of the one to destroy the words of the young man. I would rather be broken off in the middle. I would rather last only half as long.

I want death to be earnest, I want death to be dreadful and most dreadful where only nothingness is to be dreaded.

It would be even harder to die if we knew we would remain; but were obligated to silence.

Everything one *records* contains a grain of hope, no matter how deeply it may come from despair.

1944

The greatest intellectual temptation in my life, the only one I have to fight very hard against is: to be a total Jew. The Old Testament, wherever I open to, overwhelms me. I found something suitable to me at almost every point. I would like to be named Noah or Abraham, but my own name also fills me with pride. I try to tell myself, when I am about to sink into the story of Joseph or David, that they enchant me as a writer, and what writer have they not enchanted! But that's not true, there's more to it. For why did I find my dream of the future longevity of men in the Bible, as a list of the oldest patriarchs, as the past? Why does the psalmist hate death as only I do? I scorned my friends for tearing loose from the enticements of many nations and blindly becoming Jews again, simply Jews. How hard it is for me now not to emulate them. The new dead, those dead long before their time, plead with one, and who has the heart to say no to them? But aren't the new dead everywhere, on all sides, in every nation? Should I harden myself against the Russians because there are Jews, against the Chinese because they are far away, against the Germans because they are possessed by the devil? Can't I still belong to all of them, as before, and nevertheless be a Jew?

What should a Bible have been like to hold up the self-annihilation of mankind?

The random things in most convictions are becoming more and more unbearable to me.

Not to speak anymore, to place words next to one another mutely and watch them.

The resistance to the age requires its sharp utterances, or it will remain dull and helpless. It is hard to keep the utterances to oneself once they are found, once they are sharp. But only the ideas no one knows about keep you alive.

The many meanings of reading: the letters are like ants and have their own secret state.

A sentence by itself is clean. The very next one takes something from it.

It is not shameful, it is not selfish, it is good and right and conscientious that we are now filled with nothing but the thought of immortality. Do we not see them, people, being sent to death by the trainload. Don't they laugh, don't they joke, don't they brag, to sustain each other's false courage? And then hosts of airplanes, twenty, thirty, a hundred, fly over us, laden with bombs, every quarter of an hour, every few minutes, and we see them peacefully returning, glittering in the sunlight, like flowers, like fish, after exterminating whole cities. One cannot say "God" anymore, He is marked forever, he has war's Mark of Cain on his brow, one can only think of one thing, the one Savior: immortality! If it were ours, if it were here already, how different it all would be! Immortality! Who would want to kill then, who would even dream of killing *if nothing could be killed?*

The old ruins are saved, and we will be able to draw comparisons with the new ones.

Don't be dazzled by the glory of victory. Germans can be bribed with victories; but you?

Progress has its bad side; from time to time, it explodes.

One would have to determine by experiment which games in which people face one another hostilely can help develop hatred, and which calm it down.

It is bizarre and disquieting that after two thousand years the basic ethical question is the same, only more urgent; and the man who now says "Love one another!" knows there isn't much time left for it.

The language of my intellect will remain German—because I am Jewish. Whatever remains of the land which has been laid waste in every way—I wish to preserve it in me as a Jew. *Their* destiny too is mine; but I bring along a universal human legacy. I want to give back to their language what I owe it. I want to contribute to their having something that others can be grateful for.

Mistrust of pain: it is always a pain of one's own.

The slowness of plants is their great advantage over animals. The religions of passivity, such as Buddhism and Taoism, want to help people to a plantlike existence. They may not fully realize this character of the virtues they recommend; but the life of action they struggle against is eminently animal. Plants are not wild; the preparing or dreaming part of their nature is far superior to the voluntative. But within their sphere, they have certain things reminiscent of us. Their blossoms are their consciousness. They got there earlier than most animals, whose actions leave them no time for consciousness. The wisest people, whose time of action is way behind them, bear their mind as a blossom. Plants, however, blossom in large numbers and always anew; their mind is plural and seems to be free of man's dreadful tyranny of oneness. We will never be able to emulate them again in that respect. Oneness has grabbed us, and now we are trapped forever in its teeth. The scattered works of artists have something of blossoms; only the plant always brings forth the same, whereas modern artists are racked with the fever of variety.

Man acquired his plantlike nature in architecture. His buildings quelled his fear. Now he has succeeded in filling them too with fear.

Literary histories sometimes read as if all names were interchanged and the author were discussing totally different things from the topics he mentions, and as if we could just keep interchanging everything while the judgments remain as they are.

One lives in the naive notion that *later* there will be more room than in the entire past.

Soon no ancient writing will remain undeciphered, and no new writing will turn up to be deciphered. Writing will thus lose its holiness.

You become everything you loathed the most. Each loathing was a bad omen. You saw yourself in a distorting mirror of the future, and didn't realize it was you.

What if you hadn't looked? Would you then not have become this?

If you knew more about the future, the past would be even more difficult.

To the extent that we think or even claim to think, nearly all of us are now moving in the sphere of psychology. Yet we are thus owning up to a poverty that could not be drearier. Truly, we have become modest and humble. It is a matter of intellectual cleanliness today that we do not know too much. Gone is the age of the thinkers who were after everything. Their names have remained great, their solutions are no longer taken seriously because they weren't specialists. Now and then, we run into ambitious people who want to know at least everything there is to know for sure. But is that what counts? Isn't it exactly the opposite that counts? Uncertainty ought to be the true province of thought. The mind should ask its questions in uncertainty; brood in uncertainty; despair in uncertainty.

However, things have overwhelmed us. By mass-producing them, more massively every day, we have gotten used to taking seriously only that which is materialistic enough. All we now see and hear is: objects. We feel objects. The visions of the courageous are filled with objects. Everything aims at producing and destroying objects. The earth, a round object, is to come into the hands of the greediest, and that's all. Objects, mass-produced, are to be justly distributed; that's all. These two ideas, extreme enough, offer a welcome inducement to destroy all life together with all objects.

Where is the man who does not scorn things merely because he wants to have them? Where is the man who marvels, marvels from afar, marvels at what he will never touch? We have laid hands on everything and then believe that it is everything. Even the animals were better, for how great and far was everything remaining beyond them! They had no inkling, we have seized the inklings. Seized, murdered, mangled, choked down.

Bad writers wipe away the traces of metamorphosis; good writers display them.

As soon as the word "love" occurs, a woman believes anything. Men reserve the same gullibility for fighting.

They talk of instincts as though they were albatrosses.

A growing passion for all sects no matter what religion they come from. It gives me great intellectual enjoyment to study their differences and fix the point at which they deviate from the stream of the main religion. I am convinced that I will some day succeed in finding deeper laws governing these break-aways of religions. But even the question of faith per se, the greatest and uncanniest human issue, can only be answered in terms of its diversity.

I have all the qualities of a religious man, but also the deep, inner drive to escape the enclosure of any faith. Perhaps I could practice these two contradictory qualities by mastering the sects.

One wants precise knowledge of everything men were ever ready to die for.

The taciturn brother: a man you haven't seen for years had gone mute and as such suddenly comes towards you.

Dreams always have something young about them; they are new to the dreamer. Even if he thinks he recognizes them, they never have the repeated and worn-out quality of waking life. They glow with the colors of paradise, and in their terrors we are baptized with unheard-of names.

That woman who admitted at a gathering that she had never had a dream; and instantly she became a monkey to everyone.

The man who goes to dream-diviners is frittering away his most precious possession and deserves the inevitable slavery.

A gathering of all the gods that ever existed; their strange differences, their tongues, their costumes; and the way they—gods!—have to touch one another for mutual understanding.

An Egyptian meets a Chinese and trades a mummy for an ancestor.

Never despise a man for what he believes. What you yourself believe does not depends on you. Receive every belief naively and without hostility. This, and only this, allows the very faint hope of your getting to the nature of belief.

The man who doesn't believe in God takes all the guilt of the world upon himself.

In one's own speech, one becomes too noble, one imagines one has the finest sentiments. One misuses the caricature of ordinary baseness, as expressed in false and filthy words. The religions all suffer because the preacher can speak for a long time and with self-satisfaction. His words thus become more and more farfetched and warm *his* vanity instead of striking the hearts of the listeners.

1945

They love war so much that they have pulled it into Germany; and there too they refused to yield it.

Come spring, the grief of the Germans will be an inexhaustible well, and little will distinguish them from the Jews.

Hitler has turned the Germans into Jews in just a few years, and "German" has become as painful a word as "Jewish."

The abandoned earth, overtaxed with words, choking in knowledge, and with no living ear left on it to listen into the cold.

You can't do anything nastier to a person than occupy yourself exclusively with him.

In love, assurances are practically an announcement of their opposite.

In some people, the word "soul" sounds like the epitome of everything one fears and hates, and one would like to change into a locomotive and zoom away with a hiss.

Countries, islands, places are alive for me when I meet someone who comes from there. But then their life turns quite uncanny in me, as though I came from there myself.

Nationalism cannot be overcome by internationalism, as many people have thought, for we speak languages. The answer is plurinationalism.

The chaos of voices and faces in which I used to be at home has become hateful to me. I like to experience people individually. When there are several of them, I want to have them sitting next to one another, in an order, as in a train, and I wish to decide what to look at first. Chaos has lost its attraction. I want to order and form and not lose myself in anything anymore. The time of promiscuous devotion is over. Chaos stands for war. I despise war more than I hate it. The many people who move about in the center, on leave, or in everlasting quest of pleasure strike me as deserters from a very lofty cause. They are ready to return to their obedient cowardice, or else they have constantly feigned ignorance. They only have more truth at night as shadows, outside the pubs; they are like dead men who do not realize they are dead; from the tiny sidestreets leading to Piccadilly, I watch them on and on in great excitement. They reach for one another, and so I know there are female shadows among them. A few shouts interfere, they feign more life than is their due. Did I once listen only to voices? My uncanny strength lay in chaos; I was as sure of it as of the whole world. Today, chaos itself has exploded. Nothing was structured so senselessly that it could not collapse into something even more senseless; and wherever I sniff, everything is heavy with the stench of extinguished fire. Perhaps we'd be better off if everything had burnt up. The bewildered survivors will make themselves comfortable in the ruins. They will cook their soups on the volcanoes and cheerfully spice their food with the sulphur. But for those whose hearts were open to this, to the least little thing that has happened, no chaos will ever be beautiful again, and they will tremble hardest in the face of the most impossible, in honest knowledge and hopeless fear.

One should not study things too thoroughly too soon; there's no benefit in treating the moment as exhaustive. It may very well be that at times, but it should not be permitted to know it. The vain moment is a lost moment. Its beauty and its strength are in its innocence. The divided moments, those divided over the years, spent in contemplating an object, add up in a mysterious way, and suddenly everything becomes deep and unified.

One can be passionately fond of several people at once, and things go with each one as though he were the only one, and you are spared nothing, no fear, no ardor, no fury, no grief, and at times the whole thing grows to such vehement proportions that you act like several different people at once, each with his own purpose, and yet all at once, and no one knows what's to become of it.

The prophets predict old things with a wail.

The fact that the gods die makes death more brazen.

The gods, nourished by worship, starving to death in unnamedness, recalled in poets, and only then are they eternal.

Everything happening in the world today moves between two opposite basic judgments of mankind:
1. Everyone is still too good for death.
2. Everyone is just barely good enough for death.
There is no reconciliation of these two opinions. One or the other will win. There is no way of telling which.

The hardest thing: to keep discovering what you know anyway.

The analytics believe they have the Ariadne clew for the labyrinth into which they lead us. All they have is the knots on which the clew, torn a hundred times, was bound together again; between these knots they have nothing. There are countless labyrinths; they believe it's always the same one.

Motion is most likely a remedy for incipient paranoia. The intensity of this kind of confusion makes you static. You act as if a certain place were threatened, the place you're standing in, and you cannot leave this place no matter what. The overestimation of this random stand-ing-place is often very ludicrous; the place can be worthless and wrong. You'd be much better off and much safer elsewhere. But you force yourself to be exactly where you are; to defend yourself at all points of this specific perimeter; not to yield an inch of it; to draw upon any devices, the most abominable and despicable, for this de-fense: in a word, you act like a nation defending its homeland. The similarity of this private condition to the politics of a state is striking. The unity of a nation consists mainly in its being able to act, when necessary, like a single paranoiac. In either case, a piece of earth is at stake, the ground you need for your feet so that they may carry you erect. This kind of rootedness, which can become so dangerous, is often healed the moment one destroys the roots quickly and harshly;

and it ought to be said that the forced migrations of whole nations, which one so greatly pities or despises, can also lead, under favorable circumstances, to curing their homeland paranoia.

There is something hopeful about the fact that the whole earth has the same name as every piece of it.

Germany, destroyed early in the year as no land has ever been destroyed. And if it is possible to destroy *one* land in this way—how can Germany remain the only one?

The cities die, men hole up deeper.

I was in many of the destroyed cities when they were still flourishing; but I was never in many more cities that were also destroyed; and thus for everyone of us, in our lifetime, there are things that we shall never be able to see again, for anything in the world, so suddenly, so ruthlessly.

Things will be better. When? When the dogs rule?

In Germany, everything happened that can exist as a historical possibility in man. The entire past at once came to the fore. Sequences were suddenly simultaneous. Nothing was omitted; nothing was forgotten. Our generation was allowed to realize that all the better efforts of mankind are futile. Evil, the German events say, is life itself. It does not forget, it repeats everything; and we don't even know when. It has whims, these are its greatest terrors. But its substance, the gathered essence of millennia, cannot be influenced; if you press it too hard, the pus spurts in your face.

The collapse of the Germans affects us more deeply than we like to admit. It is the extent of the deception they lived in, the hugeness of their illusion, the blind power of their hopeless faith that keep haunting us. We always loathed the people who tacked together that disgusting faith, the few truly responsible ones, whose minds were just barely sufficient for that; but all the others, who did nothing but believe with as much concentrated energy in a few years as the Jews mustered in thousands of years, who had life and appetite enough to really want their earthly paradise, the control of the world, to kill anyone else for it, to die for it, everything in the shortest time, these countless, flourishing, radiantly healthy, simple-minded, marching, decorated guinea-pigs for a faith, drilled for a faith, trained like no Mohammedan—just what are they now when their faith collapses? What is left of them? What else was prepared in them? What second life could they now begin? What else are they without their dreadful military faith? How greatly do they feel their impotence since nothing existed for them but power? Where else can they fall? What will catch them?

Perhaps because we dare not even catch our breath between this war and the next, the next will never come.

One invention still lacking: how to reverse explosions.

There are two kinds of people; one kind is interested in the positional aspect of life, the position one can achieve as a wife, school principal, manager, mayor. They keep their gaze riveted on the point they have put in their heads, they can view their fellow men only in terms of such points, and all that exists is position, anything else doesn't count and is unsuspectingly overlooked. The other kind wants freedom, especially the freedom from positions. The'y're interested in change; the leap through apertures rather than up. They cannot resist any door or any window, but their direction is always out. They would fly from a throne, from which nobody in the first group, once he were on it, could raise himself for even a millimeter.

The enormous vanity in any concentration on God, as though someone kept shouting: His own image! His own image!

We are coming from too much. We are moving towards too little.

The degree of definiteness in news keeps changing according to the way it's transmitted. A messenger came running, his excitement infected the receiver. They had to act instantly. The excitement became the faith in the message. A letter is calm, if for no other reason than because it was secret during its transmission. One believes it, but with reservations, and one doesn't feel impelled to act. The telegram combines certain features of the letter with those of the old oral messenger. It is secret, unknown to the deliverer, but one is served alone with it; it is even more sudden than the messenger, it has something of death and therefore inspires more fear. We believe a telegram. Nothing is more disconcerting than to learn that a telegram lied.

It is so lovely to tell someone: I'll always love you. But then if you really do it!

You learn the most from the least of men. What he lacks, you owe him. Without him, this debt can never be evaluated. Yet it is the very thing you live for.

On beauty. Beauty has something very familiar, yet very remote as though it could never have been familiar. That is why beauty is exciting and cold at once. As soon as you get it, it is no longer beautiful. You have to recognize it, however, otherwise it won't excite you. Beauty always has something remote. It was once here and then far away for a long time; thus, it is unexpected when you see it again. It can't be loved, but you long for it. It is richer in the mysterious ways of remoteness than anything you have within yourself.

Beauty must remain *outside.* There are lunatics who think they are beautiful; but even they know that they can only be beautiful on the outside. "Inner beauty" is a contradiction in terms. Mirrors have brought more beauty into the world; they even feign remoteness; much in the most ancient beauty may have come from a gaze across water. But mirrors have become too frequent. So they usually yield only what's expected. Only the grossest people claim that beauty contradicts itself. A man can find anything beautiful that was long familiar, became remote, and then, unexpectedly, returns. The beloved dead man is beautiful when you see him but do not know he is dead, and you still cannot love him: in a dream.

Any ancient thing has an easier time being beautiful because it was long buried and gone. The traces of its disappearance as a patina contribute a great deal to beauty; it is not oldness per se that we treasure here, but the oldness that was out of sight for centuries. Beauty has to be found again after long distances and long periods of time.

The arrogance of a concept as the basest arrogance, for it has a huge hoard of coins to buy more, but it is too tightfisted to change them.

A Chinese steals an Oedipus complex in Cambridge and sneaks it into China.

The nations ought to lend one another their dignitaries for two months at a time, and they ought to travel a lot and give the same speeches in many languages and settle war and peace in sleeping-cars.

The conversations of Confucius are the earliest complete intellectual portrait of a human being; it is astonishing how much one can give in five hundred jottings; how well-rounded a man thus becomes; how tangible; and yet how intangibly whole, as if the gaps were merely deliberate folds in garments.

After a game of twenty years, China is at last really becoming a homeland for me. It is wonderful that nothing is lost in a mind, and would not this alone be reason enough to live very long or even forever?

The word "civilization" seems nowhere so apt as in everything connected to China. Breeding and counter-breeding in their interplay can be most accurately studied here. What human beings can at best become without turning inhuman; what they can at worst remain without losing their earlier gains; becoming and remaining occur here in a very unique way and exist in that way even today.

One feels quite at home in the pious texts of the Chinese, as in childhood: they talk so much about heaven.

I think another reason I love the Chinese is that they include the relationship between an elder and younger brother as one of the five main human relationships.

The silkworm is a deeper expression of what is Chinese than even the script.

A real Chinese revolution would be the abolition of the cardinal points.

Good words are so colossal! How one can soothe when one forgets oneself, one's vanity, one's dogmatism, one's bossiness, one's thousand and one mirrors!

Oh, if only I might be the man who can be fooled by all people and calmly puts up with it, and is none the less for it, and likes them all, and yet sees them as they are, and does not plume himself on that!

There are times when people who are very much in love accuse one another of any and all crimes, which they are certainly not capable of. It's as though they *owed* one another the worst things and felt only scorn because no one is about to make any of it come true. "You robbed me" they say, with the pleading underneath: "Why don't you do it." "You've destroyed me," which means: "Destroy me, finally, won't you." "You've killed me," which stands for an ardent plea: "Kill me! Kill me!"

Perhaps this expresses the wish for a true passion from the other, a passion that would not cringe from anything, not even the consequences of a murder; and the proper feeling for the tremendous size of a love that wipes out its own object and will always be aware of that.

The falsest manners of speaking are the most entertaining, as long as there are people who use them earnestly.

A man who can never be neutral. In wars that do not involve him, he is on both sides.

One cannot breathe, everything is full of victory.

The terrible events in Germany have given Life a new responsibility. Earlier, during the war, he stood all alone. Whatever he thought was thought for all people; he would certainly have to stand judgment for it in a future time, but he did not have to explain his conduct to anyone living today. It had become too much for all of them, they contented themselves with disconnected blasts of life; it was impossible for them to breathe amply, they had failed. At the time, it didn't seem to have any deeper meaning that he thought and wrote in this German language. He would have found the same things in a different language, chance had given him this one. It was flexible, he was able to use it, it was still rich and dark, not too glib for the more profound things he was tracking down, not too Chinese, not too English; pedagogy, morality, which he was naturally also after, did not block the path to knowledge, they flowed from knowledge. The language, of course, was everything in its own way; but it was nothing, measured against freedom.

Today, with the collapse of Germany, all this has changed for him. People there will soon be looking for their own language, which was stolen from them and deformed. Anyone who has kept it pure during the years of utmost madness will have to hand it over. It is true, he will keep living for everyone, and he will always have to live alone, responsible to himself as the highest authority; but he now *owes* the Germans their language; he has kept it clean, but he now has to hand it over, with love and gratitude, with interest and compound interest.

To read all utopias, especially the old ones, in order to seek what was forgotten and omitted, to compare it with what we have forgotten.

Superlatives emit a destructive force.

Today it is no longer possible to save even the names of all the ancient gods. The immortals, the immortals, how they have deceived themselves about life on earth!

It is hard to plan only a *little*. But success depends precisely on that. Much is pleasant; little is good. The wind is outside, a delightful motion. The capable breath is inside. But the man fighting for his breath knows precisely what work is. The tides of the breath designate the permitted piece. Only the sick, of all those who take in air, know how little they keep, and they live for this little bit.

No one forces me to stay alive. That's why I love life so much. It is true that later men, among whom death will be taboo, will not know this huge tension, and they will envy us for something we would gladly have foregone.

There is a dangerous force in mistrust: it leads one to believe that one can think alone, judge alone, decide alone. It leads one to believe that one is alone. It forces others, who belong to one, to humiliate themselves and behave as if they had sinned. It removes the borders between what has really happened and what might happen, and it makes the suspects guilty in any event.

To have been everywhere. Tell no one where you were. That's how you preserve the fear of all places.

The false foreigner: Someone takes an oath to live disguised as a foreigner in his country until someone recognizes him. He dies, deeply embittered, as a foreigner.

A specialist: He seeks learnedness without movement; his doubts are to be directed in such a way that they endanger little. He needs a good, safe ground, but only a few people are to stand on it with him. He sees himself higher in small groups. He seldom leaves his ground for fear he might not find his way back. He exerts his control through the small group he belongs to. It's easy for him to despise everything because no one understands anything of his subject, and nothing else really interests him. He is never seriously in danger so long as he keeps himself narrow. This uniqueness is heightened by his nobility for he has chosen something remote, useless, and futile; who could ascribe selfish motives to him? If his knowledge remains dead, he feels good. He gets nervous when it suddenly begins sprouting, he knows he has breathed too deep and he presses his chest with a severe grasp. He keeps a wife chiefly to remain quite alien to her. She embodies, for him, the unteachable stupidity of the world. He needs a double, in his own image, who rummages in the same stuff as he does, a second specialist, to whom he can show respect as though that man were himself.

The first will flatter the last, and it will be delightful to hear what they have to think up.

In eternity, everything is at the beginning, a fragrant morning.

August 1945

Matter is smashed, the dream of immortality is shattered, we were on the verge of making it come true. The stars, so close, are now lost. The closest and furthest things have become one, under what lightning! Stillness alone, and slowness, are still worth living. They have little time left. The fun of flying was brief. If souls existed, this new catastrophe would have struck them. So one does not wish that something exists, for what is unattainable? Destruction, certain of its divine origin, reaches into the very marrow of things, and the Creator smashes both the clay and his own shaping hand. Survival! Survival! Ignoble word! Trees were the wisest form of life, and they fall with us atom-robbers.

If we survive, a lot more will be at stake. But the thought that we may not survive is unbearable. All certitude came from eternity. Without it, without this wonderful feeling of some permanence, albeit not one's own, everything is insipid and futile.

All time was not white-hot for us with possibilities we never suspected—what a blessing! Paradise *was* at the beginning, and now it's come to an end. The thing that pains me most is the fate of other creatures. We are so guilty, that we almost don't matter anymore. One can only sleep now so as not to think of it. The waking mind feels guilty, and it *is* guilty.

The *succession* of discoveries in our history is really a tragedy. A few slight changes, and everything would have come out differently. A few decades for this or that, and it wouldn't have overtaken us. Of course, like everything, this misfortune too has its laws. But who is interested in the laws of a world that will certainly not survive.

It is not that we do not see anything ahead of us. But the future has split; it will be thus or thus; on this side, all fear; on the other, all hope. One no longer has the weight to decide, not even in oneself. Double-tongued future, Pythia restored to honor.

The sun dethroned, the last valid myth destroyed. The earth has come of age; on its own now, what will it do with itself? Until now, it was the unchallenged child of the sun, totally dependent on it, unable to live without it, lost without it. But light is dethroned, the atomic bomb has become the measure of all things.

The tiniest thing has won: a paradox of power. The road to the atomic bomb is a philosophical one: there are roads leading elsewhere, no less enticing. The time, oh just the time to find them; you may have lost fourteen years in which something could have been saved. Thus nothing distinguishes you from the people who worked on the destruction during those fourteen years.

Gratitude for joint melancholy. We spoke of life as of a dead man. The things we hear about pre-war days sound paleolithic. The same thoughts are no longer possible. But in what splendor do words now stretch. All doors suddenly open, and each man shows what he has been carefully guarding for today. Hope for salvation by exposing the ultimate secret.

Now the final avarice has been crushed: the store of finagled years in a future beyond our lives. Nothing can rob us of a pure joy in life since we no longer save it for immortality. Living for no purpose, not even for eternity; this is the new freedom.

The religions knew, but they also helped create it. Astrology with a reversed end: *we* will now make planets and suns. The closed season for stars is past, we have overtaken them.

The ark is growing, when will it be full. We build and build, but the floor is thinner than air. The daring, the squandering, the light hand of mankind are things of the past. Mankind must be cautious if it wants to survive.

There is no end for the creative thinking of man. This curse contains the only hope.

The first pictures and words from my real home town were both happy and terrifying. To think that the Prater is destroyed, the ghost train with the earthquake of Messina as the deepest impression of my childhood; that this gaudy life survives only in my comedy, where no one knows it; that I thus am the preserver of the Prater until it exists again, and in a form containing its destruction: this is certainly a bizarre fate for someone who sees transformation and play as the essence of man.

The souls of the dead are in the others, the survivors, and there they slowly die out.

Fame is venal, but only for the moment. In the long run, it is unpredictable, and that is the only thing to reconcile us with it.

Anything you may ever have thought of death is no longer valid. With an enormous leap, he has achieved a power of contagion such as never before. Now he is really omnipotent, now he is truly God.

The "you" gives the lonesome man the warmth he needs in order to speak about himself without the braggadocio of the "I" and the hypocritical indifference of the "he." One puts one's graven image across from one like an intimate friend, its strengths and weaknesses are long familiar; without rancor or worship, one tells the image what it already knows, but it ought to *hear* it too, and, on this occasion, one hears it oneself.

Every work is a rape, through its sheer mass. One ought to find different and purer ways of expressing oneself.

Hitler ought to live on as a Jew.

The thing that puts our minds at ease about history is its falseness. It is a story about history, for what if we knew the truth!

The satirist who can no longer turn against the outer world will perish as a moral being: Gogol's fate.

Gradually he becomes aware that his hatred of his characters is hatred of himself. Whomever he despised, he despised *himself*. He seeks a severe judge who threatens him with hell. He does not succeed in completing *Dead Souls,* his own office of judgment. He throws it, himself, into the fire and remains as ashes.

Fear avenges itself. Every suffered fear is passed on to others. The degree of a man's development shows in whom he gives his fear; whether he cares about who receives it; whether he builds houses for it; or lets it flow freely; whether animals suffice; whether he needs people for it or only very special people, who receive it from him in a certain way.

Praying as a rehearsal of wishes.

It is a serious goal of my life to really get to know all myths of all peoples. However, I want to know them as though I had believed in them.

A tormenting thought: as of a certain point, history was no longer *real*. Without noticing it, all mankind suddenly left reality; everything happening since then was supposedly not true; but we supposedly didn't notice. Our task would now be to find that point, and as long as we didn't have it, we would be forced to abide in our present destruction.

All creatures are antediluvian, from the time before the atom bomb.

This would be the time, Dante, for a precise world judgment.

The attempt at keeping memories of people alive in their stead is nevertheless the greatest thing that mankind has heretofore accomplished.

Keeping people alive with words—isn't that almost the same as creating them with words?

I'm haunted by the thought of a last man, who knows everything that has happened before; who knows, treasures, loathes, and loves all varieties of these people who have died out; who is as filled with it as I would like to be; but who is truly alone and quite certain of his death. What can this last man do with himself, and how can he force the preservation of his precious knowledge? I cannot believe he would vanish without a trace if only he is given the time to orient himself. His pain will soon turn to skill; he will raise animals as people and give them his riches.

I'm only forty; but hardly a day passes without my learning of the death of some person I knew. With the years, there will be more of them every day. Death will creep into every last hour. How can one help being at his mercy?

Guilt feelings towards my father: I'm now nine years older than he became.

Oh, who could drain the bitterness from the future so that he alone swallows it and everyone else will be happy!

You are still so naive that you actually expect the very best from every new person; and your greater maturity comes out in the fact that this expectation quickly turns into distrust and scorn. Basically, all that counts is the strength of this naive expectation, which has such a hard time asserting itself against the growing experience of life. As long as it exists, anything can be expected of you.

Cynicism: expecting nothing more from anyone than what one is one-self.

He has preached so much that he now believes in nothing. How often can you assert your faith without endangering it? Find the right proportion.

The sufferings of the Jews had turned into an institution, but it out-lived itself. People don't want to hear about it anymore. They were amazed to learn that one could exterminate the Jews; now, perhaps without realizing it, they have a new reason for despising them. Gas *was* used in this war, but only against the Jews, and they were help-less. The money giving them power earlier was useless. They were degraded to slaves, then cattle, then vermin. The degradation worked; the traces will be harder to wipe away from those who heard about it than from the Jews themselves. Every act of power is double-edged; every humiliation increases the lust of the presumptuous man and in-fects others, who would like to be just as presumptuous. The very an-cient history of how others relate to Jews has changed fundamentally. People do not hate them any less; but they no longer *fear* them. For this reason, the Jews can make no greater mistake than to continue the laments at which they were masters and to which they now have greater inducement than ever before.

Why aren't more people good *out of spite?*

Everything became faster so there would be more time. But there is always less and less time.

War has moved into outer space, earth is heaving a sigh of relief before its end.

It would be strange if among all the forms of life that may exist else-where, we on earth were the only ones to know war.

The most dangerous thing of all is to fight with someone weaker; this windy, useless, empty feeling of superiority before the fight, during the fight, afterwards, this incessant "Haha! I could devour you!" I could derive all bad feelings from this situation, in which one is, unchallenged, the superior, the superior by far, and yet one *does* fight.

The last animals ask men for mercy. That same moment, men are blown up. The animals remain alive. What glee at the thought that the animals could survive us.

The war began with guilt. It ended with guilt. But the guilt is ten thousand times greater.

She wishes he knew everything; but it would be dangerous for her if he knew everything. On the few days he really trusts her, a word of hers makes him distrustful and nervous. Thus she can hope that he will ultimately know everything. She endures cheating him, but she cannot endure his ignorance; for his alleged omniscience is what gives her the strength to life, which includes the strength to cheat him.

The sharpest and most ruthless hierarchy is in art. There is nothing that could ever wipe it out. It rests on the utterance of experiences that are real and inevitable. In art, everything still has to happen. It is not enough to have something or be somewhere. One has to *show by doing;* something must be done.

All knowledge has something puritanical about it; it gives words a morality.

The best person ought not to have a name.

The virtue of English historians, English scholars altogether, is also their greatest drawback; it is their goal to instruct, which hardly any of the writing scholars can ever quite forget. They transmit their knowledge as if to children; they leave out the obscure parts of their knowledge; and they round off its cruel points. It is particularly the latter that distinguishes the friendly clarity of the English from the precise clarity of the French. Thus, Gibbon was a Frenchman by nature. The Englishman doesn't like to nail his youth to overly profound impressions. He would rather protect it through subdivisions, he would rather prohibit than terrify. But he also tends to stay like that as an adult. His civilization, one of the strongest, is unbrokenly naive, and perhaps that's why its figure of a judge has remained intact.

I would like to become tolerant without overlooking anything, persecute no one even when all people persecute me; become better without noticing it; become sadder, but enjoy living; become more serene, be happy in others; belong to no one, grow in everyone; love the best, comfort the worst; not even hate myself anymore.

The woman who wins is not the one who runs after, not the one who runs away, but the one who waits.

Ah, if one could only watch life with a cloak of invisibility over one's mouth, without ever saying anything, without ever expecting or fearing anything from one's vanished mouth.

To jot down all the things one yearns for, jot them down for just one day, without explanations or connections, nothing between then, really only the things one yearns for.
On another day, jot down all the things one fears.

A different kind of scapegoat, in which one finds all one's worst traits, only stronger. Instead of improving oneself, one expends all one's energy on the scapegoats; for this is futile, the goat will never become better. One's own improvement would succeed with much less effort; and that's the very thing one wishes to avoid.

Philosophers, though unmarried, have offspring with one another. Their family relations are bearable because they take place outside any family. Their dislikes are directed against one another rather than against a wife. They defend their peculiarities more consciously than other men, with less guilt feelings and with a claim to never going silent as long as there are others. They brook no rebuttal, although they themselves like to practice this imaginary business. The obnoxious ones among them are those who refuse to forget anything. A few pretend to be forgetful. The most singular really forget most things, and then, in their gigantic darkness, they are as lovable as stars.

In the philosophical thoughts of the Greeks, the thing that keeps frightening me is that we are still all caught up in them. Everything we desire seems Greek. Everything we justify sounds Greek. The scattering of what has come down to us makes the impact all the more striking. Does our world look the way it looks today because there doesn't exist a totally new, totally original thought? Or does it look that way because there are things that are too different from the Greeks.

The metamorphoses of Socrates, which he himself would not permit, all suddenly existed, in his disciples: the posthumous drama of an anti-dramatic character.

1946

True writers encounter their characters only *after* they've created them.

Learning has to be an adventure, otherwise it's stillborn. What you learn at a given moment ought to depend on chance meetings, and it ought to continue in that way, from encounter to encounter, a learning in transformations, a learning in fun.

In reality, *every* faith is close to me. I feel at peace in any faith so long as I know I can go forth again. But doubting is not my goal. I am enigmatically prepared to believe, and it's easy for me, as though it were my task to represent everything that was ever believed. I cannot impugn faith itself. It is strong and natural in me and moves in all kinds of ways. I could imagine spending my life in some secret haven containing the sources, myths, disputations, and stories of all known forms of belief. There I would read, think, and gradually absorb all faith.

He himself can never be simple; to be simple, he first has to change into a very poor and afflicted man, love for this man will make him simple.

The time of defending himself against something is the most important time for a writer. As soon as he surrenders, he is no longer a writer.

I enjoy all systems if they are perspicuous, like a toy in your hand. If they get complicated, they make me nervous. Too much of the world has come to the wrong place, and how shall I get it out of there again?

Fame always wants to hang from the stars because they are so far removed; fame always wants to find safety.

Man must learn to *be* many men consciously and to keep them all together. This latter and far more difficult task will give him the character he imperils with his plurality. Instead of ruling others, he will have to rule over his own personae; they will have names, he will know them, he will be able to order them about. His lust for power will no longer want other people; it will seem despicable to want others when one can be as many people as one controls.

The world might be governable with just a few stories. But they would have to be the right ones; we would not be permitted to confuse them with one another; and many others, most, could never be told. The superstitition of writers.

I cannot indemnify myself with anything; everything has its own value for me, its own meaning; if things could be traded for one another, that would make life easier for me; I never trade; even when buying something, I like to feel that two people happen to be giving each other presents at the same time.

What you made up in *dismay,* later turns out to be the bald truth.

How easy to say: find yourself! How scary when it really happens!

In love, you have a stronger wish to do what you would have done anyway. Love merely brings everything to a higher pitch, you want to fully cover the other being with yourself, and one of the wiles you employ to that end is disguise: you act as though you wanted to absorb the other without endangering him, without doing anything to him. He is to feel fine, but unchanged, in a cloud of fragrant admiration and sonorous tenderness; when venerated, he remains the same, for he could not be more splendid than he already is. The dungeon that love has actually prepared will turn visible only gradually. Once those clouds float away, the naked walls can be seen, and no one has ever recognized them at once.

To read until the eyelashes are almost audible with fatigue.

One always pulls oneself together with an ancient myth; there are so many of them; something for everything. Is that the reason why nothing truly creative has occurred in the world for a long time? Did we deplete ourselves with the ancient myths?

The danger of prohibitions: one relies on them until one no longer reflects *when* they might be changed.

In an astronomical book, I read the date: Novemember 24, 1999. Huge excitement.

No new earth will come, this was the only one. Ardently it survives its tortured end. Watch over it? Who may watch over it? If One Man were totally the earth, his heart precisely the earth, he could watch over it. It would then take the form of his heart. Towns, mountains, rivers would have different places on it. People would know that the earth had become a precise heart and it will beat. It is the beat they expect. It is the beat they hope for. It is the beat of the earth become one.

One survives so much that one mistakenly thinks one can survive anything.

You place your hope in any omen of any faith that happens to come your way: a graveyard on a slope, a peculiarly marked cow, a fireball over a tombstone, an unusually shaped building, smoke from a train, a jerking hip, your departed mother's birthday.

Everything around you becomes more and more significant; your environment fills up. It's not really an environment now. Things once captured in pictures and frames emerge and swell up before your eyes. You see so much in them and you also see through them; their enlargement makes things transparent. You have room for everything; in you, the most outrageous and most beautiful things interpenetrate one another.

The letters of one's name have a dreadful magic as though the world were composed of them. Is a world without names conceivable?

A dispute between two men who lust for immortality: one wants continuity, the other wants to come back periodically.

The most tormenting notion: *all* dramas have been played out, and only the masks keep changing.

Every space must be acquired through powerful experience; feeble spaces are like corridors and only good for connecting.

A passion can be ineffably beautiful if it turns from restraint, order, and consciousness and becomes blind and unreflected again. It saves itself by threatening destruction. The man who lives without passion does not live; the man who always masters it is only half alive; the man who perishes from it did at least live; the man who recalls it has a future; and the man who exorcizes it has nothing more than the past.

For each trait a man has a special hopelessness.

Unused knowledge wreaks vengeance. There is something awfully intentional and restricting about knowledge. It wants to be utilized, directed, and handled. It wants to be indispensable. It wants to become custom and habit. It will not let itself be degraded to shining and faraway stars. It wants to hit. It wants to kill.

The uncanniest things have never been conceived, much less depicted.

The slightest obnoxious event grows into a catastrophe if one meets it with a writer's full and unspent force. One flings mountains of figures and interpretations at it, yet it could be captured with a paltry and practical word; only strenuous efforts make it wild and huge. A writer doesn't have the aptness and smallness of the commonplace institutions which other people's lives consist of. He is too far gone in the vastness, in the swelling of breath and stories. He doesn't want the tried-and-tested magic that works. He wants to increase the danger himself until there is no way of stopping it; and then tries remedy after remedy, desperately and futilely.

This need to be *good* when one feels guilty; a passionately strong need when one is alone in knowing one's guilt, when nobody one could submit it to could recognize it; when others regard one as good at a point where one is least good, that diabolically tormenting need to *really* be good, as though every life, every single life, depended on you alone, on nobody else, even the lives of people you don't know, through the lives of people you do know; as though you had killed and failed, failed and killed, and as though, after more than half a lifetime, one could still become really good.

If you were alone, you'd cut yourself in two, so that one part would shape the other.

I want to know more about men than anyone, even writers, have known up till now. I therefore have to get deep into my own few people, as though I had to *make* them very accurately myself, as though they weren't alive without me, my word being their breath, my love their hearts, my mind their thoughts.

The mystery of these bonds, which I can never fully exhaust, *justifies* me.

His head is made of stars, but not yet arranged into constellations.

Since he never prays, he has to *say* something about the gods every day, even if it's only a joke. The believing man, in this disrupted time, can find no faith anywhere, and so he borrows the dried-out names of the ancient gods.

One has to seek one's ethics in an endangered life, and one should not shrink from any consequence so long as it's the right one. One can reach a conclusion and decision that sound fearful in the usual language of others and yet are the only correct ones. It makes no sense living by the lives and experiences of others, whom one did not know, who lived in a different age, under different circumstances, in totally different relationships. One has to have a rich and receptive consciousness to attain one's own ethics. One has to have grand goals and be able to stick to them. One has to believe that one loves people very much and will always love them; otherwise these private ethics will turn against others and will be nothing but a pretext for one's own naked interest.

It is simply good to hate oneself occasionally, not too often; otherwise one needs a great deal of hatred towards others to balance one's self-hatred.

Dislike of a person can reach proportions that make one feel good; but then you really have to watch out for him.

Savor powerlessness, after power, in every phase that matches it precisely; replace every old triumph with the new defeat; strengthen yourself on your weakness; win yourself back when so very lost.

Glee at one's own defeat, as though one were two.

Beauty is given the power to multiply itself; thus even it dies.

You can experience so much with the same few people that you come to recognize neither them nor yourself and only dimly recall that it's you, it's they.

Usefulness would not be so dangerous if it were not so reliably useful. It ought to stop very often. It ought to be unpredictable like something living. It ought to turn against you frequently and vehemently. With usefulness, men have called themselves gods, although they must die. The power over usefulness deceives them about this ludicrous foible of theirs. Thus, in their self-conceit, they grow weaker and weaker. Usefulness multiplies, but men die like flies. If only usefulness were more seldom useful; if there were no possibility of precisely calculating when it would definitely be useful and when definitely not; if it had jumps, moods, whims—then no one would have become its slave. People would have thought more, prepared themselves for more, expected more. The lines from death to death would not be erased, we would not be its *blind* prey. It could not mock us in the midst of our security, like animals. Thus usefulness and our faith in it have left us as animals; there are more and more of them, and we are merely all the more helpless.

One can be lonely only if one has people waiting at some distance. Absolute loneliness doesn't exist. There is only that cruel loneliness in regard to the people waiting.

Literature as a profession is destructive; one should *fear* words more.

Leonardo's aims were so manifold that he remained free of them. He could undertake anything because nothing took anything from him.

His contemplation was not split off from his vision. Natural forms could be important to him because they did not yet have their full liveliness. He took nothing over; or if he did, it thereby became new to him. Most conspicuous about him is his intellectuality: he pointed the way to our destruction. Our scattered strivings were all together in him; but are no less scattered for it. His faith in nature is cold and terrible; it is a faith in a new kind of dominion. He certainly sees the consequences for others, but does not fear anything himself. It is precisely this lack of fear that has passed into all of us; technology is its product. The adjacency of machine and organism in Leonardo is the eeriest fact in intellectual history. Machines are usually just drawings, his games, his tamed whim. The anatomy of the human body—his addiction, his chief passion—allows him his lesser machine-games. The discovery of purpose in this or that faculty of the body whets his appetite for a purposeful apparatus of his own inventing. Knowledge still has that peculiarly fermenting character, it won't allow anymore to calmly transcend it, and it shrinks from any system. His restlessness is that of a contemplation that does not wish merely to see what it believes; it is the *fearless* contemplation, an always ready fearlessness and an always ready gaze. The process in Leonardo's mind is opposed to the process that the mystical religions aspire to. They want to reach fearlessness and restfulness through contemplation. Leonardo, however, uses his peculiar fearlessness to achieve a contemplation that signifies, for him, in regard to every individual object, the goal and the end of his strivings.

To see all the conceptual hairsplittings and systems of philosophers come true, that nothing is forced together gratuitously, nothing is thought gratuitously—the world as a torture-chamber of thinkers.

Recognition is the sole relaxation of the mind. Faith in transmigration provides as many points of recognition as possible, and no matter how humbling many of them may be, they are even more reassuring.

What an astonishing hierarchy among animals! Man sees them according to how he stole their qualities.

The forms of human faith are composed of circles or directed straight lines. Progress, say the cold, the bold, and wish to have everything like arrows (they escape death by murdering); recurrence, say the tender, the persevering, and burden themselves with guilt (they make death tedious through repetition). Then, in the spiral, people try to fuse the two into one, thereby taking over both attitudes towards death: the murderous and the repetitive. So death stands many times more powerful than ever before, and if anyone opposes death as the one-time thing it really is—that man is bombarded with arrows, circles, and spirals.

Only the dead have lost one another completely.

My hatred of death implies an incessant awareness of it; I'm amazed I can live like that.

It is said that death comes to many as a deliverance, and there can scarcely be anyone who has not wished for it at times. It is the ultimate symbol of failure: the man who fails on a grand scale comforts himself with the thought that there can be further failure, and he reaches for that huge dark cloak that covers everything evenly. Yet if death didn't exist, no man could ever fail at anything; every new effort would make up for weaknesses, inadequacies, and sins. Unlimited time would inspire unlimited courage. From the very start, we are all taught that everything comes to an end, at least here, in this known world. Boundaries and closeness everywhere, and soon a final, obnoxiously ugly narrowness, which we cannot expand ourselves. Everyone gazes into this narrowness; whatever may come beyond it, the narrowness is regarded as inevitable; everyone has to bow to it, whatever their plans or merits. A soul may be as vast as it likes; it will be squeezed together until it suffocates, at some point that it does not itself choose. Who fixes it depends on whatever opinion happens to be prevailing and not on the individual soul itself. The slavery of death is the core of all slavery, and if this slavery were not recognized, no one could wish for it.

If a man is very personal, then the impersonal becomes his greatest attraction, as though, because so much else exists, he had gathered up the world but left himself out.

The beauty of the figures on Greek vases also comes from their spanning and holding together an empty and mysterious space. The darkness inside makes their circle brighter outside. They are like hours for time, but rich and various and articulated. While contemplating them, one can never forget the hollowness that they frame. Each vase is a temple with an undisturbed and uniform holy of holies, which is never spoken about, although contained in the very name and form. The figures are loveliest when representing a dance.

The reverse Zeus: changing into a dozen different shapes in order to *prevent* a woman from loving.

If only the hell of feelings at least had some order; if penalties and places were at least fixed, if something represented something, if something stood on something; but in the hell of feelings everything is indefinite, it has no boundaries, its paths are illusory, everything is incessantly changing, in every dimension, and yet there is no chaos; it is a hell, full of shapes, in which there are new arrivals daily, from which no one is ever released.

How preposterous is the route from the many gods to the one God. They don't get along with one another; instead of trying again, as human beings do, they give up and reduce themselves to *one;* he then gets along with himself.

My thoughts keep turning to faith. I sense that this is everything and that I know very little about it. It is belief itself, and not a special contents, that occupies my mind. But when I vehemently feel I cannot get any closer to this, the great central enigma of my life, and to its solution, I reach for some particular faith and toy with it, and I cannot say how happy and secure I become and how greatly I trust in a future solution to my enigma.

The true Don Quixote, an unsurpassable fool, would be one to wage the struggle against a woman's desire with words, with *sheer* words. She feels this desire for others. The fool, who once loved her and who cannot face the way she is now, decides to fight with words. He is too proud to seize her at the one point she really can be seized at, and to offer her greater pleasure. What he wants to give her flows into the words he finds for her. She soon learns how to swim in his ocean, where she likes to be, she is a creature of his element; but nothing can dissuade her from pursuing her experiences in seaside caverns. He lures her out again, she keeps swimming to shore and then back to him. He enlarges the ocean, she devises islands. He floods the islands, she learns how to dive and sets up her love-bed on the ocean bottom. His passion changing him into a Poseidon, he shakes the ocean and destroys her bed. She finds fish in which she can make love and talks her lovers into being swallowed up with her. So the fool makes up his mind to dry out the sea of words. He makes no ocean, he keeps silent, the waters flow away, the woman thirsts, the last lover vanishes, the woman dies of thirst alone.

Without words, he could have accomplished everything.

To figure out what animals might find praiseworthy about you.

There is nothing uglier than instincts. The affable veneration with which people look at one another's drives, tenderly cultivate them and so deeply admire them—it all reminds me of the loyalty in a club of criminals. What most people like to do most of the time seems human, and the few others who are sometimes different appear inhuman. One fears or despises those who want to be better, for how could their behavior come from anything but a defect? Those, however, who always have their mouths greedily open or full are the good ones. Oh how disgusted one is by this recognized uniformity of the drives! They are the reason and they are the goal, nothing can prevail against them, for they are strength too. Wasn't it better when people were ashamed of them? When people were hypocritical rather than boastful about their baseness? Today the instincts are acknowledged as gods; anyone trying to resist them is committing blasphemy; anyone calling them by name has accomplished something; anyone wanting more than them is a fool. I'd rather be a fool.

I shall always own a few people only, so that I can never get over losing them.

I would never really have gotten to know power if I hadn't practiced it and if I hadn't become the victim of this my own practice of it. Hence, power is thrice familiar to me: I have observed it, I have practiced it, I have suffered it.

Only now, in bizarre accounts and abstruse books, are the gods interpenetrating, the gods of peoples that never knew one another.

Perhaps anything could be bearable in solitude. But one speaks of it and others hear you. If they don't hear, then you speak louder. If they still don't hear, you shout. It is then more of a furious aloneness than lonesomeness.

Pictures as the positives of the *windows* among which we go about and live. A walk through the streets and you've passed perhaps a thousand windows. There was something to expect in each of them, you saw nothing in scarcely any of them. In distinct outlines, they slice out a piece of expectation and you carry it further unfulfilled. But in art galleries they are suddenly there, the contents of all windows, the outlooks and insights; and it is odd how genuine, how correct, how accurate the views appear in rooms you'd certainly have seen, as tiles, tables, chairs, and as people sitting there in quiet performance.

The satiated person. He sates himself before he even gets hungry. He's afraid of his hunger. He's been told stories about hungry people, stories that filled him with profound horror. When he walks past ragged, emaciated people, he is so afraid that he instantly goes to eat in the nearest, most expensive restaurant, and there he calms down his trembling innards. He is a very sympathetic person and in every hungering man he sees himself. He is more sympathetic than most people, which is why he cannot endure seeing a hungry person. Generally, he avoids these wretched souls, but there are times he is so sated as to be disoriented, and then he has to find a hungry man somewhere. The thought that such people stand there with empty bowels disgusts him. He cannot comprehend how there can be hungry people. A conversation in which someone tries to enlighten him as to the reasons for the existence of the hungry will end with a large meal. But he has his own arguments. Why, he asks, don't the hungry steal? Why don't they sell themselves? Why don't they use bad checks? Why don't they kill? He would do anything rather than feel hunger, much less go hungry for even one day. He justifies his endless meals by saying he couldn't be responsible for himself in case of hunger.

He finds lovers ridiculous. He makes fun of them for sharing their very last things with another. "The very last" is his most horrible thought. When he hears someone say "the last piece of bread," he has to weep. In his dreams, he sees people eating in and out of windows. He knows houses by their kitchens. When he passes through streets, he can sense where the kitchen lies in every building, and woe unto the houses that mislead him. People like to invite him over because his way of eating is unforgettable. He wants to get through life without ever having felt hunger; he subordinates everything to this lofty goal. If he had no money, the accomplishment of this life would be admirable, but he must have a great deal of money. Once, he invites a hungry man to a meal and explains why he must never go hungry again. He succeeds in tracing all the evils of the world back to hunger. He considers himself a decent and model human being. Tables should never be eaten clean. While vanishing, the food has to be replaced, he makes sure that everything is always there in splendid abundance. He needs the hungry, but he hates lovers. He would respect them if they used their love to roast one another. But when could that happen?

The satiated person has a family that inspires him to eat and to delimit the food. Each member divides off what belongs to him, and small pots and jars stand around on the table like toiletries, next to the general courses, as separate condiments. The personnel changes according to the food. When certain servants appear, in a certain livery, he knows what's being served today and he can slowly, not overhastily, look forward to it. The satiated person sometimes goes shopping. Stores are his brothels, he takes a long time choosing, the bigger the store the less he purchases. He would love to have a huge special store for every meal component he shops for, a store with many floors and countless people inside. He talks a lot while making his selections, but he prefers having people talk to him. He likes being convinced of splendid things, he wants to be treated with exquisite friendliness, care, and love, and here it is easy to steal into his heart. His minions put special morsels aside for him. The satiated person is neither a man nor a woman. According to whim and need, he uses the qualities of either sex. He kisses food in various ways, he inhales fragrances. "Give me this chair or that," he says, according to the food he hankers for. There are meals for which he goes to bed, others that he consumes walking up and down. In some restaurants, he stands at the window and, while eating, gazes at the passersby as though they were walking through his eyes into his stomach. He has a sense of the various estates and nations among men, special foods have developed within them, nothing authentic in this area eludes him, but he prefers the embassies of towns and peoples and doesn't much care for traveling himself. Ever since boyhood, he's had a warm spot in his heart for monasteries since monks are said to be gluttons. In wartime, he breaks up into several people and knows how to obtain their rations. He likes to invite guests who bring something. But he also likes to be a guest himself. He wants to keep meeting new people, for the sake of their kitchens. Smells are his kingdom of heaven. He falls in love with a skinny person who eats no less than he and yet never gets fat. Anything he doesn't eat haunts him: he never takes his eyes off little children. When they scream, he sees them on a spit, and he hates their mothers for watching over them.

Human outlines are different for the satiated person. A gorged python fills him with envy. He regrets that his tissue cannot yield any further, that he cannot devour ten times his weight, that his shape pretty much remains the same, that he only gains weight slowly, through weeks and months, instead of in an hour, that he has to yield a good part of what he has so quickly ingested instead of nurturing it for weeks. He likes to sit among people who are eating. He then dreams of how to take the best morsels from their lips and talk them into not doing the same thing to him. He keeps dogs because of their teeth and can never get his fill of watching them crunch up bones and suck everything out. He wants to know what's eaten in the beyond, and he adjusts his faith accordingly. The reports on this are not very promising, and so his interest in the beyond is minor. Nor does he care much for the pills of the future, he considers himself lucky to be living today. He is asked whether he isn't troubled by the hunger of so many millions after the last war. He reflects and then says honestly: "No." For the more people there are hungering, the more he feels his life is correct. He despises those people who have failed to keep eating no matter what.

People love as self-recognition what they hate as an accusation.

The brevity of life makes us bad. We would have to test whether a possible longness of life wouldn't also make us bad.

One would have to find the system of one's contradictions by being calm. If one *saw* the bars, one would have gained the sky between them.

Dreadful persistence, holding fast to people, things, memories, habits, old aims, an awful burden, with new ones added constantly, viper of heaviness, malice of ownership, frenzy of loyalty, less of that, oh, less of that, and we would be light, and we would be good. But we won't let go, we will never let anything go, finger by finger has to be loosened, tooth by tooth removed from the intractability we would rather love forever.

Each man ought to attain his fundamental asceticism: mine would be silence.

The cure of the jealous man. Of all the difficult undertakings in this world, nothing is so difficult as curing a jealous man. Unless you carefully reflect on what jealousy is, you will scarcely be able to cure it. It is a confinement of thoughts and air, as though one had to live in a small room from which there is no escaping. Now and then, a window is opened, she, the object of the jealousy, quickly peeks in, disappears, and closes it again. While she goes about freely and at will, the man himself is locked in and can never go anywhere. Jealousy arises because one can't go anywhere. The roads one should have taken, together with her, have not been taken. Thus there are many unprotected roads, they weren't taken, they are free, anyone can take any liberty there. Someone addicted to the many roads seems absolutely born to arouse jealousy. How would it be possible to be present everywhere, at every mood, every step, one would have to become a satellite, a dog really; dogs do it best, they want nothing but to be always there on their master's roads. A man, however, can't very well be a woman's dog. If he makes even the slightest move in that direction, he will no longer be himself, and the slightest move can't help him at all.

Now there are poor wretches who like to remain at home, amid books or music; for these unfortunates, who spin themselves into a quiet existence, no woman is suitable. For if they keep a woman, then so much for the quiet; and if they keep her away, they soon won't know what she's doing. The men who seclude themselves are forced to seclude their women even more than themselves. The woman secluded far away has a long road, and sooner or later the road comes alive. The air has its temptations and forms into manly words. For every time the man turns down an invitation to share a road, another road will come later with another man, and as tired as she may get of these new roads, they are nevertheless the beginning of a different life, that no one can hem in. The place where one secludes oneself must remain a secret from the woman one wants to protect oneself against. For if one lets her come there, she will bring her waverings along, and the place will be done for. But if one never lets her come there, she will be unable to picture the place and will look for other places instead. The victim of jealousy has a much harder time of it in the modern age. He can telephone and establish the guilt of the absent woman at any moment, so that no doubts remain; he cannot even cherish the hope of being mistaken. His misfortune is always obvious, there is no hedging, there is no solace.

Does it help the jealous man to love many women, to dole out his love? No, it doesn't help, for his love, if it *is* love, will always be great. Either the people he "loves" do not matter to him, that is, they do not really exist for him, and then it doesn't matter to him what they do. Or else he loves, that is, he totally absorbs the people; there can be as many of them as he likes, each is a whole person, and each, in his precinct, can grieve the lover mortally. The doling out is useful only if it altogether banishes the seriousness of one's feeling. It's not worth living for that. Better alone, all by oneself, hotly venerating a god beyond any ken. The many are simply multiple grounds for jealousy.

But might it help to love in a different way? Without the decision over death and life, without the responsibility, without the fear for the other person's life, which is in constant jeopardy. Jealousy is worst in the heart of the responsible man, whose anxiety is always awake, and these are usually the men who stay secluded, anxiety doesn't always leave them on the road. If it weren't for death, jealousy would be bearable. For a man would know that the disappearing person is somewhere, and perhaps he'll run into that person again, perhaps that person will come running back. Death, however, can have a different aim. The creature one loves may perish once he or she is out of sight, and when he or she is dead, who will bring it back? One couldn't watch over death; could one have prevented death? What love is so brief as not to think of death, what love is so weak as not to try and subdue death?

Without death, there might be a way to cure the jealous man, but it's pointless to talk about it. There must be a way to be found in this bounded life.

Sticking to conventional people only makes them slyer and petty and mean. They learn to get around you, to scorn big words, which are only big, after all, because one uses them for all people and not for individuals. The conventional people are so sure of their place that it bores them. So they simply go away and leave behind scarecrows of themselves, which have just enough life to guard you and keep you. The man who really loves (the conventional know this soon enough), will dote on even the semblance of the beloved forms. The wind can feign motion and sounds for him, and he will regret, rather than see through, the rags in which the scarecrow is dressed.

It is not the lovely face one loves, it is the face one has destroyed.

The eeriest thing about distrust is its justification. In real life, there is a justification for distrust, which is dreadful and basically makes up three quarters of normal worldly wisdom. One needs only think of the institution of money. How greatly one relies on money and with what fanatic distrust one must protect it! How deeply one takes for granted that everyone else wants to take it away. How one hides, how one distributes it to make it more secure. Money alone is a lasting and ineradicable training for distrust. Older forms of distrust are more conspicuous, and, when speaking of distrust, one thinks only of them. But everyone has to deal with money; whether there's much of it, or little, everyone holds on tight to it, everyone husbands it, everyone keeps it a secret. One can't buy anything without knowing the price, and how densely and doggedly people cling to prices. There would be no prices if there were no distrust; prices are quite simply its measure.

A worshiped being who always carries his little temples around with him.

The immortals ought to be able to grow old, otherwise they can never be truly happy. Everyone should be allowed to abide in the age that suits him.

People's fates are simplified by their names.

At times, when one is drained by a sense of one's badness, one's bad attitude, one's bad effect, one then tells oneself that there is nothing left to justify oneself, and without knowing of any god to justify oneself to, one feels damned; more damned than if one had this god; for his sentence would consist of words; one's own sentence, however, has no form, it is nothing but a soft rain of despair, there will be no end to its drops.

The blows are no longer so serious, one is familiar with them, there is nothing astonishing about them, they are merely a frequently interrupted rule. One may cringe when they come, out of habit, but one doesn't properly fear them. Is this, then, the age and end of man: that he no longer takes his suffering seriously?

I like reading everything pertaining to imperial Rome. That Rome was like a modern city, we know a lot about it, it is not all that remote. Familiarity with a name that is still valid today and once again alive today animates the feeling of that earlier age. Of course, I'm irritated by the costume they wore back then; I don't like thinking about it, it is the only thing that sometimes alienates me again. On the other hand, their words and relationships, their actions and games, seem to me like a literary creation that was meant to explain us to ourselves and imbue us with hope. The religious circumstances have something of our modern freedom; the party structure, which we might be ashamed of, is far more mechanical there and hence informative. The nations lying outside are not yet too close together; there is something like elbow-room there, which we really don't have anymore. One knows at every instant of dealing with the Roman Empire that it ultimately perished; but Rome still exists. So we comfort ourselves on the far more serious dangers of destruction threatening us today, as though this destruction too might just be temporary, as though we too were merely facing barbaric enemies that want to plunder whole, perspicuous objects, as though we weren't confronted with the disintegration of every tiny bit of matter that every last one of us consists of.

To live as if our time were unlimited. Appointments with people for a hundred years hence.

1947

Any page of a philosophy, no matter where we open it, puts us at *ease:* the dense coherence of a net, that was so obviously woven outside of reality, the disregard of the moment, that grand scorn for the world of feelings, which keeps ebbing and flowing even in the philosopher, that security of semblance which sees through itself in counterglow, *gegenschein,* and yet will not cease, that incessant intertwining with all previous ideas, so that one reaches out and senses: this kind of mat, this very kind, has been woven for thousands of years now, and only the patterns change; what handicraft has survived this well, what pottery was ever practiced uninterruptedly in the very same way? Whatever philosophy one deals with, whether because one knows it better or because one doesn't know it at all, it is basically always the same: an emphasis on just a few selected words, saturated with the juices of all others, and their meandering continuation.

A decree making *misers* pay double for everything.

Avarice is regarded as a moral disease, those suffering from it are publicly declared to be misers and have to wear a special mark. Instead of by origin, people are distinguished by their social qualities. The mark of avarice can never be removed. Misers wear it in the street; they grow accustomed to it; what they do not grow accustomed to is their treatment in shops. They have to enter in such a way that the proprietor cannot possibly doubt their avarice. They have to watch as customers standing next to them pay only half the price for the same articles. They cannot grumble; otherwise, by law, they have to pay extra. These severe measures against avarice have the strangest effects. Some misers try hard to become spendthrifts and, above all, to prove it. Their efforts have an athletic character: when they throw away their money, they look as if they were hoisting heavy iron dumbbells to hurl at other people's heads. Some are so despondent over the higher prices that their avarice seems more and more justified to them, and they buy less and less from day to day. They soon run about like wretched shadows; they replace the poor, but such paupers are loathed with good reason.

A religion in which the sinner has to fix his penitence himself, otherwise it's ineffective.

The tantrum of a thief who is *given* everything.

Myths signify more to me than words, and that's the greatest difference between Joyce and myself. But I also have a different kind of respect for words. Their integrity is almost sacrosanct for me. I am reluctant to cut them up, and even their oldest forms, those that were really employed, command my awe, I don't like to take them into disastrous adventures. Their is something eery *in* words, and I do not want to tear out this heart of theirs like a Mexican sacrificial priest; such bloody ways are hateful to me. The eeriness should only be depicted in characters, be presented in terms of them, never in terms of words as such. There is something deceptive in words alone, without the lips that uttered them. As a writer, I am still living in the age before writing, in the age of *shouts*.

We look better to ourselves in foreign languages; that's why we quickly, and immediately, learn their curse words.

When he hasn't read for a long time, the holes get bigger in the sieve of his mind, and everything goes through and nothing, except for the grossest things, seems to exist there. What he has read serves to catch his experiences; and without reading, he doesn't experience.

I like any scornful statement I find about the general character of writers; for instance, recently, in Pascal: "Poète et non honnête homme." I fully realize how onesided and unfair this judgment is, even in Plato, but something inside me says: "Yes, yes, dammit, a poet." It's probably the writer's vanity, his thirst for fame, his conceitedness that make me uncomfortable; whereas I certainly don't reject his vast possibilities of metamorphosis. A good number of living writers that I have met were people I didn't like for some reason or other; but perhaps it was because one might prefer being the only one. Yet what I read about earlier poets almost never displeases me; it can be any of myriad things, but it always moves me; even Baudelaire, whose life style was hardly attractive, has been dear to me ever since I learned *more* about him. Even the poet's unsureness and tentativeness towards anything concrete has something that captivates me. The thing that takes me by storm, however, is the richness of their illusions about everything that happens to them. Usually, in order to think all sorts of things, they imagine the wrong thing about what concerns them. What is so lovely, so captivating about that? The wealth of illusions or their failure? I can't decide. But I know that in "normal," in ordinary people, who adjust to everyday life, the most disconcerting thing of all is the way everything fits in with everything else from hour to hour, the way everything is right for them in the short run. They climb into a tram and reach their destination. They are employed and actually get to the office. Something has a price and they know the price. They like a woman and they marry her. They have certain streets, but only to get somewhere; not like people like us, who prefer only streets leading us nowhere. If the poets merely always got lost, you couldn't say anything against them. But the fact that they turn this into something distinctly admirable makes their getting lost not as serious as it ought to be. Poets who die young are not sufficiently experienced in spreading their tails; hence, what we know about them remains lovable. The others, who rise to a bird's-eye view of themselves become more and more repulsive and despicable from year to year. One would like to knock the handicraft, which makes them so conceited, out of their heads, and the superfluous years out of their lives.

Each man is meant to be the keeper of several lives, and woe unto him if he fails to find the lives he has to keep. Woe unto him if he does a bad job of keeping those he finds.

Oh night and two lights, four lights, eight, until each has gotten the other to think.

To feel death constantly without sharing one of the comforting religions. What a gamble, what a dreadful gamble!

Even if not having to die were physiologically possible today, it could well be that no human being would have the moral strength to elude death—simply because there are so many dead people.

Freedom is every new face, so long as it cannot speak to you. Freedom is everyone before you who doesn't know you. Freedom is the populated space that does not yet contract, in which you do not suffocate. You are free as long as you do not enter other people's reckonings. You are free wherever you are not loved. The chief vehicle of unfreedom is your name. Whoever doesn't know your name, has no power over you. But many people will know it, more and more; to remain free against their united power is the almost unattainable goal of your life.

To become better? Even if you succeeded, you would not be better in a different situation, hence you would not have become better, merely cunning.

God, if God existed, would be the being without fear; acting without fear, resting without fear; creating and commanding without fear; punishing and rewarding without fear; promising without fear; forgetting without fear. That would be God, that would be an immense, a powerful God. The others, the alleged gods, writhe and collapse in fear. What do they have over us?

God's yearning for the world as it was before he created it.

Death has his own way of sneaking into his enemies, undermining their will to fight, demoralizing them; he keeps offering himself as a radical solution, he reminds us that there is not a single real solution outside of him. The man who lives with the rigid stare of hatred upon him grows accustomed to him as the sole zero point. But the way that zero grows! The way one suddenly trusts it because one cannot trust anything else! The way one thinks to oneself: that is left when nothing else is left. He topples whatever stands near you, and once you're almost ready to give up in pain, he says with a smile: You are not as powerless as you may think, you can throw yourself, and your suffering, over. He causes the suffering from which *he* then can save you. What torture judge has ever understood his office better?

When I read about sacred things, their memory takes hold of me only because they were sacred, and so long as they breathe within me I remain calm. Oh, the peace they must have had when they were unchallenged, whole golden apples, deeply fragrant and round. I seek after all holinesses, and they break my heart for being past. I find nothing for later, I have called death naked, woe unto the man who has summoned him naked. The sacred things were his garments; so long as he was garbed, even men, those eternal murderers, lived unruffled, and nothing would have happened to them if they had not torn off his garments, those plunderers, those brigands—wasn't murdering enough for them!? I myself was one of the worst. I wanted to be bold, so I said: "Death, death, and nothing else." What is boldness, and how much more was caution. But we have become powerful, so we have dragged him forth, we have pulled death out of all hiding-places, there is no hiding-place we do not know now. We scorn hell, but didn't it at least come *after* death. What suffering would not be better than nothing. Boldness, oh stupid boldness, we have fallen into the shears of your vanity, nothing, nothing has remained unshorn, and no dying man knows where he is going.

A God who keeps his Creation a *secret*. "And lo, it was not good."

Most of all I dislike ideas if they turn out to be correct too soon. What's the use of saying something if it turns out to be right within two years?

The words you fail to find with some people come to you later, after leaving them. These words derive from the daze caused by a person's presence. Without this daze, those words would never come; but one feature of them is that they cannot be here at once. I believe it is these vehement but delayed words that make up the poet.

The shrieks ought to be over; but I still hear the silence of the executed.

To depict a man in whom everything instantly *passes*, every impression, every experience, every situation. A man in whom nothing persists. Today and yesterday and tomorrow are not connected for him in any way. Everything has happened to him, nothing has happened to him. His freshness. His mortality driven to such an extreme that it too is meaningless. He knows everyone and can't remember anyone. He lives in a world without names. He is unafraid, but no one is afraid of him. His age and sex are unclear. He has neither goals nor plans, one never has the feeling he is reaching for one. He can't become obnoxious. He lacks any religion. The instants he consists of are incalculable. Anyone looking for him will always find him somewhere else.

I hate people who build fast systems, and I will see to it that mine never fully closes.

All the places that words have been to! In what mouths! On what tongues! Who can, who may know them all, after these wanderings through hell, after these dreadful abysses. Words have a twofold existence: each word is trapped and squeezed together inside us; but we are squeezed together inside each word. The many words, and each one double: tortured and torturing, a victim and victimizer, dense and hollow.

To think that no one has yet heard the true words, the words for whose sake people hear at all, that all people hear and hear and wait for these real words. Until someone finally hears them, his ears will change into wings, and so will the ears of others.

The astonishing thing about distrust is the distrust of the completed event, of the *fact*. One can distrust the ill will of a person close to one, his betrayal, his two facedness, his trickery, for a long time without evidence. One can then suddenly hear the dreaded things from his own lips, as a confession in a dream, for instance, so that not even the shadow of a doubt is possible. The lover may drop the pet name of the lover she is deceiving you with. But the moment it is certain, it no longer seems true. As long as you lacked proof, you had to believe it. As soon as you had proof, you couldn't believe it. It is as though faith were only there to make something true, as though the thing made true were no longer of interest; as though you released the air in your fist as soon as this air hardened into stone.

A man who is immortal by the millimeter.

Fear has something that wants to hear, no matter what, hear desperately. Everything to be heard is all right then, the good, the bad, things avoided, things feared. When fear is greatest, one would accept a command to murder simply in order to hear.

When there was war, we had to hold our tongues; shame and despair seemed legitimate. The war is over and now we know the full measure of our own impotence, which, back then, we ascribed to violence and isolation.

If one knows a lot of people, it seems almost blasphemous to invent more.

The soothing aspect of Antiquity: its not being a *threat* to modern man. Its threats have long since recollected themselves; they cut off nobody's breath. We are an instrument on which Antiquity can keep playing; it knows us and plays us properly. We have been thought up by Antiquity, unstrenuously, one of its many flukes. It despises us and is no longer domineering.

The days of the year as a pack of cards. One can pull out one or the other, keep it, play it, and then reshuffle. No day is the cause of a coming day; they begin arbitrarily next to one another, each time differently. They repeat themselves, but one recognizes them in a different sequence each time. How much more intelligently one would treat one's days if they were repeatable; if one would understand them, how close one would get to them, validly, in their constantly changing forms. Now, however, with our custom of progressing and unrepeatable days, one remains their sad dilettante.

Kafka truly lacks any writer's vanity, he never boasts, he cannot boast. He sees himself as small and proceeds in small paces. Wherever he sets his foot, he senses the uncertainty of the ground. It does not carry anyone, when you are with him then nothing carries you. Thus he forgoes the illusion and delusion of poets. Their brilliance, which he certainly felt, is lost for his own words. One has to walk the small paces with him and one becomes modest. There is nothing in modern literature that makes one this modest. He reduces the swelled head of every life. One turns good when reading him, but without being proud of it. Sermons make the moved listeners proud, Kafka forgoes sermons. He does not transmit his father's commandments; a strange obduracy, his greatest gift, permits him to interrupt the chain of commandments handed down from fathers to sons. He eludes their violence; their external energy, its animal quality, wafts away. He deals all the more with their content. The commandments become qualms for him. Of all writers, he is the only one never to be infected by power; he never exercises any kind of power whatsoever. He has stripped God of the final vestiges of fatherliness. What remains is a dense and indestructible net of qualms concerning life rather than the demands of his begetter. The other poets imitate God and act like Creators. Kafka, who never wants to be a god, is never a child either. What some people see as terrifying in him and what disturbs me too is his constant adulthood. He thinks without commanding, but also without playing.

God is supposedly not a Creator: supposedly he is, above all, an enormous resistance, protecting the world against us; slowly he yields; we human beings grow more powerful; until we have become so powerful as to destroy the world, and ourselves, and him.

Lecture by a blind man. A blind pianist, married to a singer, and whom I've known for a long time, gave a lecture on blindness yesterday. He emphasized how satisfied he is with his condition. All people are friendly to him and his wife; that's the reason for the confidence and good cheer of blind people. He spoke with a propriety and modesty that seemed familiar; it occurred to me that his were the general characteristics of the Englishman. He never looked to the right, he never looked to the left, he never looked around or forward—if one could say that about him; however, he saw his definite goals as well and as surely as a seeing Englishman. He wasn't curious, he wasn't arrogant; he wasn't the least bit thrown by his wife's later crisscross talk. His acknowledgement of the rest of the world, to which he had to adjust— the world of the seeing—was as practical and natural as the acknowledgement of the world around him is for any normal Englishman. He incessantly performed proud small bows to the others and apologized for almost nonexistent offenses. He stressed the pleasure of his independence, he was as free as anyone else; he earned his living honestly and by himself.

I would like to describe him and his lecture very accurately. But what I want to depict now are a few strange features in the life of the blind, features that were new to me. For him, a strong wind is what fog is for other people. It makes him feel totally disoriented and lost. Loud noises pour in on him from all sides, streaming into one, and he simply doesn't know where he is. For while walking he always relies on a sure sense of the nearness of objects. He senses the nearness of a wall or a table. He always halts right in front of it and never bumps into it. This faculty must somehow be auditive, for it always ceases when he has a cold and his ear is out of commission.

He does have *one* pleasure over people who can see. He can listen to several conversations at once and pluck out whatever he enjoys. The seeing, who rest their eyes on the people they talk to are, he said, therefore unable to eavesdrop on other conversations next to or behind them.

He can tell a person's mood and character by his voice. They had already done this as a game at the school for the blind; they would judge people on the spot solely by their voice and the way they talked, and whatever they managed to find out later always fitted in with their first judgment. Blind women, he said, have a harder time than blind men. A man who can see is seldom willing to marry a blind woman, it's too much trouble.

It's difficult for blind people to have *gestures*. He had once performed in a play, and they had to teach him every single movement artificially. It was incredible how awkwardly he acted. But here too he saw an advantage for blind people. They save energy that other people squander on useless gestures.

The deaf are far worse off than the blind. They are, so to speak, blind in all directions. Towards the back, the side, and the front. The blind man, however, is blind in only one direction, since he can hear anywhere.

He cannot imagine colors at all; but he is deeply interested in everything concerning the fine arts and likes to hear about them. His inner vision is neither dark nor light, something peculiar in between, which he cannot really describe.

If no one could see, then the blind too would be lost. But since everyone would be blind, all would be lost. One wonders how long people, if an accident struck them all blind, could get along with the memories of the seeing time. A hoard of old experiences would have to be carefully guarded and handed on. It would gradually assume the character of a religious revelation; just as the followers of a faith tell about the miracles experienced by its earliest founders. One could imagine that the memory of people who could see and the things they saw would hold the blind together for many centuries. It would be strange if suddenly a single one of them could see again and told all the others about the truth of their old faith.

The cardinal question of all ethics: Should we tell people how bad they are? Or should we let them be bad in their innocence? To answer this question, one would first have to decide whether the knowledge of their badness would give people the possibility of becoming better, or whether this very knowledge would make their badness ineradicable. It could very well be that badness had to remain bad once it is separated and designated as such; it could then conceal itself, but it would exist forever.

Three basic attitudes of a man when wooing: the boaster, the promiser, the mother-beggar.

The man who is accustomed to his own thinking can be saved from despair by only one thing: the communication that he deprives others of, that he registers only for himself and forgets, that he rediscovers later and only in amazement. For everything he consciously continues, about which he keeps thinking daily, consistently, increases his entanglement in the world, which afflicts him. He can remain free only by thinking to no avail. His contradictions have to save him, their diversity, their unfathomable absurdity. For the creative man becomes the victim of his precision; his poison is the continuation in which he entangles himself; even reading becomes his *own* continuation, as though the pages he turns were modeled within him. Only one thing can help him: the self-created chaos of his thoughts to the extent that they remain isolated, uncontinued, forgotten.

One needs friends mainly in order to become more impudent, that is, more oneself. One practices one's boastings in front of them, one's highhandedness, one's vanities; in front of them, one acts worse and better than one really is. One is not ashamed of any untruth: the friend who knows one, knows how true it could become. The general rules and customs one usually has to observe bore the friend, who in orderly moments of his life practices them as well as anyone. So long as he is with you, he will ignore them; the freedom he grants you is something you give back to him. He is quite satisfied; he too likes to be himself.

It is very odd to think that there are people among us who view human bodies in all details day by day, ugly, unclothed, deformed bodies, of every sex and age, and they never have enough of them: doctors. In between, they sit among us, with innocent faces and speak to us like other people, and we don't fear them, we greet them and amicably shake hands.

How much I would like to listen to myself as a stranger, without recognizing myself, and only find out later that it was I.

To see all the people we know as twins: each person has his twin aspect, each seeks himself as another; since he is different from everyone else, he seeks himself in a different way. For most people this search is a healthy thing. For those who are really twins, however, the search is confused: what they could be looking for already exists, as a false compulsion.

To invent a new music, in which the notes are in sharpest contrast to the words, thereby changing the words, rejuvenating them, filling them with a new content. To remove the danger from words, with music. To give words new dangers, with music. To make words hateful, make words popular, with music. To smash words, unite words, with music.

If man were better, he wouldn't need music. It is also the wickedness in people that makes them like music so much. What might they think of themselves if they didn't have music? A murderer would manage to comfort himself if he got to listen to the right music. During music, all values and judgments are different, erased, raised, refilled, fulfilled, whatever we think signifies less or more; above all, new connections are possible, and under such auspices they seem everlasting.

There is no great wish that we do not have to pay for. But its highest price is that it comes true.

One can want to know more and more; but there is a point at which this knowledge becomes unbearable and takes revenge for having found so many things already there.

To get to know countries as if no others existed; but to get to know many.

In order to live, one has to be aware of various injustices; some of them have to have been committed and concluded; others, still open, have yet to be committed. The amount of injustice resulting from both directions must not be too large or too small. A saint has to devise artificial sins. The man who can honestly tell himself: "I haven't done any evil," is lost. For evil exists and has its claim; and there are sound reasons why the faith in original sin has gained such prestige.

The disappointing thing about languages: they seem so obliging with their sounds and words and rules, and yet one can say just about the same thing, in a completely different way, in another language.

The only interesting thing about translating is what is lost; to find it, one ought, now and then, to translate.

The countless countries one longs for still exist, the shape and hardness of their mountains, the windings of their rivers, and the transparent cities, full of chatty people, who die at different times, not all at once, not all suddenly; one can still be confused by the supposed meanings of their words and the absurdity of their destinies; everything is still richer, gaudier, more varied than ever, right before it becomes all one and comes to an end.

It's best to be among people you'll never see again; you can stand them as long as you think they'll never do anything to you.

You can't keep living in a truly beautiful city: it drives out all your yearning.

There's nothing harder to control than learning, the passion for meaningless learning, as though one were the first man and had to store the knowledge of all coming people for them. One fails to get used to the thought that one is actually the last rather than the first man.

To undo something as though it had never happened, a single event, a single tiny incident, almost nothing: the story of a man who wants to undo such a nothing. His desperate efforts; just as others go after a specific goal in enigmatic concentration, something they have to gain or have, so too this man has a negative goal, to remove something from the sequence of his experiences and throw it aside.

But it has to be something nugatory, not a sin; for sins have definite atonements.

Old threats, like boiled fish—you can take out the bones.

When you've made a lot of words, you lose your sense of how much they mean to others. Thus begins the actual wickedness of the word-man.

Ever since I saw a human stomach, nine-tenths of a human stomach within less than two hours after it was cut out, I know even less why we eat. It looked just like the pieces of meat that people roast in their kitchens, it was even the size of an ordinary schnitzel. Why does this like come to like? Why the circuitous route? Why must meat incessantly go through the bowels of other meat? Why must this in particular be the condition of our life?

A town in which the people become as old as one loves them. Like and dislike balance each other exactly, and the result decides the length of a life.

Sometimes a man leaves his best on the street, like an old newspaper, and someone else comes along, notices it's a newspaper in a language he doesn't know, and he stomps on it angrily in order to make it dirtier.

There is a point at which one dare not experience anything else if all earlier things are to have a peaceful and unequivocal meaning. For those earlier things are changed by further events and influences; they aren't totally lost, but they change so greatly that their uniqueness is lost. Metamorphoses make use of what already exists; nothing is really changed back. The ability to recognize the stations at which only looking back and expressing are allowed may be considered the acme of the poetic art of life. In reality, one misses most of one's works because one is after more things. This hunger for an immensity in oneself, for a store of the living world, which store would remain in existence even if the world didn't—this hunger is wonderful and quite worthy of a human being, and yet, once aroused, it cannot be sated, and the man who is driven by it has no choice but to outwit it from time to time and lull it to sleep.

In the stillness, at night, when all the people he knows well are asleep, he becomes a better person.

The resurrected suddenly begin accusing God in all languages: the true Last Judgment.

One could wish for a world that is completely untouched; whose existence we never suspected; on which we had no influence; we as unknown to it as it to us: unapproached by any legend: nowhere expected; and yet comprehensible to us when it suddenly comes to our aid, giving us, the suffocating, giving us new souls together with the eyes to make that world visible for us.

There is nothing more dreadful than the sight of a dying enemy; I will never understand why all the enmity in the world hasn't ended for that very reason. One sees the dying man's face, but one doesn't see the place where one has hit him. Yet how one feels, how one feels the slightest pinprick one has ever given him, and how one feels that, but for the pinprick, he might perhaps have lived for three more full instants.

The deepest meaning of asceticism is that it engenders compassion. The eating man has less and less compassion, and finally none.
    A man who wouldn't have to eat and yet thrives, who behaves like a human being, intellectually and emotionally, although he never eats— that would be the highest moral experiment conceivable; and only its fortunate solution could make one seriously think of overcoming death.

The stupidest things are *complaints*. People are always grumbling about someone. Someone or other has been presumptuous. Someone or other has done us wrong. How dare they, what's the meaning of this, and that's one thing we won't put up with. This petty nonsense gyrates in your head, petty, for it concerns you yourself, and really only the least part of your person, the ever artificial border. These complaints fill up one's life as though they were words of wisdom. They take over like vermin, they multiply faster than lice. You go to sleep with them, you wake up with them; that's all that human "business life" consists of.

How is it possible that we put torn things in our mouths, tear them and tear up some more, and then have words coming from the same mouths? Wouldn't everything be better if we had a different aperture for food and used our mouths only for words? Or does this intimate blend of all sounds that we form, with lips, teeth, tongue, throat, the very parts of the mouth that serve eating—does this blend express the fact that language and food must forever be connected, that we can never become anything better or nobler than we are, that basically, in all disguises, we always say the same terrible and bloody things, and that we feel nausea only when there's something wrong with the food?

Then along came a man who proved that all experiments, from the very first, precisely because of the very first, were wrong; that later, they were right in themselves, in their sequence, and no one had noticed the mistake only because the first experiment had gone un-challenged. Thus the entire technological world was exposed as a fic-tion, and mankind could awaken from its worst nightmare.

A man lives in the belief that everything going through his mind is poisoned and must be avoided forever as of this moment. Reducing all existing things to the unknown is his only salvation. To protect the unknown against himself, he invents a method of *thinking nothing*. He succeeds in realizing it; the world around him blossoms again.

Each of your words turns into a swarm of mosquitoes in her; and you're surprised when they return to you as bites.

An exchange of habits: I'll give you this one, you give me that one; the result is supposed to be a marriage.

The moral kitsch of the Puritan: in his deepest and most contrite self-accusal, he still presents himself a hundred times better than he is.

How many habits does one need to move about in the unhabitual?

A country in which giant women run about with their tiny husbands in their pockets. When these women get into arguments, they sud-denly pull their husbands from their pockets and hold them towards one another like tiny scare-gods.

He imagines he has to change each sentence he ever spoke or wrote. It's not enough to change the sentences within reach; he has to find all the lost ones too; track them down, grab them, bring them back. He cannot relax until he has every last one. An infernal punishment for all who had a wrong faith.

The last of the month, I climb down into my ruins, a ridiculous lamp in my right hand, and I tell myself the deeper I go: it's no use. What faith can lead to the core of the earth? Whatever you, whatever another, whatever each of us does—it's no use. Oh, vanity of all strivings, the victims keep falling, by the thousands, the millions; this life, whose holiness you want to feign, is sacred to no one and nothing. No secret power wishes to maintain it. Perhaps no secret power wishes to destroy it, but it does destroy itself. How should a life that is constructed like a bowel have any value? Among plants, everything may have been better constructed—but what do you really know about the torment of suffocation?

Oh, nausea reaches out everywhere, and nausea comes from feeding. Everything is infected by food, everything is addicted to food. The peaceful day that some people experience is hypocritical. The torn-up things are more true. The peaceful ones envelop earth with the leaves and slowness of plants, but these nets are weak, and even where they are victorious, the fleshly destruction continues under their green covers. The powerful man swaggers about with his biggest stomach, and the vain man is iridescent in all the colors of his innards. Art plays a dance for the digesting and suffocating. It gets better and better, and its legacy is guarded as the most precious good. Some people delude themselves with the idea that things could come to an end, and they calculate catastrophes on top of catastrophes. But the deeper intention of this torment is an eternal one. The earth remains young, its life multiplies, and new, more complicated, more distinct, or more complete forms of wretchedness are devised. One man pleads with another: Help me, make it worse!

The people one relies on, and the people who rely on one: a comedy.

To think that there could be another life behind this one, and ours would be the relaxing one, in which those people rest up!

To find a comet for all the fear in the world and then send it, thus charged, into the wilderness of the universe, a scape-comet.

1948

The self-hater. A character who comes on with a furious speech against himself. There is no evil, no meanness that the self-hater does not charge himself with. He thereby arouses all people's unanimous love. Anyone hearing his speech runs after him, his thrall. But he merely keeps raging more and more, to keep the pursuers at bay. He starts to be like his claims. His self-accusations come true, his success grows. His dangerousness is directly proportional to his attractiveness. His success makes him breathless, he is totally at sea. In his despair, he forgets himself once, and a few *good* words about him slip out. Instantly, everyone defects and he is redeemed.

Deus ex machina: God has waited patiently, and now he steps forth from the atom.

There is something terrifying about the exhaustion of gods.

A place where people love only from afar, without ever seeing one another. A lover must never find out what his beloved really looks like. Indiscretions in this direction are severely punished, like rape in our country. There are tragedies in the lives of these people too: for instance, when someone learns that the woman he chose to love is someone he already knows from somewhere. He is then as horrified at himself as an Oedipus here. It is sometimes not easy for lovers to avoid one another. But they know that everything is over with the first meeting. It is impossible for them to love someone they know; they are good observers and they can see through anyone they have spoken to even once. How can they possibly develop any love for such a creature? The nicest thing of all is to think of foreign countries, whose customs they do not understand; those places might still have things to admire. They conjure up images of the foreigners and write them incomprehensible letters.

There are very many people everywhere, whom I see: they do not feel it. Very many everywhere who feel me seeing them: I do not see them.

To live in a city until it becomes alien to you.

Porcelain as the grace and elegance and distribution of the fear of catastrophes. If a man has a great deal of porcelain around, little can happen to him. And how lovely are his myriad little fears! How he can watch over them, lovingly tend them!

A plea by Ananda, at the right moment, could have extended Buddha's life. But the plea was not spoken, and Buddha resolved to enter Nirvana within three months. In the account of Buddha's final days, nothing moved me more than this unused opportunity. The master's life lay in the hands of the disciple. If Ananda had loved him more, his love would have been even more attentive. Buddha would not have died at that point. This shows the importance of the precision of love. Such an emotion has meaning only in its precision, thus saving or maintaining the beloved's life.

In a religion like Buddhism, where death is accepted, discussed and varied in all ways, intensified to a multiple superdeath, nothing moves one more deeply than any stirring of life, *against* the doctrine as it were, a spontaneous flame, since everything is supposed to be extinguished. The eighty-year-old Buddha, recovering from a serious illness, speaks of the beauty of the places he has wandered through; he named them all, secretly hoping that his disciple will try to keep him alive. He repeats his words three times, but the disciple fails to notice anything, and the mute sadness of Buddha's renunciation of life is more eloquent than any sermon.

To be God and then renounce it, as though it were nothing. Have we been thus renounced?

From time to time, all one's past life concentrates in a terse sequence of similar situations: people who once meant a great deal to you emerge, gather, corresponding to their real sequence in you, repeat themselves and fortify themselves, and suddenly, albeit briefly, they exist so intensely that the day and the night blaze with their words. In such moments, you learn to hate your life most. For those who were closest to you should never have been close to you. Those you respected were not worth your respect. Those you thought beautiful are ugly, perhaps they always were. Those who helped you, now begrudgingly take back their help. Those you helped, now testify that it happened against their will. Everything was, if not futile, then certainly wrong. And if it was that way back then, and you took it very seriously back then, what will guarantee that it's not that way now too?

Love in Bosch's millennium is detached from the world of values and prices. Instead of cold evaluations and estimations, there are strange plants and animals; fruits are giants and *they* express the value of love. Every animal, every fruit is something special. One would not always care to know what it stands for: one feels that it always stands for a lot. Its appearance is sometimes more than its meaning. The painter proves superior to words. All conceptual systems live from refilling just a few words at whose expense others were emptied. The painter who ignores natural dimensions has a more powerful device in hand. A strawberry can be made bigger than a man.

The astonishing thing in Bosch is the *colorlessness* of lovers. The color wealth of his animals and fruits, the fantastic inventions of rock formations and crystal wells, the shapes in which he puts his couples, the tortures he devises for hell—all these things have something licentious, voluptuous, about them, something rich and abysmal, compared with the pallid, unchanging figures of humans. Never have human crowdedness and egalitarianism been so convincingly expressed in art. Human beings, for Bosch, are like mirror images, the moment they are naked. In clothes, they have their distinctive faces; naked, they are all Adam and Eve. True Adamites, the people in the center picture have budded away from the primal parents. They all love one another, but where is there a pregnant woman? Even in the punishments of hell, nothing is linked to pregnancy. Love is there for itself; released from the world of values and prices, detached from the world of consequences. In this, it is really the millennium of Joachim da Fiore; these are sexless beings who love each other. Their tools are outside their bodies, in tropical plants, prickles, and fruits. They are the opposite of East Indians: for in Indian art, every single body has the sensuality of a thousand.

A principle of art: to rediscover more than has been lost.

We can only imagine great men alone, a single one in a generation: envy and lowness of the great, even in our image of them.

No language has absorbed so much arrogance as English. It would be good to make comparisons and learn how the Romans spoke after a few centuries of their power; we will never find out. However, among those who exist today, the language of the English is arrogance itself. Their words are strung together as if on bars; they fall neither too high nor too low. The sentences can be broken off anywhere, like bars; a species-sense of security and superiority emanates from them, a feeling that has nothing to do with the merits and qualities of the individual. Arrogance can only be something taken for granted, otherwise it is taboo; the man who has a private arrogance along with the general one will hide it, the general one is so much more important. Every statement, in its seeming dryness, is a verdict; judgment has eaten up the language. The respect due every individual and his sentence is respect for the *judge*. Passion in speech arouses distrust; how could it be impartial? Yet all these judges are ready to condescend to children and explain different things to them; their friendliness knows no bounds. The person giving judgment has patience here; the execution has time. It may be put off altogether; it's enough that the judgment was pronounced. Whatever else has to be pronounced has little significance; it may just be a feeling, a mood, it is provisional, and it passes in any case. Integration in a whole caste's sense of superiority does, however, remove all vanity from the language; the private and malicious shimmer of French is totally lacking. Englishmen utter little malice about others; or more precisely, the malice they do utter could just as well be uttered by anyone else, and hence does not sound as hateful as elsewhere. The cold pretentiousness of the Englishman in his language is inimitable; all or at least very many take part in it; and one has to live among these many for a long time in order to make it one's own.

To keep thoughts apart by force. They all too easily become matted, like hair.

The people who can breathe deeply only when *all* are imperiled.

And what if only the worst survived? A Darwinism in reverse.

What is truly historical is killed in prehistory. Prehistory deals with mythless objects; it talks of them as though they were created by us. Our modern divorce of faith and production is thus transfered back to a period for which it does not hold. The way such objects are put side by side in museums robs them of the best of the time and patience that went into producing them. So many things, such different things lie close together; order *deprives* objects of their history.

The many towns we see, landscapes, spaces, and roads! Somewhere they all meet, forming a new paradise.

A father feels that parental education destroys children. He sends his three small children out into the world and wears a disguise in order to observe them. Their life under the eyes of the unseen father.

God was a mistake. But it is hard to decide whether too early or too late.

To think that the cruelty of the Assyrians, that systematic cruelty of all things, could fade, and we ourselves experienced that fading. The moral fulcrum of history has shifted forever, and the Barbarians we read about as horrified children were we, our time, our generation, but we were far more barbaric.

The sudden contraction of conditions and relations, going on for years of a lifetime, a contraction into a single scene in reality: everything is repeated in a few moments, everything that once took weeks and months; everything seems familiar without your properly knowing why; the rhythmic and temporal change removes it from knowledge. But then, when the scene is over, you suddenly feel relieved and you notice the sinister concentration: in one or two hours, years have passed, years that one knows very well because they are so painful. Perhaps it's the only way to free oneself from past suffering, and perhaps that is the origin of drama.

How many credible utterances of hope and goodness must we find to balance the utterances of bitterness and doubt we generously threw around! Who can dare think of death knowing he has only increased the sum of bitterness, albeit with the finest motives? Had one always kept silent, one could at least die. But one wanted to be heard and one screamed loud. Now it's time to say the other things and yet be heard, for it can't be screamed.

1949

A race that is interrupted every evening at a certain time. A signal is given. Everyone stops; sinks down; falls asleep. In the morning, the signal to continue. Everyone gets up and starts running. In the evening, they stop again and nod off wherever they are. Thus it goes day after day; week after week; month after month; year after year. Some give up sinking down in the evening and sleep standing. These people have a head start.

Those who are secure on the rotting earth; and the rot slowly reaching their legs.

The impudence of man: he pretends to be alone.

Jonah has two important features of the prophet: the fear of this office, which drives him into the stomach of a whale; and the wrath at the failure of his prophesy. This latter trait is the most repulsive and dangerous thing in prophets. They have to desire the worst once they have foretold it. Their dogmatism makes them merciless. They take God's threat more seriously than he does. A prophet has a hard time of it: he is taken seriously only when his prediction comes true; thus he cannot forgo that moment. God, wresting away his triumph, has deceived him; and the prophet, speaking about the most fearful things, can be anything, but not ridiculous. Thus, the feeling that people have, namely that he in his way embodies the evil he threatens them with and helps to bring about, is not altogether groundless; if they could *force* him to predict something else, perhaps something else might happen; they always keep trying to exert this force on him. A further conspicuous, but unusual feature of the Book of Jonah is the presence of animals; they have to do penance with the people by fasting like them and being wrapped up in sacks like them. God, however, takes pity not only on the people in Nineveh, of whom there are more than 120,000, but also on the many animals.

114

Do animals have less fear because they live without words?

It pains me that the animals will never rebel against us, the patient animals, the cows, the sheep, all the creatures in our control and unable to escape our control.

I can imagine a rebellion in a slaughterhouse, spreading from there throughout a whole city; men, women, children, old people ruthlessly trampled to death; the animals pouring over streets and vehicles, smashing down gates and doors, dashing furiously up to the highest floor of the buildings, subway cars crushed by thousands of oxen running wild, and sheep tearing us apart with suddenly sharp teeth.

I would be relieved if just one bull would send those heroes, the toreadors, into a lamentable flight—a whole bloodthirsty arena too. But I would prefer an uprising by the lesser, gentle victims, the sheep and cows. I won't admit that it can never happen; that we will never tremble before them, before them of all creatures.

Those heroes! They always know who's watching.

They never pass, the things we eat daily, they sing like the men in the fire.

Everything gets more meaningful from year to year: the aging man will drown in meanings.

He burned all his books and withdrew as a hermit into a public library.

Hobbes. Thinkers not bound to any religion can impress me only if their thinking is extreme enough. Hobbes is one of these; at the moment, I find him to be the most important.

Few of his thoughts strike me as correct. He explains everything through selfishness, and while knowing the crowd (he often mentions it), he really has nothing to say about it. My task, however, is to show how complex selfishness is; to show how what it controls does not belong to it, it comes from other areas of human nature, the ones to which Hobbes is blind.

Why, then, does his presentation so greatly impress me? Why do I enjoy his falsest thought as long as its expression is extreme enough? I believe that I have found in him the mental root of what I want to fight against the most. He is the only thinker I know who does not conceal power, its weight, its central place in all human action, and yet does not glorify power, he merely lets it be.

True materialism, both for invention and investigation, began in his time. He respects it, but without giving up earlier human interests and qualities. He knows what fear is; his calculation reveals it. All later thinkers, who came from mechanics and geometry, ignored fear; so fear had to flow back to the darkness in which it could keep operating undisturbed and unnamed.

He never underestimates the dreadful weight of the State. How lamentable are many political speculations of later centuries, compared with his. Next to him, Rousseau sounds like a childish chatterbox. The earliest period of modern history to truly contain us, who exist today, was the seventeenth century. Hobbes lived through this period, consciously and thoughtfully. The sharp partisan schisms, which he had to evade throughout his long life, were binding and dangerous enough to threaten him. Anyone else would have been fully infected or broken. He knew how to see them from both inside and outside at once and to delay their declared enmity long enough to shape and establish his own ideas.

He really stands alone as a thinker. There are few psychological trends in later centuries of which he cannot be viewed as the forerunner. As I have said, he experienced a great deal of fear and articulated this fear as openly as anything else he struggled with. His lack of religious faith was a peerless stroke of luck; his fear could not be allayed by cheap promises.

His support of existing political power, first the king's, then Cromwell's, cannot be held against him: he was convinced that such power concentration was appropriate. His distaste for the shout of the crowd was something he never explained, though he did record it. One cannot expect a man to explain everything.

Machiavelli, about whom there has been so much ado, is scarcely the one half, the classical half of Hobbes. Thucydides was for Hobbes what Livius was for Machiavelli. Although frequenting cardinals, Machiavelli never understood anything about religion. He could not utilize the experience of the religious mass movements and wars in the hundred years between him and Hobbes. Since Hobbes, any study of Machiavelli can have only a historical significance.

I sensed Hobbes' importance for a long time. I praised him before knowing him accurately enough. Now that I've earnestly studied *Leviathan*, I know I'm going to include this book in my "thought-Bible," my collection of the most important books—by which I especially mean the books of enemies. These are the books on which we sharpen our minds, and not those with which we grow weary because they are long since sucked out and drained. This Bible—I'm sure of it—will include neither Aristotle's *Politics*, nor Machiavelli's *Prince*, nor Rousseau's *Social Contract*.

Mohammed is something like the fulfillment of all prophets: he is a legislator and a de facto regent, it was he who first brought the prophets truly to power; no one before him ever utilized God so consistently and successfully. Faith, for him, is obedience. He is lavish with God's possessions, the rewards he promises for the next world; he would like to be as generous as a king. He calls himself God's prophet; he could just as easily or better be named God's *command*.

He accepts only those of his forerunners who achieved great success: Abraham, Moses, Jesus. He never knew his father, his respect for other people's property is that of a well-behaved orphan; it gets him a rich widow for a wife, who worships him in every way.

In the Temple of the Caaba, he intercepts the pilgrims; a tourist-prophet instead of a tourist-guide, and he is more and more tempted to install himself there; to replace the oligarchy of the Koreishites with a tyranny. His negotiations with the people of Medina have something political from the very beginning, he secures his position with alliances and systematically prepares a war against his home town.

Mohammed's interest in *tombs*, he catches his mortal disease in tombs. Corpses interest him as objects of resurrection. For him, the Last Judgment is the utmost concentration of dominance. *All* are judged, and the decision is forever. It is the greatest crowd imaginable, the object of a definitive judgment. The heap of the dead, a true goal of war, is so great as to include all corpses. (Mohammed certainly prefers wars to healing the sick.) After the Last Judgment, when there is no more dying, all the dead become living, and the only purpose of their awakening is for them to come together under the immediate and direct command of God.

In Islam, God's command is a great deal like a death sentence. In the Bible, the "slaughter this and slaughter that!" mostly refers to sacrificial animals; God's command strikes people only occasionally as an immediate bolt of lightning. The step from Judaism to Islam is one of a powerful emphasis on and concentration of command.

The ancient Kelts had a vivid expression for the relationship between warriors and dead men—as a mass, a heap. When they went off to war, each man would take a stone and throw it, together with the others, on a heap. When returning home from the war, each man would take back one of the stones: the stones of the fallen, who could not do the same, remained lying there. Thus a stone monument to the dead was created of its own accord. This precise subtraction of the returning men from those who had gone out expresses a peculiarly distinct feeling for the heap of the dead: instead of the corpses on the battlefield—the monument of stones.

Crowds and outshouting. A significant function of the crowd is to outshout dangers: whether earthquakes or enemies. People get together in order to shout *louder.* When the other, the earthquake or the enemy, has gone silent, then the crowd has won. It is important to bear in mind that the *ocean* will not be outshouted. For even if a strong crowd succeeded in being louder than the sea for an instant, it would nonetheless never silence the sea. Hence, in the minds of those who know it, the sea has remained the greatest crowd, which no one can ever equal.

"If people would at least keep their relatives a secret," said the stranger, "so that you couldn't tell who belongs to whom. It would be wonderful having a secret family, really all for oneself, and no one could know about it, you can only reach it with great caution because no one must find out about it, a father, mother, brother, sisters, like secret mistresses!"

Words we cannot live without, such as love, justice, and goodness. We let ourselves be taken in by them and we see through them, in order to believe in them all the more vehemently.

Let each man keep his deepest sorrow a secret.

The peculiar movement of knowledge. It keeps still for a long time, like rock or seemingly dead life. Then all at once it gets an unexpectedly plantlike character. You happen to glance at it: It hasn't moved from the spot, but it's grown. A great moment, but not yet a miracle. For one day, you look somewhere else, and that knowledge is there, where it certainly wasn't until then, it has changed places, it has *leaped*. Everyone waits for this leaping knowledge. In the night, which fills us, we listen for the snarling of new predators, and their eyes glow in the dark, dangerous and greedy.

God from an egg, and the philosopher who laid it.

The most disgusting thing for my ears is the dialect of satedness.

In a fog, shapes are like *words*. Anyone coming along in the fog excites me like a new word.

A word can collect him.

There is something so despicable about cleverness that one would rather be wise as a fool.

Then the efficient will be outlawed, and anyone having success will be punished.

For weeks now, I have been perusing a book that deeply disturbs me: *Memoirs of a Nervous Illness,* a book by Schreber, ex-president of the Dresden senate. It appeared almost fifty years ago, in 1903, paid for by the author, bought up by his family, removed from circulation and destroyed, so that only a very few copies have passed down to us. One copy came into my hands in 1939 under peculiar circumstances and has remained with me ever since. Without having read it, I felt that it would become important to me. Like other books, it waited for its moment, and now that I'm ready to gather my thoughts on paranoia, I have taken it up and read it three times in a row. I do not believe that any other paranoic, interned as such for years in an institution, has ever so completely and convincingly presented his system.

What things I have found here! Support for some of the ideas that have been haunting me for years: for instance, the insoluble link between paranoia and power. His entire system is the description of a struggle for power, with God Himself as his real antagonist. Schreber long imagined he was the only surviving human being in the world; all the others were the souls of dead people and God in multiple incarnations. The illusion that a man is or would like to be the only one, the only one among corpses, is decisive for the psychology of both the paranoic and the extreme practitioner of power. This connection became clear to me for the first time in Vienna during 1932, when I attended the trial of Matuschka, the railroad assassin.

But Schreber also had in him the complete ideology of National Socialism as a delusion. He regards the Germans as the chosen people and sees their existence endangered by Jews, Catholics, and Slavs. He often designates himself the "warrior" to save them from this peril. Such forestalling of what happened later in the world of the "mentally healthy" would be reason enough for everyone to study his memoirs. But he thought up a lot of other things as well. He is haunted by the thought of the end of the world, he has grand visions of it, unforgettable visions. It would be idle to list everything occurring here; I discuss it thoroughly in *Crowds and Power*. But some aspects, interesting to me in connection with *Auto da Fe,* will be mentioned here. For instance, the depiction of the period of *motionlessness;* it recalls the corresponding chapter, "Petrifaction," in *Auto da Fe*. Likewise, the conversations with imaginary figures could also come from *Auto da Fe*.

This study of paranoia has its dangers. After just a few hours, I am seized with a tormenting feeling of being locked in, and the more convincing the system of madness, the stronger my fear.

Two things are involved here. One: the completion and isolation of the delusion, which makes any escape very difficult—no doors anywhere; everything tightly locked; no use looking for any fluid to submerge in, to float away on; even if you found it, it would be locked out; everything is like granite; everything is dark, and how naturally this hard darkness passes into you. In everything I have ever tried, I have always taken cautions against being locked in like that; apertures, space—that was my uppermost thought, so long as there's a lot of space, nothing is lost. But here, someone thought, as his delusion, something that was the easiest thing in the world for me, something I could bring about so effortlessly, so nonchalantly. Never am I more afraid of myself than in the completeness and isolation of another person's delusion that I understand.

The second and far more dangerous thing is: that I begin doubting the validity of my own thoughts. If it is possible to so convincingly depict and isolate this manifest delusion that it overwhelms one—then what could we not depict, assuming we have something of this "paranoid" power? The convincing evidence that I often feel for myself is just as available for the other person. The difference, however, is that I instantly deviate without locking up what strikes me as convincing, I shift it, put it away, begin with something entirely different, approach the same problem later from different sides; never pledge myself to any *one* method and certainly not a method of my own; leap from the confinement of established disciplines to others, like a chess knight; remove private rigidity by mastering new things; and above all, despite well-meaning friends, I draw my labor out over more and more years, so that the course of the world has every opportunity of refuting or destroying these discoveries and me.

Nevertheless, it is still true that I cannot live without the faith in these discoveries. I cannot equate them with any varieties of madness. Thus I hate myself for the danger to which I expose new ideas when I penetrate other people's confining delusions.

One can only experience a piece of this world; you, however, count nothing but the whole thing: your limitedness.

A love letter from Sweden. Strindberg on the stamps.

Love in buckets, one person pours it over the other's head.

He made a desert in her mind. That's where his ideas blossom.

That horrible story of the Sultan of Delhi! One witnesses a kind of compulsion of conscience and lets it all go down one's back; and suddenly one feels as though one were a murderer oneself; simply because one went along with it, because one didn't immediately repulse it, energetically and with disgust. The worst thing, always, is history, and I must not escape it; the fact that history has actually kept getting worse forces me to be its anatomist; I slice about in its rotting body and I am ashamed of the profession that I myself have chosen.

You cannot put up with anything more unless you force yourself to articulate it right away; there is too much here, and you are now in the river. You will never escape from this river until you reach the estuary. It is better to swim along voluntarily instead of constantly struggling against the current.

A man spoke to his wife: "It's raining, I'm going to have pleasant dreams." The start of a tale from Surinam.

He went there, evening after evening. She received him amicably. He remained for hours. He left her lying in a desert of destroyed secrets and went away.

Getting lost in another person, who lives, exists, looks at you, speaks to you; the search within him has something desperate about it: "Where is it?" you tell him, "are you hiding it? It still exists, doesn't it?" And so you investigate him and hunt through him in vain, and everything is sunken; but there is no sea far and wide in which he could have sunk it; and nothing else is important, only this search, it is the hunt for the nothingness you have become in the other.

The restorer. A cross between an actor and an archeologist. He has to play the role of the painter whose picture he is restoring. By lifting off layer after layer, cautiously and making sure that nothing is shifted, he eventually gets to the picture of the man he is playing. His awe is imbued with his expectation. But he is also active: much remains in his power. The more scarcely recognizable things he restores, the greater his success as an archeologist. This humble side of his nature can turn into its reverse if he gives free rein to his arbitrary side and presents things that cannot be completed anymore—presents them according to his speculations. He may ultimately think so highly of himself that he totally invents pictures, but he will always remain in an accepted role, like that great majority of actors who never write plays themselves.

The metamorphoses of the restorer are prescribed; art history contains the full list of his personae; he adds none himself. He likewise accepts their hierarchy; he reaps the most honor with the greatest names.

1950

I would give a great deal to get rid of my habit of seeing the world historically. How wretched is this division by years and its transfer to the life of animals and plants, when they were not yet burdened by us. The crown of human tyranny is the counting of years; the most oppressive of all legends is the story of the creation of the world for us.

Every year makes a man more impudent.

A country that hangs its scum out the windows as flags.

Human beings as ships and their disgusting freight.

The worst crowd one could think of is a crowd consisting solely of *acquaintances*.

The truly noble doctor, who invents a new disease for each of his patients.

The greediness in some disease names: meningitis.

Redeem psychiatry from itself: five hundred or a thousand precise accounts, and not a word of division or explanation!

He imagines how people would have stood their own against an evil god. They would have become good *against* him. They would never have expected anything of him or prayed for anything to him, they would always have fought against him. Some would have hidden from him—cave artists; others would have hunted him down—bold sportsmen.
    Their faith that they could once succeed in improving God.

Perhaps every breath you take is someone else's last.

The city in which no one weeps. They built their cathedral around the millennial tear, as a relic.

Even in the best satirists, I am bothered by their reasonability, the shallow pond from which their enormous ideas emerge.

A philosopher getting through life without a single answer. But oh how he asks!

Women on stilts, throwing themselves from high up into the arms of the unsuspecting men they have chosen.

History portrays everything as if it could never have come otherwise. Yet it could have happened in a hundred different ways. History is on the side of what has happened, detaching it in a stronger context from what has not happened. Among all possibilities, it banks on the one, the surviving one. Thus history always seems as if it existed for the *stronger,* for what has actually happened; it could not have *not* happened, it *had* to happen.

Ranke recognizes power, and the fulfillment of power is history for him. Historians who do not worship power cannot write a coherent history of states. Rome sufficed for many of them long after it ceased existing. Of the four great periods in history, such as Voltaire saw it, Louis XIV's was the last: the adversary of a history of kings and battles was no less influenced by power than any normal chronicler of wars.

Ranke's peculiarity as a historian is his pluralism; he is a polytheist of power. Since, during the centuries before him, as in his own, there were a number of great powers, he has to announce them all. For those who were no longer great, Spain and Turkey, he seems to have felt something like embarrassment.

How much will men kill when they can revive everything?

He has so much money that the bombs eat out of his hand.

Now hanging has all the gentleness of fishing.

It turns out that there is no such thing as the atom. Yet the atomic bomb remains.

"How can one be just to someone with no notion of justice?"—"Does one thereby destroy justice? Is justice so sensitive?"

For everyone you love, you need someone to take your abuse; and in order to save on people, you would have to properly combine the couples of abusing and loving.

This urge of mine to know everything about all people, no matter when or where they lived, as though my salvation were contingent on each one, his peculiarity, uniqueness, the course of his life, and then what they should be together.

To become a town, a whole country, a continent, and not conquer anything.

A special lightning-bolt for misers, taking everything of theirs at once.

The best man would not be the one who needs the least, but the one who gives away the most through what he needs.

The notion that the earth is under observation is the best-deserved fiction it has ever gotten.
     It well may be that we are being observed by several observers, and it may be that they are fighting over possessing the earth.
     Overseers of an alien star for the earth, hearing us, but to whom we cannot possibly speak.
     To think that the technological development of the earth could have drawn the attention of aliens to us; that they have regarded us as a real danger ever since the first atomic bomb went off; that they have since conferred about our destruction, which may be imminent very shortly.
     A few remaining primitives will then be the only ones who do not distinguish between us and the aliens, who understand *nothing* of what has happened, the last ingenuous earth-dwellers, natives, lost and innocent at once.
     Amazement and disgust when the discoverers open the first stinking human skin, performance of a feeding, illumination of a digesting.
     Assume they had light units instead of persons, and all boundaries, even between people, disgusted them, light instead of fat.
     And what if they had chosen the earth as *their* graveyard?

1951

The thing that repels me most about philosophers is the *emptying* process of their thinking. The more often and more skillfully they use their basic words, the less remains of the world around them. They are like barbarians in a high, spacious mansion of wonderful works. They stand there in their shirt sleeves and throw everything out the window, methodically and steadfastly, chairs, pictures, plates, animals, children, until there's nothing left but whole empty rooms. Sometimes the doors and windows come flying last. The naked house remains. They imagine that these devastations make it *better*.

The wise man forgets his head.

All that's left of the beyond is nothingness, its most dangerous legacy.

Diver, you plunged tirelessly into the confusions of others. Can you still learn from them? Can you help them? Are they more to you than the seal of your own confusions?

A dream is like an animal, but an unknown animal, and you cannot see all its members. The interpretation is a cage, but the dream is never inside.

A person who never meets you without *asking* for something. That's how sublime you seem to him; that's how little he thinks of himself, and he wants so much. The figure of demanding. Most enigmatic are the people who lay claim to everything, use a great deal, and yet have no regard for themselves.

The most lamentable man I ever knew was a storekeeper who was cast away under words; he put them in his mouth grain by grain and, ruminating, indited a poem.

The ambitious, who are after power, are always in quest of *slogans*. They pick up what someone has casually said in a company and arrange it as a kind of omen. The unknown person who answers their question makes no difference to them. They do not even wish to see him again; often they do not know what he does, and they may even forget his name. He is "a Pole" for them, or "a psychologist." All they need from him is a word that strikes them, enigmatically, as useful. They will tend to withdraw from the company as soon as that word has been mentioned; it could easily lose some of its power if others follow it. As soon as they are alone, they completely detach the word from its original user and twist it about at length until it has something absolute; as though it came from a higher power in order to serve them.

The anxiety of the stars seen and registered by us.

Each war contains all earlier wars.

Rome and Paris and London will be forgotten. One ocean will cover them. No one will understand English. A few horses will read a mass for Epsom Downs. The graveyards of Verdun will light up the bottom of the sea.

The realization that one has no more power over a person can make one happy. The more intensely one controlled him, the greater this feeling of happiness. Freedom, I keep thinking more and more, is a freedom to *let go,* a giving up of power.

If I know people well, I like hearing them tell the same stories over and over again, especially when they concern the central events of their lives. I can stand being only with those people whose stories are somehow different each time. The rest are actors who have learned their parts well, I don't believe anything they say.

Very beautiful eyes are unbearable, one has to keep looking at them, one drowns in them, one loses oneself, one is totally disoriented.

People always ask you what you *mean* when you rail against death. They want the cheap hopes from you that are droned about in religions ad nauseam. But I know nothing. I have nothing to say about it. My character, my pride consist in my never having *flattered* death. Like everyone else, I have sometimes, very seldom, wished for it, but no man has ever heard me praising death, no one can say that I have bowed to it, that I have acknowledged or whitewashed death. I find it as useless and as evil as ever, the basic ill of all existence, the unresolved and the incomprehensible, the knot in which everything has always been tied and caught and that no one has ever dared to chop up.

It's too bad about everyone. No one should ever have had to die. The worst crime did not merit death; and without the *recognition* of death, there could never have been the worst crime.

We would have to think of a world in which murder had never existed. In such a world, what would all the other crimes be like?

You carry the most important things in you for forty or fifty years before you venture to articulate them. For this very reason, you cannot reckon what is lost with those people who die early. All people die early.

The behavior of martyrs strikes no one as despicable, although everything they did was done with a view to *eternal life*. How despicable those same martyrs would seem to the followers of Christianity if they had wanted an eternal life *here* instead of somewhere else.

The very idea of a transmigration seems more meaningful than that of the afterlife. The advocates of a faith in the hereafter do not realize that they are concerned with something they don't even mention by name: a *togetherness* in the hereafter, a crowd that never disintegrates. Once gathered there, they do not want to be forced apart.

How about a paradise in which the blissful never saw one another, in which each one lived for himself in a kind of hermit bliss, remote from the others, so that no voice could reach them; a paradise of everlasting solitude, without physical needs or complaints; a prison without walls, bars, or guards, from which there was no place to escape because there was no place to go. Each soul would give speeches to himself, as his own preacher, mentor, comforter, and no one else would be listening. A blissful existence, with many people preferring the torments of hell.

128

I cannot explain why my clear sense of the evils in this life always goes hand in hand with an ever-waking passion for it. Perhaps I feel it would be less bad if it weren't arbitrarily torn and cut off. Perhaps I am prey to the old notion that the *permanent* tenants of paradise are good. Death would not be so unjust if it were not destined in advance. For each of us, even the worst, has the excuse that nothing anyone does can even begin to approach the evil of this predestined doom. We have to be bad because we know we will die. We would be even worse if, from the very start, we knew when.

The religions are all satisfied. Is there no religion of ever-acute despair? I would like to see the man who cannot look *any* death calmly in the eye, even his own; who, acting on this hatred, has dug a constantly full bed for the permanent river of his dissatisfaction; who does not sleep, because during his sleep some people do not wake up again; who does not eat, because during his meal some are eaten; who does not love, because during his love others are torn apart. I would like to see the man who is only this one feeling, but always this feeling; who, while others enjoy themselves, trembles for their joys; who grasps the trivial regret for "impermanence" as a sharp torment, the torment of death, death everywhere, and breathes only in this torment.

The blind man speaks about the great men he knew when he could see, and he explains that he now knows them better, having gone blind; they are not harassed by anything, disguised, discolored, distorted, or sullied. He rejects anyone else's memory of the same people, it has no part in the purity of his own sphere.

When his eyes closed, he began to live. He saw nothing more. He didn't bump into anything. He went from one to another, and didn't know who he was. All the false things that were said came from no one. When he was sad, he held on to a table. When he got angry, he pulled off the tablecloth. Women slid off him like water; he didn't see them and let them run. His blindness always found the goal, which then changed its place and came towards him. He said thank you, sat down at the piano and played a Sumerian waltz for the friendly goals. "It was so cheerful in the world even back then," they said in amazement.

The most surprising thing is the precipitous increase of wisdom in a person who was always with you, in whom that increase was never noticeable, of whom one expected many things, but just not wisdom. You thought you knew him thoroughly, in every way, and yet there was something more concealed in him. This secret content of a human being is the best thing about him—so secret that it does not reveal itself to anyone, no matter how close or how remote, unless he has achieved the blossoming of his form and suddenly blooms, opens up, forever. We seek stubbornly for this secret content, but usually in the *wrong* people. What we looked for so arduously *there,* always existed *here,* the reverse side of all disappointments, reward, grace.

Square tables: the self-assurance they give you, as though one were alone in an alliance of four.

What's the meaning of this, you're made of clay, said Adam to Eve, and threw her away. I am your rib, she said, my clay comes from yours. He didn't believe her and bit into the apple. Then he knew that she had told him the truth, he picked her up and gave her to the serpent.

Men naked on leashes of sumptuously dressed women: lap-men like Pekinese.

All the advice he has ever given, and the people he has advised appear in person. They act as he advised them, but with one another, a lively community. Finally, seeing all of them together, he realizes what he himself was after.

The man who only looks at women who he particularly dislikes, but in such a way as if he liked them. His destiny.

The gesture of the true idiot, who cannot be anything else, touches me more deeply than that of the Almighty.

His dream: to know everything he knows and yet not know it.

Reckoning up his friends, he finds *himself;* after adding, subtracting, multiplying, dividing—the result, the sum is unexpectedly *he.* Did he select them in such a way that nothing else could come out of it? *So many,* and this *old* result?

The sea is never lonesome.

How he wishes he were in a world in which he didn't exist.

There are some English expressions that I hate from the bottom of my soul, for instance when you call a person a "failure," because nothing impressive has become of him. Just look at the people to whom this word is applied! P., who is full of such English peculiarities, once said to me about Benjamin Constant: "He was a failure." Well, who wasn't? Didn't everyone live in vain? And didn't everyone die.

The tall waitress whose finger movements recall orders she might forget. "I'm coming," she nods and glances stealthily at a pair of splayed fingers. Other fingers then confirm what the first have remembered, and she is very happy about this agreement with herself. It is not the strangers who send her about and order her around, she hears something and confers quietly with herself; she decides when one finger replies to the other and makes sure they don't fight. When customers become impatient, she spreads her entire hand, and then they know there's nothing: the fingers simply refuse to confer with one another.

The stupidest women: those who come and report everything right away; to the nearest ear; it hasn't even fully happened yet.

The man with whom flattery will get you everywhere—you only have to tell him often enough how good he is. He is ready to commit murder in order to be considered good.

Only the unexpected makes us happy, but it has to meet with many expected things, which it disperses.

I am still attracted by everything in *Hobbes:* his intellectual courage, the courage of a man filled with fear; his highhanded learning, which senses with a peerless instinct what it has to confront *in itself,* and what it has to leave aside as empty and drained; his restraint, which allows him to hold mature and powerful thoughts back for decades, determining their moment by himself, uninfluenced and ruthless; the joy in that closed ring of enemies around him—his being his own party, letting some people think he can be used, but knowing how to defend himself against abuse, and without ever going after low power, doing only what creates an audience for his ideas; his constancy through so much liveliness and freshness of his mind; his distrust of concepts (what else is his "materialism"?) and also his great age. I sometimes wonder whether my liking him is overly affected by those ninety-one years he reached. For I almost never agree with the results of his thinking: his mathematical superstition says nothing to me, and it is his conception of power that I want to destroy.

But I *trust* him; the processes of his life and thought strike me as unadulterated. He is the adversary whom I hear; he never bores me, and I admire the terseness and power of his language. The notional superstition of later philosophers is a thousand times more unpleasant to me than his mathematical superstition. I trust him and I trust his years. It's true that I wish I could have as many years as he did, for how else can I achieve the same constancy, the same testing, affirming, confirming of *my* fundamental experiences—which are today the same for all, one only has to give them time to permeate one totally.

A man who has never gotten a letter.

The thief's hell is the fear of thieves.

Throughout dinner, the old, old woman spoke about poltergeists. The meal was a long one. I tried to envy her for her experiences. Why didn't any poltergeist ever come to me? I tried to change the topic, out of pure defiance. She wouldn't let go. A telephone book had moved, moved from the spot. Shoes had been gathered on a bed. I found this poor. I would have preferred a poltergeist confusing the names and addresses in the telephone book, for I can give the thing a simple little kick all by myself. But I was downright embarrassed for the shoes gathered on the bed. Why hadn't they all gone strolling in different directions? I didn't care to listen. The poltergeist was unimaginative. The old, old woman, sensing my disappointment, began to speak of other things. I finally left her, she was tired. It took hours for me to realize that she herself was the poltergeist. She was preparing for her future career. She was talking about her plans.

A nightbook, a "nocturnal," no line of which was ever written by day. Parallel to it a real daybook, a journal, always written by day. To keep the two apart for a few years, never comparing them, never confusing them.

Their ultimate confrontation.

1952

Every few weeks, the "Numbered" pounce upon him. How quietly they continue their lives in him! How thankful they are to him for giving them time! They know that he'll never neglect them, that he can never forget them. They want to drain their existence in him, and for this they request a little time. He likes all of them, every one of them, and he thinks in amazement of that period in his life when he flung out his characters with hatred and bitterness. What has given him so much tenderness for these phantoms?

One may have known three or four thousand people, one speaks about only six or seven.

You notice some things only because they're not connected to anything.

The events of 1759 in Everton make clear that *John Wesley's* sermon and that of his wild followers created *crowds of dying people,* damned people, squirming in fear of the consequences of their deaths. The description in the *Journal* reminds one of a battlefield, but an imagined or pretended one, a provisional battlefield so to speak, which is played in order to escape the real one. To that extent, Wesley can doubtless be compared to a general, one who issues the commands and gives the signals for the battle, a one-crowd battle, however, which, of its own accord, turns into a massacre. Yet this condition is dominated by the notion that the spectacle of massacre has a salubrious effect, saving people from actual destruction.

When they saw heaven open, it was so full that they had only one wish: to find a place in it.

Can one personally feel all fanaticisms? Don't they exclude one another?

He pokes his nose into all sects, perhaps he's a quite ordinary inquisitor.

Historians on the day of the Last Judgment.

What forks, what flesh, and who is it who roasts us?

The psychiatric observation of people has something wounding, which lies more in classifying the abnormal than in merely establishing it. There is really no such thing as a norm anymore; people having judgment and experience are now convinced that everyone and everything is abnormal in some way. The value of this insight is in the feeling of the uniqueness of every person that this insight helps; one would thus like to love, respect, and protect every single one, even if his behavior is neither understandable nor predictable. The psychiatrist, however, who creates categories of the abnormal, who aims at classifying and then curing, robs the frequently humiliated man of his uniqueness too. This power, of *grouping* others, is felt to be painful not only by its victim; it is also oppressive for the involved observer to see this power functioning and to be unable to reverse it.

As of a certain age, every intelligent person seems dangerous.

He always knows in advance what the newspaper will say and that's why he has to peruse it thoroughly.

He knows how to arouse even a mosquito's hatred.

History, consisting mainly of diabolical cruelty—why do I read it if I have nothing in common with any of its cruelties—torture and killing, killing and torture, and I keep rereading it in myriad ways; always the same. Without the dates that stick in it like pins, you could never tell all these things apart.

He is waiting for a word that will rehabilitate and justify all words for him.

I want to keep smashing myself until I am whole.

Perhaps it was lucky for me that I never let myself be overwhelmed by my material in earlier years, that I always kept it detached from me. Thus every single part had its own, lasting effect. I could think about things which would otherwise have suffocated one another. Many things had time to meet and link up in memory, whereas otherwise they would have had a short and turbulent existence on the surface. Thus I can understand why the enormous material I have looked at during the past few months has not inspired any truly new ideas in me—it has only confirmed older ideas and given me new—I would say—*scientific* courage.

Oh, sentences, sentences, when will you join together and never come apart again?

I am surrounded by enemies who want to comfort me. They want to break my defiance, in two ways. On the one hand, they say, in regard to the abandoned woman, for whom no salvation seems possible: Since it *has* to be, it would be better to *be*. Or else they shriek: *I* am dying! *I* am dying! But I have never acknowledged that it *has* to be—for anyone, may the tongue that acknowledges it wither away, and I would rather dissolve into stinking vapors than ever say yes to that. And I know that all the others will also die, I take it seriously enough, but I am furious at them for *threatening* me with that, in order to have my fear for themselves alone and take it away from someone else who is threatened *now*—I will forgive no one for that.

Is sentimentality the love for everything we know well? So many familiar things gather during a lifetime that everything then seems coated with sentimentality. The more familiar something is, the more sugary layers pile up on it. It takes a long, long time for the sediments of familiar things to harden fully. Until then, no one can escape sentimentality; one can only make sure that the areas of familiar things lie far apart from each other; many still *astonishing* things will then remain in between. Only coherent familiarity, the closed continent of the familiar is dangerous. If a man settles there—where else can he go, what strangers can he possibly reach?

It is necessary not always to elude earthquakes. The grief for undeserved and blind destruction is unappeasable, and no life is long enough to be fully reassimilated in the sediment of the familiar things that appear secure.

Some people manufacture their own earthquakes, daring souls who are eaten up with fear. Others find their way to endangered places, as in a dream: *silent* prophets. But there are also victims who go too far in the violence of their lives, who wander weakly, far away, until the misfortune comes upon them *alone,* and everything is then senselessly over for them, senselessly because there are no witnesses.

Every eruption must have something mendacious about it! The dynamics of eruption demand that its cause be magnified. You feel wild, certainly, but what things don't you get from far away to stoke this wildness and justify it. The moments of wildness make sense only if they are *full,* if the entire person and all his reserves suddenly go up in flames. Anyone too chary or too fearful for this and unfamiliar with this experience is unfortunate. Everyone needs the memory of his own fire; you can't get by with borrowed fire.

The game of chance in which everything is gambled is a kind of wrath. It seems different only because it takes place within an established ritual, a cold wrath, but a wrath.

Some people prefer this form, because the high price feigns a vestige of reason. It appears as though one wanted to *have* something special. In reality, one wants to risk something special, for which one needs the fire of wrath. The seeming cold is for the anticipated loss. One abuses what one has; the more it is, the stronger one's anger; the man who gambles everything is the most furious.

The thing I find hard to understand is the greatest gamble: life itself. Perhaps I'm too curious, too hungry for miracles; I always expect the unexpected. Whatever I know or want is valuable to me mainly when it is canceled or refuted. At the end of each direction, the *other* waits, concealed, in regard to which I only feel that it will be surprising. I *know* in order that it suddenly may know itself as *other.* I *want* in order that the will be *deviated* from me. Everything has such a wealth of expectation that a conclusion, of whatever kind, is inconceivable. There is no end, for everything keeps increasing. The real human being, for me, is the one who acknowledges no end, there shall be none, and it is dangerous to invent one.

What religions do seems useful to some people. It is true that they mellow the dreadful edge of parting and give hope to those who are less affected, the ones remaining alive. However, religion's chief sin is against the dead, over whom they decree as if they had the right to do so and possessed some knowledge about their destiny. I approve of any fiction that makes the living behave better to *one another*. But statements about the completely vanished dead strike me as unscrupulous and frivolous. By accepting anything claimed about them, one abandons them totally, and they cannot defend themselves in any way. The defenselessness of the dead is the most incomprehensible fact. I love my dead too much to locate them anywhere (I already find it degrading to lock them away and bury them). I know nothing about them, absolutely nothing, and I am resolved to continue loving them in the full torment of this uncertainty.

Photography has destroyed the image.

Oh, lightness, lightness, will he grow old and lighter and lighter, until he understands all people without saying it, loves all people without wanting it, holds all people without their feeling it?

There can be no Creator, simply because his grief at the fate of his creation would be inconceivable and unendurable.

The satiety of the victor, his voraciousness, contentment, his long digestive comfort. There are many things one shouldn't be, but the only thing one must *never* be is a victor.

Yet one is a victor over every person one knows well and survives. Victory is surviving. How can one keep living and yet not be a victor? The moral squaring of the circle.

As a premise for *The Numbered:* I don't understand why people do not focus *more* on this mystery of their lifespan. All fatalism basically deals with this issue: Is a human lifespan predetermined or does it only come out of the course of a life? Does a person enter the world with a specific life quota, shall we say sixty years, or is this quota uncertain for a long time, so that the same person, after the same youth, could go on for seventy or only forty years? And at what point would the limitation be *clear?* The man who believes the former is, of course, a fatalist; the man who doesn't believe it endows humanity with an amazing measure of freedom and an influence on the length of life. One lives vaguely, as though this second assumption were the correct one, and one comforts oneself about death with the first. Perhaps both are necessary and would have to operate alternately, so that fainthearted people could endure death.

Most religions make people more cautious, not better. How much is that worth?

The heavens want to be *seen through,* and remind people of this with lightning.

People (one person every few years) with whom one *sums up;* to whom one has to present all earlier things, as though from a vantage point. People who stand for mountains with a vast, free view, who themselves see as little as the mountain on whom *one* sees.

1953

Everything about *The Numbered* is mysterious to me. I cannot calculate the effect of any scene on life. I fear *immediate* connections, as if I were in the middle of a network of rigorous shalt-nots, which I offend with every new scene. To make up for my sins, I would have to devise a new scene each time, balancing the earlier one, i.e., outweighing it. How can I tell if such balancing scenes will be successful?

Perhaps all thoughts until today have revolved around one that still waits to be thought. Perhaps everything depends on this thought's really being thought. Perhaps there is no certainty that it will be thought.

A man who can only stray his way home. Each time, he has to find a *different* route.

It is a dreadful peacefulness that comes over one when more and more people fall around one. One becomes quite passive, one does not hit back anymore, one becomes a pacifist in the war against death, and one turns the other cheek to death and one's neighbor too. Religions profit from this, this fatigue and feebleness.

A man becomes a mass murderer because a disease which felled the person he loved most became curable shortly after his death.

I cannot read about any primitive nation anymore. I myself am an entire primitive nation.

He reads in order to remain rational, intelligible to himself. Otherwise—what might have become of him by now! The books he holds, regards, opens, reads, are his leaden weights. He clutches them with the strength of an unfortunate about to be swept away by a tornado.

Without the books he would live more strongly, but where would he be? He wouldn't know his place, he wouldn't orient himself. Books are his compass, memory, calendar, geography.

God as a preparation for something more sinister that we do not yet know.

Passersby and "eternal" ones. I am haunted by the thought of a bizarre world in which the people *halt* at a very specific age, each at a different one. One man hurriedly becomes thirty, and stays there. Another hobbles along till seventy, and then remains seventy. Some run around as children of twelve, and never get any further. There are two classes of people, some are en route to their goals, the others have reached it. Some children may pass through their twelfth year, but there are others, *eternal* twelve-year-olds as it were.

These *eternals* come in all shapes and sizes, children, men, women, old people. They have a certain sense of superiority, nothing else can happen to them. They lose interest in their years; once they reach the second main period, they no longer calculate, they *remain* what they have become. They have the privileges of their permanence, they recognize one another and greet one another in a uniquely respectful way. Their actions are suitable to what one might call their basic age. They are models for the others, who are known as "passersby." Each of the passersby has an "eternal" as godfather, and *he* determines the passersby's goal.

Passersby and "eternals" all live together and are not separated. Intermarrying is not forbidden, but does involve difficulties. An "eternal" can fall in love with a passerby, his love for her is then exposed to all of *her* changes. She may have to pass through a number of years before reaching his class; from that moment on, she will no longer interest him. In contrast, a passerby may be seized with the ambition of loving only "eternals," and seducing one such woman after another, until he finally comes to rest himself as an "eternal." And only this world can offer the kind of happiness which we thoroughly ephemeral mortals sometimes long for: one "eternal" can find another "eternal," and they never change, together they can remain the same. They can exhaust their feeling for one another without the influence of time eroding it. They can find out whether they truly belong together; they, and only they, can test and prove their feelings.

Whoever regards love as important in this intensified way may find it and keep it. Whoever is excited by a change in the other, even though he has achieved constancy for his own nature, can, as an "eternal," court a passerby. Whoever wants to live in flux but has to worship what remains even and palpable, he, as a passerby, will look for an "eternal." Those, however, who, in their own changeability, can endure only changeable things, can be passersby sticking to other passersby.

In this world, everyone could find what he needs for his happiness.

A land in which the people weep when they eat.

The pious friend thinks that God lets a new human being be born for every good deed and someone die for every bad deed.

He believes that there are angels who stop up your ears at the right moment.

Assume that the promises are cut off for *everyone else* as for you, that no one senses anything further, that everything is over for everybody the moment he dies, that people have become thoroughly *secular,* here, everywhere, and for the future. What, exactly what, would then change in their life together? Would they be less enterprising or more? More cunning? More closed-off? Would it be enough for them to conceal their wickedness, till the very last moment, fully aware that they will then be rid of it at one swoop? Or would the memory they leave behind replace the afterlife fully?

I do not believe that this can be precisely decided, since remnants of faith in each person help to shape this opinion. But I could imagine that the desire to do good becomes a true passion in every faithless person, as though he himself stood for a wise supreme power and for everything one awaits from it.

Human. Will they never succeed in driving out the word for them? Is there such a thing as an unshakable human being?

Nothing is more boring than to be worshiped. How can God stand it?

What often bothers me about Montaigne is the fat on the quotations.

The mellower. A man who mellows other people's statements, wishes, and actions until he manages to create an environment in which nothing irritates him. His gestures, his caution, the calm he radiates. His fearless good-cheer, his freedom from curiosity. Even though he mellows everything, he *knows* about nothing, he goes about like a blind man. He senses only what can be enfeebled, and his measured activity focuses on that exclusively. He does not walk too fast or too slow; his words are like notes, each of his sentences a few measures of carefully selected music.

He is always able to make the individual aware of the universal: a man loves—as all men love; a man has died—like all men. The intellectual substance he operates with is very small; which also helps make him effective. He neither judges nor condemns, because it always affects the individual; he never accuses anyone, and he is never amazed.

Whatever happens, it has happened so often that there is nothing special about it. Powerful people no more exist for him than do poor people. He sees people as leaves, they are as similar to one another as leaves, transparently friendly, their lot is gentle. Their case is considered only something of the common run. Just what is the individual leaf that falls?

He never suffers hunger, he denies himself nothing, and if ever he wants anything too greatly, he imperceptibly veers away and forgets it. The mellower never has an accident. If he happens to witness one, he will not acknowledge it. If someone confronts him and forces him to take a stand on it, he proves, with a smile, that it was all for the best. Anyone who suffers poverty would have been destroyed by wealth. Anyone who dies has been spared a protracted suffering. Anyone who hates is ill. Anyone who loves too much is likewise ill. Any account of old terrors, nay, all human history is a fairy tale. For never could people have done what history says they did; people don't do it now either.

I know very well how the mellower acts, but I don't know what he looks like.

One should see "great" people harshly. One has to act towards them as they act themselves. They are "great" only when harsh. The mercy they do not know must not shine upon them, it puts them in a false light. Cruel the way they fight with one another, cruel the way they tread down; that's how one should experience them, everything else is deception.

The first effect of adjusting to other people is that one becomes *boring*.

The unerring hallmark of a great book: one is ashamed, when reading it, of ever having written a line; yet afterwards, one must reluctantly write again, and in such a way as though one had never written a line.

The rocking of the writing, as though it had been written on water.

Could it be that her death has cured me of jealousy? I have become more tolerant towards the people I love. I watch over them less, I grant them their freedom. I tell myself: Do this, you people, do that, do whatever you enjoy, so long as you live, do anything possible against me, if you have to, hurt me, cheat me, push me aside, hate me—I expect nothing, I want nothing, only this: *that you live*.

He tore his heart to shreds. It was pure velvet.

The chief mourner, who has inherited a hundred friends. He is satisfied with that.

In order to tame wild beasts, he blows into their noses. When the tamer told me that, it reminded me of how mellow and addicted I became when someone blew into my *ears*.

Dangers of pride: One becomes so proud that one does not measure oneself with anybody anymore. One does not confide in anybody one fears. One confides only in people who admire one. One does less and less and finally one does nothing, in order not to endanger the attitude of pride.

How can relinquishing the dominated be learned? How can one open one's hand without shrinking in one's emotions? How can one yearn for the familiar without inducing its approach? How can one forgo one's property without destroying it?

1954

A world in which no person *recognizes* anyone else. The main activity of these people would be to convince each other *that they are who they are.*

Only the non-believer has a right to miracles.

Which of the sentences in an aphorism collection does one write down?

For one thing, the sentences that confirm one: things that one feels are right, that one has often thought, that go against conventional opinion, that justify one. There is much dogmatism in this urge to be confirmed by great or wise men. But it can also be more: a pure joy in meeting a truly congenial mind. For if many sentences by a single man accord with one, then mere dogmatism turns into astonishment: in a totally different time, among totally different people, a man sought to grasp himself in exactly the same way as oneself; the same form, the same definiteness and definition came to him. One would be happy if one's best were equal to his best. Only timidity keeps one from falling into the arms of the older brother: the feeling that many things in one could frighten him.

Then there are two kinds of sentences that do not refer to oneself; one kind is funny, they amuse one with an unexpected turn of phrase or with terseness; as sentences they are new and have the freshness of new words. The others arouse an image that lay ready in one for a long time, in the clarity that permits it to rise.

The strangest effect is perhaps that of the sentences that put one to *shame.* One has many foibles one never worries about. They belong to one, one takes them for granted like eyes or hands. One may even bear a secret tenderness for them; they may have gained one the confidence or admiration of other people. Now, suddenly, one is harshly confronted with them, they are torn from any context of one's own life, as though they could occur anywhere. One doesn't recognize them in-

145

stantly, but one is taken aback. One reads a second time and one is frightened. "Why, that's you!" one suddenly snaps at oneself, pushing the sentence on like a knife. One reddens at one's entire personal image of oneself. One even promises to turn over a new leaf, and though one hardly gets any better, one never forgets these sentences. They may drive out an innocence that might have been attractive. But man's initiations into his own nature take place in such cruel cuts. Without them, he never can see himself *fully*. They have to come unexpectedly and from outside. By himself, man adjusts everything to his own comfort. By himself, he is an irresistible liar. For he never says anything truly unpleasant to himself without instantly counterbalancing it with something flattering. The sentence from the outside has an impact because it comes unexpectedly: one does not have any counterweight ready for it. One *helps* it with the same strength one would have *met* it with in other circumstances.

There are also the untouchable or sacred sentences, like those by Blake. One is embarrassed to find them among other sentences: for these can be wise, but in the light of the untouchable sentences they appear false and stale. One does not dare write down the untouchable sentence. It requires a page or a book for itself, where nothing else is written and nothing else will ever be written.

There is an embarrassing malaise that is unmistakable, a condition in which one cannot undertake anything because one doesn't feel like anything; in which one opens a book only to close it again; in which one cannot even speak, for every other person is a bother, and one is another person to oneself as well. It is a condition in which everything that once constituted one will now fall away, goals, habits, paths, divisions, confrontations, moods, certainties, vanities, times. It is a dark and tenacious groping within one by something one doesn't even know; one never senses what it will be; one can never help it in its blind motion. One is always surprised when it finally becomes obvious; one does not grasp that one was struggling with that, with that of all things, and one heaves a sigh of relief, not without bewilderment at the untamable world one carries inside oneself and that prefers not to manifest itself for a long time.

The superstition that one can catch up in one day with what one has missed in a hundred and a thousand days. One could also call it the thunder-and-lightning superstition.

Noteworthy in the journals of Ludwig II of Bavaria (first published in Liechtenstein in 1952) is the significance of certain commemoration days, especially the days of the execution of Louis XVI and Marie Antoinette. Those are the days of *his* martyrs, they are lugubriously emphasized every year and used for oaths in his most private domain. His future is dominated by a *single* number, his forty-first year, which he wants to reach; anything that happens or should not happen is seen in those terms.

Periods, definite lengths of time, the recurrence of certain days are of cardinal significance in paranoia and serve to absorb fear. The paranoic seeks a guarantee of the future in the calendar with its fixed commemoration days. When everything falls apart, the one thing that remains as a single, a final certainty is the calendar with its special days.

How prudent Buddha's father was! And how humiliating the legend of Buddha's first meeting with age, disease, and death!

Would everything have been otherwise if, from Buddha's earliest childhood, his father had kept an old man, a sick man, and a dying man for him, like playmates and pet animals, like dancing-girls, women, and musicians?

London after Marrakesh. He sits in a room with ten women at different tables, all unveiled. Slight irritation.

The roundness of all events in Marrakesh, like the eye sockets of the blind; nothing comes to an end, nothing breaks off totally, the most abrupt things continue in repetition.

The stammering of your ear when it heard so much and understood nothing.

To think that every day since you left, they have kept calling, to think, that the blind are calling now, while you sit here: Alláh! Alláh! Alláh!

The floating of the blind, who are not disturbed in any observing. What does a blind man see in himself, how *long* does he see it? Do his visions change *more seldom?*

What is it one loves so much in closed cities, in the cities wholly contained within walls, not running out into streets gradually and unevenly?

147

Above all, it's the density; you can't get out everywhere, you always find walls and are forced back into the city. This keeps recurring in a city with many dead ends, like Marrakesh; you come deeper and deeper into the city and suddenly you're standing before a front door and you can't get through. The house is closed to you; no path leads inside, no path leads past, you have to double back. The tenants of these end-houses—even though there are scarcely any windows—are so familiar to one another that they would have to notice a stranger. There is no inducement for passers-by.

Strangers are more strange here, and tenants more at home.

Some people so greatly feel the torment of others that they feel nothing else. Yet they keep living, avoid any torment of their own whenever they can, and even consider themselves good. Would those be the *most cunning* people? Could their sensitivity to torment merely serve to keep it away in time, through a finer scent. Torment antennae?

Languages fail, the constantly employed words do not count. When I had to speak to Englishmen in Morocco, I was ashamed for them merely because I spoke to them; they were very alien to me there. Even more alien were the French, who are the masters there, and indeed masters in the moment before being thrown out. The others, however, the people who have always lived there and whom I didn't understand—they were like myself to me.

He imagines God as a polyglot, politely answering every worshiper in his own language.

Here too, since my return, nothing has been wiped away. Everything is actually increasing its radiance. I believe, through a simple presentation of events, with no change, no invention, no exaggeration, I can erect something like a new city in me, a city in which the halting book on the crowd will thrive once again. I am not after the immediate, which I now intend to write down; I am only after a new foundation: a different, unexhausted space in which I may be; a new breath, an unnamed law.

For the lover of invention, it is wonderful to suddenly become very plain and true to memory and to forgo any invention.

Dirt as the *worthless* thing, everything one can no longer do commerce with. But one doesn't remove it right away; perhaps—who knows?—there might still come a possibility of selling it.

Since my trip, a number of words have been charged with so much new meaning that I can't utter them without evoking major turmoil inside myself. I say something to someone about "beggars," and the very next day I can't write another syllable about beggars. I read the name "Marrakesh" in a strange book, and the city conceals itself and will not emerge anymore. It is very unpleasant for me to talk about "Jews" because they were so strange there. Everything I saw has an energy, that wants to save itself, in order to discharge itself in *one* single possible and specific way.

A coward, a true coward, is only the man who fears his memories.

All language is permeated with and animated by creatures who are the object of utmost scorn. One speaks of toads and vermin, of serpents, worms, and pigs. What would happen if all words and objects of scorn were suddenly lost to us?

What if every man sensed how many people saw through him!

In England, no man is praised to his face, that's why people keep dogs. Praise is permitted for anything one undertakes with them.

There the people never go anywhere singly, only in groups of four to eight, their hair inextricably intertwined.

Religions infect one another. No sooner do you enter one than the other comes alive in you.

Twosome and threesome people. Some people seek the most important moments of their lives in twosome situations, others in threesomes. There are also other popular constellations—a well-known one is that of the single person—but most people are twosome or threesome people. The latter cannot imagine love without counting on a child; the former can least stand the thought of a child when they are in love. Threesome people like to bring strangers together and regard themselves as judges between them; twosome people keep strangers apart and only like being alone with each single one of them. Threesomers think of their parents together and despair of ever separating them and appropriating them singly. Twosomers have a father *or* a mother, and one parent is neglected or ignored for the other.

Keeping these conditions in mind, one could easily find the structure of a life and even foretell probable events.

1955

To the administrator of words, whoever he may be: Give me dark words and give me clear words, but I want no flowers, you can keep the fragrance for yourself. I want words that don't fall away, words that don't wither. I want thorns and roots, and occasionally, very occasionally, a translucent leaf, but I do not want any other words, you can distribute them to the rich..

How much have I forgotten that I thought I knew; how many things am I perplexed about, which once were as clear to me as sunlight?

He kept turning the other cheek until they stuck a medal on it.

She decided to tell him in advance if she deceived him. He was happy at her confidence.
    Then she told him so often that he died of boredom.

How often can one break off with the same person? Breaking off itself has something that rescinds it. Jumping away makes you want to jump back; the main thing is this energy of jumping, and it binds you again.

Each week, new figures were put up, and everyone could pray to them. Everyone came and was relieved. They made sure that at the end of each week, the figures were removed and new ones brought in. These new ones had different names. No name was ever venerated for more than a week, and the same name never came to be venerated twice.

The heavenly constellations were meant as advice, but no one understood them.

"When camels are sold to a stranger they get sick, out of disgust at the price."

151

Ever since it entered technology, all magic has become such a bother that one can't even bear reading about it in the Cabbalah.

Magic has succeeded, it has spirited itself away. *Nothing* else has succeeded, and hence *everything else* has become more interesting and more important than magic. When he goes among people, he is dressed in the thick coat of goodness, so he is never cold. He would rather give away the shirt off his back than this coat of goodness. Sometimes he imagines with dismay that there might be a prohibition against being considered good. The sweat emerges on his brow and, a harried man, he dashes among his victims, who receive him gratefully and radiant with happiness. If he has done something good for two people who do not know one another, he makes sure that they meet. He then pictures them sitting together and talking about him. Later, he hears a report from each side on what was said, and he compares precisely. For he is willing to be cheated of anything, but not his goodness.

He acts most modest when he does the very best, the effect is thus greater. He likes to think back over his life and ascertains that there was never a period when he was not good. He can see no funeral without feeling his way into the head man's situation, and perhaps he envies him a little, because everyone has something good to say about him. But he comforts himself with imagining what they would say about him if *he* were the dead man.

One day, he takes his imagination seriously and spreads the news of his death. He subscribes to a press agency and punctually receives all obituaries. He spends a few happy days pasting these clippings into an album. He is a fair man, however, and does not suppress the obituaries that strike him as too brief. He puts the stately volume on his bed as a pillow and sleeps on it. He dreams of his funeral on the next day and, when all are done with it, he throws another shovelful of goodness into his grave.

Dogs have a kind of pushy readiness for feelings that eases dried up people.

In Haydn's *Creation,* God has succeeded in everything, even with the first human couple. The Fall of Man has yet to come. God is still innocent. The praise of the creatures does not sound hollow, none is aware of its misfortune. God himself does not yet know what he has done, and he *believes* that everything is good.

The finest statue of man would be a horse that has thrown him off.

His vanity grows on him every year like a new skin. He feels unsure of himself while slipping out of the old skin, when no one has yet seen the new one.

A wasps' nest as a lock on the opening to the men's house. (New Caledonia)

How often does one have to say what one is until one really becomes that?

There is a "modesty" in science that I find much more unbearable than arrogance. "Modest" people hide behind methods and turn divisions and delimitations into the most important part of experience. Often, they seem to be saying: "It doesn't matter what we find. What matters is the order we put into what we don't find."

A new thought wants to look about from time to time among the old of its kind; otherwise it will die of thirst.

I have not committed enough portraits of the powerful to paper. How many of them have I not dealt with! But rather than compressing and recording my impressions of each one, I have mostly used them as a kind of energy source. Over and over again, they have kindled my hatred for power; over and over again, they have warned me against my own power over people.

How far do the things we learn drive us towards a faith? It could be that we change, unknowingly, through the force of the very words we absorb; something that used to be strange is ultimately obligatory.

It is good that we have always been interested in many mutually exclusive beliefs.

The proudest man would be the one who hates any leader; who goes on ahead *without being followed*.

The lowly man, by following, creates a following for himself.

She limps so beautifully that people who walk seem like cripples next to her.

All the natural apertures in the human body as *wounds*.

He has created a new homunculus, the sting of command. That's a good word, but the word alone can't do it, one has to put it in circulation and observe it in action.

The people have a strongly alternating life there: they are awake and active for two years, then they have to spend ten years sleeping without dreams. This is repeated for a whole lifetime. After ten years, they always come to new people and conditions, and no sooner are they accustomed to them than they fall asleep again. All houses have rooms for sleeping kin; but some, who do not want to be a burden to their families, go to *sleep monasteries*, where cells can be rented for ten years. Upon awakening, they find themselves exactly where they were earlier and they need not fear the strangeness of the first moment.

Friendships can break off quite suddenly. When somebody vanishes from one day to the next, people know he's asleep. In this society, death would no longer be terrifying. Often, people don't realize for years that someone has died; when he is carried off in his sleep, he simply shrivels up, like a bat. The amazing thing there is the return and not the disappearance.

People are not permitted to talk about *when* they shall go to sleep; and thus the length of each friendship and each relationship is always uncertain. Nothing lasts over two years, for nothing survives ten years of sleep. Even the tenderness of mothers is less powerful, and some children grow up almost by themselves.

The lives of most people ultimately consist of nothing but directions that they senselessly give themselves or others.

He gets drunk on other people's faults, a drunkard of morality.

Ambition distorts a man's entire horizon. One has to be able to *leap over* one's ambition, if for no other reason than to see it.

A land in which no one dares to look at the sky, and if someone goes outdoors, he bows his head.

All intellectual people also live by theft and are aware of it. But they react to this in very different ways. Some effusively express their gratitude to the victim; they praise his name to the skies and mention it so often that he becomes a bit ludicrous as the object of their exaggerated worship. Others *resent* him the moment they have robbed him; they never mention his name; and if his name is mentioned in their presence, they attack him insidiously. Since they know him intimately as his personal thieves, their attack is accurate and does him great damage.

The pauses in decline.

Retroactive dictators, a new way of looking at history.

For years now, I have been unable to stop my fascination at primitive conditions. I don't know with what mother's milk I have taken in this predilection. A strong faith and an even stronger expectation drive me to any depiction of primitive life; and whenever I read about these things, even in the cautious and watered-down interpretation of modern authors, I think I have truth itself in my hands. Everything becomes confidence for me, I no longer doubt; here, I think, I have what I have always looked for in vain; and when, after years, I reread the same book, it has the exact same effect on me as the first time, an unalterable, ever-living revelation. It is not, as I sometimes suspected, the names of exotic peoples and gods alone whose magic never wanes. It is the mirage of the greater clarity of relatively simple conditions; for as complicated as they seem in the light of modern research, the belief in their actual simplicity always remains alive in one. And there is always an accompanying feeling of their remoteness and isolation: Whatever one thinks of them seems free of the purposes and prejudices of our life today. Their cruelty is less cruel, we are not to blame for it. Their beauty has more merit, it does not rely on the confusing wealth of *our* legacy.

What I have learned from them is inexhaustible, but sometimes I feel as though I had exposed myself to their enormous energy in order to prove to myself how little I am. They force me to do little, for nothing is creative for the man who knows them, everything already exists in them. Man began as a poet whenever he began; and as a poet, he has since grown less.

A man can measure himself only on his contemporaries. If he ignores them, then he does not *want* to measure himself. It is possible that I want to sidestep any sort of competitiveness, because it could distort what is truly important to me. But probably, I have sidestepped it too far and too thoroughly, going back to an overwhelming origin, in which everyone vanishes.

It takes many words to become enthusiastic; they have to reach the surface quickly and in a certain tumult. No sooner has a word risen, no sooner is it erect, than it is seized by the next word and flung back down. Words are like wrestlers, and it is always the later one who wins the match, its closeness to the origin gives it the greater power.

But it is a special kind of word that kindles enthusiasm, the kind that contains space and future, a vastness in every direction. Things that were locked up in a man, twisted and futile, suddenly stretch out at an enormous speed every which way; in his words, he touches a crisscross of the beginning and end and center of the world.

The power of false ideas lies in their *extreme* falseness.

A fear of Aristotlizing my thoughts; of divisions, definitions, and similar empty games.

To find the old power that grabs its object and contemplates it for the first time. Who will give it to me? The great enemies, Hobbes, de Maistre, Nietzsche?

De Maistre sees through the rules of the game in human society. The horror of the slaughter-house on which everything is based is as present with him as with me, but he accepts it, he acknowledges it, and once he has made up his mind to accept it, he becomes its eulogist.

I respect de Maistre, but I find it upsetting that he intends the very opposite with the same thoughts and experiences as mine.

Eschbach, president of the Strasbourg Commercial Court, told my friend Madeleine C. that in his youth he had visited an old gentleman, who lived in the castle of Sulz. The man was already somewhat confused and he once said: "In my youth, when I was in Russia, I killed someone in a duel. But I can't remember who it was."

It was Pushkin.

The nations exchange their recollections, and each owns up to having been the worst.

A dog is trained to bring deprecatory objects to each person.

Gerard de Nerval would strike me as a poet, if for no other reason than because he thought he was descended from *Nerva*.

All arithmetical connections, proportions, elliptical destinies and paths are of no interest to me, all connections by names seem exciting and true.

My god is the Name, the breath of my life is the Word. Places do not matter for me when their names fade out. I have never been to any place whose name did not attract me there.

I fear the analysis and explanation of names, I fear them more than murder.

It is strange that one comes closer to truth only in the words that one no longer fully believes. Truth is a reanimation of dying words.

One must also learn how to give *senselessly,* otherwise one will forget how to give.

The mad sleeper: One who can sleep only in highly dangerous places, on an eave, in a cannon, among tigers, in a burning house, during an earthquake, on a sinking ship. His adventures in finding sleep.

All that has been can be bettered. The heart of historiography, concealed from it.

1956

Every year should be one day longer than the preceding one: a new day, on which nothing has ever happened, a day on which no one has ever died.

On names in history. There are only powerful names, the others die. Thus, for one thing, the strength of survival can be measured on a name. Even today it is the only true form of survival. But how does a name survive?

The peculiar voraciousness of a name: a name is *cannibalistic.*

Its victims are prepared in different ways. There are names that dig in only after their bearers are dead, they have no prior appetite. There are names that force their bearers to eat anything they come upon in their lifetime, insatiable names. There are names that fast at times. There are names that hibernate. There are names that have to live in hiding for a long time only to suddenly emerge ravenous—very dangerous names.

There are names that nourish themselves at an evenly increasing rate, sturdy names, boring names. Their sensible hygiene does not promise them long lives.

There are names that feed only on colleagues, guild-names as it were, and others that thrive only among strangers.

Some *cut their teeth* among strangers and then find their nourishment among their own.

Names that live because they want to die. Names that die because they only want to live.

Innocent names, that live because they have refrained from all nourishment.

Perhaps it wouldn't be so bad to die happily, so long as one has never happily witnessed someone else's death.

Since her death, he has been turning his head away from every bud.

Voices—such that one could take for granted, as though they will always be the same. Piercing voices. Caressing voices. Wounded voices.

As long as there are any people in the world who have *no power whatsoever,* I cannot lose all hope.

Cold archeology: things without people give me no real pleasure. Resentment against the things that have outlived people.

The object of archeology is a whole new kind of future. It is retrograde; every new step it takes into the past, every older grave it finds, become a piece of *our* future. The ever-older becomes what lies ahead of us. An unexpected discovery could change our own, still uncertain destiny.

They could pull in their heads and peep out through a tiny hole in their chests.

Paralyses. There is the helpful paralysis from a feeling of one's own inadequacy. But there is also the dreadful paralysis from a feeling of someone else's inadequacy, someone to whom one is chained, and one is paralyzed because one is precisely the person who can never change him. To be chained to another person's corpse until one dies oneself.

Every spoken word is false. Every written word is false. Every word is false. But what exists without words?

Thoughts about dead people are attempts at bringing them back to life. We care more about bringing them back than *keeping* them alive. The mania for reanimation is the germ of all faith. Now that we no longer fear the dead, we feel a single immeasurable guilt towards them: the guilt of not succeeding in bringing them back. On the liveliest and happiest of days, this guilt is the worst.

A play in which all the dead belonging to one appear. Some of them meet again, others meet for the first time. There is no grief among them, their joy at appearing is so enormous. (What shall we say about the joy of the person who lets them appear?)

But when the gods lay on their knees before him, he was terrified and asked them to stand up. They did not dare, they wanted to remain on their knees until he had forgiven them.

He did not forgive them. They had outlived too many people, had become too old and yet remained too young. He left them on their knees and turned vehemently away.

Being alone is so important that one has to keep finding new places for it. For one gets to feel at home too quickly everywhere. The most dangerous thing of all, however, is the concerted strength of books.

The sun always drives him to everything that looks ugly. The hope that it could now look *different* in the sun.

Feet alone would be enough for a whole lifetime, the feet of unknown people.

When I saw the gait of a cheetah, this intoxication of walking came over me. We experience all physical beauty in animals first. If there were no animals, no one would be beautiful.

To spend the rest of one's life only in completely new places. To give up books. To burn everything one has begun. To go to countries whose languages one can never master. To guard against every explained word. To keep silent, silent and breathing, to breathe the incomprehensible.

I do not hate what I have learned; I hate living in it.

He is at the mercy of the observers. When he feels their eyes upon him, he turns into everything they see.

Dogs couple differently there, while running.

The ludicrous thing about *order* is that it depends on so little. A hair, literally a hair, lying where it shouldn't, can separate order from disorder. Everything that does not belong where it is is hostile. Even the tiniest thing is disturbing: a man of total order would have to scour his realm with a microscope, and even then a remnant of potential nervousness would remain in him. Women ought to be happiest in this respect because they make order the most, and always in the same place. There is something murderous in order: nothing is meant to live where it is not allowed. Order is a small, self-created desert. It is important that it be confined, so that the tenant can pay strict attention to the order. A man feels poor without such a desert-realm, in which he has the right to choke everything in a blind rage.

Since I cannot be without words, I have to maintain my trust in words, and I can do that only if I do not disguise them. Thus, every external demand based on words is impossible for me. I can write them down and keep them somewhere. I cannot throw them at anyone's head, and I cannot do commerce with them. It goes against my grain to change anything in them once they are written down. All talk about art, especially by people who make art, is unbearable to me. I am embarrassed for them as for quacks, only the latter are more interesting. Books are holy for me, but that has nothing to do with literature, and certainly not my own writing. Thousands of books are more important to me than the few I have written myself. Actually, *every* book is the most important for me, in some physical way that I cannot quite explain. The blameless beauty of conscious prose is something I despise. It is true that some of the most important things have been formulated in good prose, but that happened virtually despite the writer; those things were really important, and so the prose was good; they were so firmly and deeply rooted that their measure could not be taken too early. The beautiful prose that moves in the sphere of what is acquired by reading is something like a fashion show of language; it keeps gravitating around itself, I cannot even despise it.

Music, the measure of man's capacity.

It is wonderful to *study,* namely to take up and contemplate names and things one has never yet contemplated; to tell oneself what one notices about them; what one would like to retain about them; to register it in the large, casual hoard of one's experiences; register it in such a way that one may never think about it again. One thereby creates a realm of personal adventures and discoveries, and the things one re-encounters *within* this realm have a twofold character: each is both a discovery and a piece of oneself.

He was forfeited to all the people to whom he gave good words.

In the *Secret History of the Mongols,* I found something that concerns me very much: the story of a great wielder of power, who was *lucky* to the very end, *from within.* Not every word of this may be true, but the whole thing has a deeper truth, whose existence I never so much as suspected. Odd as it may sound, I *recognize* the words that Genghis Khan's mother spoke to him. I can smell their smell. I am so close to him that I can see and hear him. There is an enormous difference between this kind of oral tradition and the historiography we usually have to content ourselves with.

More than anything, this "secret" tradition of the Mongols has all the *animals* that belong in their lives. It has all the *names* with which they used to address places and people. It has all the *excited moments,* in their excitement and intensity; instead of a mere notation of passions, it has the passions themselves. One can liken these stories only to those in the Bible, and the parallel goes further. The Old Testament is the history of God's power; the secret book of the Mongols is the history of Genghis Khan's power. It is a power over a group of tribes, and tribal feelings are so predominant that one could interchange the names and no longer know where one is.

God's power, to be sure, begins with Creation itself, and the history of this Creator's claims is what gives the Bible its uniqueness. But Genghis Khan himself is not much more modest. He too, like God, operates with death. He is as lavish with it as God is; why, he even lets fewer people survive. But he also stands out with his powerful family sense, something that does not befit God in his oneness.

Once again I am back in the world, the world of my enemies. Genghis Khan has grabbed me by the hair and put me back where I belong. From there, I can challenge him, observe him, and think about where he comes off best, in his own legend.

I have spent this past week in a kind of spell, I was spellbound by him. All these years, I had avoided him. Everything I read about him was either quite dry or superficial, and I always abandoned it in the middle. I never tried to draw conclusions from him, he was exemplary for nothing. The closest I came to him was in the madness of Senate President Schreber, who regarded himself as incarnating, among other people, Genghis Khan. But now the *Secret History of the Mongols* has fallen into my hands (a work whose first German translation was published in Hitler's Reich). Narrated as an epic for his successors, it contains the story of Genghis Khan and the Mongolian Empire. It is far more authentic and reliable than any sort of annal. It flows with time, but time has not chopped it up.

The more I read it (and I've scarcely done anything else in the last week), the more convinced I am that the laws of power can be derived from this *Secret History* alone. I had the very same feeling with another book, the Bible. But the Bible contains too much; it contains so many other things, which have become more important, that any interpretation of power processes could easily seem like a distortion. The *Secret History* has nothing else. It is the history of a rapid, irresistible power, the greatest and, within *one* life, the most stable that ever existed. It sprang up among people who could not care less about *money*. It was visible in the movements of horses and arrows. It came from an early world of hunters and brigands and it conquered the rest of the world.

Ever since I became a Mongol and have not been thinking about anything else day or night, I have seldom felt an urge to jot down anything for myself. Now I read everything else on the same topic for hours and hours on end; and when I stop reading, I feel something of a slight daze.

It is no longer the fascination exerted by *enemies,* as I sometimes thought; it is simply a striving for what I do not comprehend: the incessantly and ubiquitously shed blood from which we live. I cannot experience it myself, my hands have kept away from any blood with horror and repugnance. But how lamentable the man who is content with letting everything around him keep on in the same old way while nourishing himself from the murders that others commit for him every day! I refuse to sleep and put up with it. But I will try to learn everything about it and, with modest and persistent efforts, come close to what no sudden flash of insight will give me.

I am personally living the history of the Mongols as the history of an expansion; and although I deprecate and despise everything that happened there, the atmosphere of expansion imparts itself to me. The false conqueror goads me on to my own conquest.

It makes no sense living only in rejection. Even if one were unable to see any action one could approve, one would at least have to disapprove so vehemently and make such an effort thereby that this alone would turn into an action. Man is not born for mere defense. In some way or other, he also has to keep attacking. So ultimately, all that matters is *what* he attacks.

All the traits of the squandermania told about Ogotai, the second Mongolian Khan, fill me with great satisfaction. His scorn of treasures is so great that he constantly has to fight the people around him, who admonish him to greater caution. Mongolian *destructiveness* has become *squandering* in him. He wants people to have restored to them something of what was taken from them. What he likes particularly about ruling is the *distributions*.

It reminds me that one of the earliest and most important kinds of power derives from the distribution pack. In many tribes, distributions were entrusted to an individual, who learned how to carry them out safely. His distribution was fair. But he became more and more powerful in doing it; and in the end, it was more important for him to possess a lot rather than to distribute.

The power of killing vanishes before the power of evocation. What is the greatest and most dreadful killer compared with a man who brings a single corpse back to life?

How ludicrous the wielders of power seem in their efforts to elude death, and how grand are the efforts of shamans to raise the dead. So long as they believe it, so long as they do not merely feign it, they deserve all veneration.

The priests I despise are those who cannot recall the dead. They merely strengthen a frontier, which no one can leap across. They administer the lost so that it remains lost. They promise a migration to somewhere in order to conceal their impotence. They are satisfied that the dead do not return. They keep the dead on the other side.

There is often something oppressive and embarrassing about the death cult of *other people*. A turning away from the world of the living, and since we belong to this world ourselves, we feel offended by someone else's developed cult for a dead man, as though we meant nothing to him, as though no living person could mean anything to him.

One would have to make very sure not to lock oneself in with the dead man, one should let him go outdoors and allow many other people a connection with him. One should also, without being pushy, speak to people about him and not distort him through isolation.

Disturbances are good for the man who has walls growing everywhere. Happy the men who spring over them before the walls get too high.

It is embarrassing to see how much more practical one is—despite all contrary convictions—than most people. I have learned from every experience, so greatly and so thoroughly that I will soon consist of nothing but valid albeit intellectual practicality.

I cannot detach myself from *Islam*. My forebears lived in Turkey for centuries, and before that, perhaps for the same length of time, in Moorish Spain. Over and over again, I have approached Islam; over and over again, I have gone away from it. There is something in the fanaticism of this faith that fitted in with my earlier nature. My liberation and expansion as a human being is like a liberation from my own Islam. The God of Islam is more concentrated than the God of the Jews. He has exerted his utmost effect as a model for the rulers of Islamic countries. The things that torment me and that I hate, the things that I struggle against and strive to destroy—I keep finding them most distinct in the rulers of Islam.

There is the double generosity in *killing* and *giving presents;* the subjugation to the ritual law; the acknowledgement of the more powerful, of God, by the ruler; being steeled by God for any cruelty whatsoever; the anticipation of the overall judgment through countless single judgments beforehand. There is also the equality of human beings before the faith, which practically adds up to an equality of being killed. There is God as a murderer, who decides every single death and has it carried out; and there is the ruler, who emulates God in the naivest way. There is the command, that always flaunts its archaic character as a death sentence; the religious recognition of any power that can assert itself (God gives power to whomever he wishes, now this one, now that one) and its religious challenge, which, however, only serves the attainment of power.

There is an enormous nakedness of power in Islam, while everything else is multiply veiled and disguised by the law.

It is a control of people only, which therefore also achieves its utmost brilliance in large, cosmopolitan cities. The time of subjugating animals is long past, it is no longer an issue; animals are now only sacrificial victims.

Nietzsche's tone has something of the Koran. Had he but dreamt that!

Basically, the only days I now find valuable are the ones I have spent with any of the holy books. Just as other people once had to pray daily, so too I have to brood over some kind of ancient holiness, as though I had to find in it the evil things we could some day do to one another.

But I do not wish to warn. Nor do I wish to foresee. I hate the prophets. I only wish to *hold* what we are. I do not believe that it can be found in arguments and assertions. But I want to know all the *assertions*. All I am interested in is the assertions. I know they can be refuted. But I want to have all the assertions inside myself, next to one another, as though they were alive and unchallenged. I know they are not, and should never be again for anyone. But it is my goal, my task, to have them alive in me and to think about them.

Just who are you anyway that you have to test? How dare you? Worry alone gives you no right to test.

Your sole justification is your unshaken hatred of death. It is every death, and so you test for everyone.

With the growing awareness that we are perched on a heap of corpses, human and animal, that our self-confidence actually feeds on the sum of those we have survived—with this rapidly spreading insight, we find it harder and harder to reach any solution we would not be ashamed of. It is impossible to turn away from life, whose value and expectation we always feel. But it is equally impossible not to live from the death of other creatures, whose value and expectation are no less than ours.

The good fortune to think in terms of a remoteness, on which all traditional religions feed, cannot be ours.

The Beyond is within us; a grave realization, but it is trapped inside us. This is the great and insoluble fissure in modern man. For within us we also have the mass grave of creatures.

1957

Respect for immortality? For whom? For Caesar, Genghis Khan, Napoleon? Are not the greatest and most tenacious names also the most fearful? And what effect did Plutarch's exemplars have?

You attempt to do the right thing: you want to unmask the inevitable murderousness in a certain kind of greatness. But what kind of greatness that is *dangerous* enough do you oppose it with?

For murderousness even risks getting murdered, and its good fortune in escaping adds to its attraction. What will you give the people who have to have others dead before them, what will you give them in lieu of this, precisely this satisfaction?

If I had to say what I found most sinister in history, it would be the *models:* Caesar's Persian plans before his death, which came from Alexander. Hitler's Russian campaign in order to outdo Napoleon. There is something insane in this recurrence of great plans, and it can never be wiped out. Thus everything will recur when it is most absurd. Who will imitate Hitler, who will emulate our other leaders? Whose children's children will die for this or that epigone?

There is no historian who does not praise Caesar for at least one thing: the fact that the French now speak French. As though they would be mute if Caesar had not killed a million of them!

One fine quality of Plutarch's *Lives* is the lucidity. The lives are long enough to contain everything peculiar to a life, and yet short enough not to make us lose our way. They are more complete than our much longer modern biographies, because they also contain dreams in the right places. The most conspicuous failings of these men become clearer with their dreams, which are unmistakable and sum them up. Our modern interpretation of dreams simply makes people more ordinary. It discolors the image of their inner tension rather than lighting

167

it up. In Plutarch, I am even fascinated by the Romans, whom I have always loathed. He is by no means uncritical of his creatures. But his mind has room for many kinds of men. He is broadminded, as only a playwright can be, who always operates with many characters and especially with their differences. Plutarch therefore had a twofold effect. Some people have sought out their models in him, as in an oracular book, and lived their lives accordingly. Others have absorbed all his fifty or so men, thus becoming or remaining playwrights. Plutarch—I was not aware of this earlier—is in no way finicky. Dreadful things occur in him, as in his successor Shakespeare. But their dreadfulness is always painful. A man who certainly loves human beings as he does may see everything, and may also record it.

Sometimes I think that this continual study of the powerful is eating me up alive. It is like the Persian punishment of the troughs, as described in Plutarch, and the powerful are the worms.

How much is still left of me? What connection do I have to these horrible creatures? Why must I do it, and won't I fail like everyone else before me? Can I really get at power? Might I perhaps give it new strength with my relentless enmity?

Throughout this month, I have been thinking about the triumph of killing or of surviving. It might almost seem as though all I have accomplished in blustering rebellion is to establish that other people's deaths are bolstering and hence popular. Don't make a big thing about having to die, I seem to be saying, you'll first see a lot of people die before you.

As though every single death, no matter whose, were not a crime that one ought to prevent by any means whatsoever!

The hanged man in the Danish peat, whom I met after 2,000 years.

The sun is a kind of inspiration; hence, one should not have it all the time.

Do not overly distrust the divisions you have found yourself. If you apply them long enough, they bring a fresh aspect of reality to light; they come true, so to speak, and *renew* life.

168

I have distinguished the four kinds of pack, and then find them all together in one. However, this says nothing against the division into four kinds, it merely shows that I was filled with something that was truly there. This is merely a special way of depicting it. One can go into the concreteness of things only after separating and delimiting it. It is dangerous, however, to stick to the limits once you have found the very things you were after.

You will not reduce the "great" by even a millimeter. You will not wrest a single one of their victims away from them. They will use every breath of yours for themselves. You have not saved a single person in this life, and likewise you will not save a single one after your death. You may possibly infect someone with the same desire to save. That is the most, that is all.

The heart must beat far and away.

There is no measure for feelings, and that is why all Greek teachings about the middle range are wrong.

The responsibility that man has today: without oracles removing it from him, without a godhead sending him hither and thither, without a limitation of his knowledge, in the sole certainty of the unending and more and more rapid change of everything that touches him!

Sadnesses as weapons—they threw their sadnesses at one another's heads.

The constant rethinking of things that have often been thought about. It is the familiarity of ancient or Biblical figures that makes them so attractive. One is always with them; and since many others were with them before, every new interpretation of them continues the total essence of the world from the *inside*.

To speak as though it were the last sentence allowed you.

He has a poet in his belly; if only he could get him to his tongue!

There is an indestructible solemnity in him, as though he had already prayed to himself in the womb.

Heirs one doesn't know; they are found by lot.

A night in which all creatures bend into new shapes. The morning after.

There is nothing more wonderful than speaking seriously to a young person. By "seriously," I mean taking him seriously. One has to be uncertain for this, inwardly uncertain without showing it to him, and then gradually grope one's way ahead, as though it were the first time, until one comes close to a certainty in which one can believe for him too and not just for oneself.

Nights and days of fear. I have the strange feeling that everything I learn is turning into fear. Days in which thoughts have totally regained their life are followed by nights of fear. Will the moment ever come when I cannot absorb anything new? Is the expansion of the mind at an end?

A dreadful notion: for I want to keep on and on.

Can an enemy teach you freedom?

They travel all over the world, come back, go away, and I am still here, always the same, nothing has happened, I—always dealing with the same thoughts and people.

What is awry here, is it they, is it I, or is it the same thoughts that have been haunting me for thirty years? Will I die of them, will I ever escape them?

For I am more and more at the mercy of these thoughts, they themselves keep growing and intertwining, and their thicket seems to contain the whole world: the world I do not know.

Oh priest of signs, disquieted creature, caught in the temple of all alphabets, your life will soon be over. What have you seen? What have you feared? What have you accomplished?

The heartbeat of all those who died before their time; that is how—like all of them—his own heart beats at night.

I have not lived any moment in the world without being contained in some myth or other. Everything always made sense, even despair. Things may have looked different from one moment to the next; there was always some meaning that kept growing. I may not have even recognized it, it recognized me. It may have kept silence, later it took the floor. It spoke in a foreign tongue, I learned it. But I did not forget the ancients. I would have given a great deal to forget something; I did not succeed, everything simply became more meaningful. I came into the world in an unbreakable shelter. Do I mistake this shelter for the world?

There the young bring the old into the world. The latter keep getting younger; and when their time comes, they give birth to more old people.

Behind glass, the world is like memory, innocent and unassailable. That is how I would like them to flow past me, all the people I have known, the dead and the remote. They cannot speak to me, they do not realize I can see them. Someone or other may sense it, but the road goes downhill, pulling them along quickly. Thus they all come, they do not know one another, but I knew them all, and no one I knew is repugnant to me. For the glass separating them from me has removed all their guilt and mine.

I long for those who will come later when I am no longer behind any glass. There will be many, but each one will count. Each of them has his own gait.

Perhaps they are the same ones whom I do not know when they walk by out there among my people. Perhaps I might some day have known all of them.

In the sun, people look as if they deserved to live. In the rain, people look as if they had great plans.

His notion of happiness: to read and write quietly for a lifetime without ever showing anyone a word of it, without ever publishing a word of it. To leave in pencil everything one has written down, changing nothing, as though it existed for nothing; like the natural course of a life that serves no confining purposes, but is fully itself, and records itself, just as it proceeds and breathes, by itself.

The future was sought in animals that were cut open. And it *was* there, for the animals were cut open. If people had not cut them, the future would have been different.

There is nothing concrete and different that does not strike me as meaningful; as though everything in existence were concealed in oneself, and one could make it visible to oneself only through things that are different.

One could imagine that the lost hours slip into later ones and suddenly peep out of them. Would they thus not be lost?

The self-confidence of people who *show* themselves from all sides.

Those lovely morning instants when all personal things seem trivial and insignificant; when one feels within oneself the pride of the laws one is seeking.

A distaste for closing things together; you always keep everything open, you always keep everything apart. You really only want to learn and directly record what you have grasped. From day to day, you grasp more, but you are reluctant to *sum up;* as though it could ultimately be possible to express everything in a few sentences on some single day, but then definitively.

An undevourable wish that this day will not come until the end of your life, as late as possible.

Aix. A small cafe right across from the entrance to the prison. I once sat there late at night. There was a poor old woman with a half-dead face at my table. A young man, drunk, was courting her; he importuned her as stubbornly as possible; offered to buy her a drink; embraced her; propositioned her: mocked and teased her; and another man, scarcely any older, equally drunk, applauded him enthusiastically. The old woman stonily let everything pass over her; sometimes she shook herself and hissed: "Leave me alone!" But it didn't help. He couldn't be shaken off. Everything took place in front of the prison, which the old woman kept staring at as though her husband or her son were inside.

One advantage of traveling in new areas is *breaking through the ominous.*
New places do not fit into old meanings. For a while, one truly opens
oneself. All past histories, one's own overflowing life, that is choking
on its own meaning, suddenly remains behind as though one had put it
into safekeeping somewhere, and, while it stays there quietly, purely
uninterpreted things happen: the new.

Arrival by night in Orange. A dense southern night, but the streets
clean and clear, something Puritan superimposed on the Roman. We
sauntered to the theater: the enormous wall facing the square. The
small gate was open, we mounted the stairs, and found ourselves up on
a gallery. In front of the stage down below, lost in the empty space,
stood a few men discussing the lighting effects for a performance taking place in a few days. Thus the theater was lit up for us two, whom
nobody noticed. I was seized with a wild feeling: how splendid it
would be to write plays for a theater like this. We climbed down and
again admired the grand wall outside. A. was tired and I walked him
back to the hotel. The streets were totally deserted and rather dark.
We separated, and I walked back alone to the inner city. It was mid-
night, the cafes were shut, there was no one around, I kept walking
and walking, I hoped for some kind of life, I liked the town so much
and the theater had been so huge—when suddenly, very suddenly, I
noticed a thick swarm of people, men, women, children, very small
children, more and more kept coming, and since I couldn't understand
where they were coming from at this time, especially the children, the
whole thing seemed like a figment of my expectation. But then I
reached a large square—there was a circus here, the entrance to the
tent was open, it was over, the people were pouring out. I walked
around the circus, the whole town was going home by families, and a
few paces further on, I found myself back in front of the mighty wall of
the theater. Now the square was crowded and lively with people head-
ing home.

Thus the crowd had found me again. I was very deeply moved. The
first southern town, the Roman theater empty, and at the same moment, as I walked through the dead, mute city late at night, its people
streaming towards me as a crowd from the circus.

To think that someone can see through life and yet love it so much!
Perhaps he has an inkling of how little his seeing through it really
means.

A ball that keeps getting hurled aloft in order to annoy the heavens: the earth.

A room occupied by three different people who do not know and never see one another.

Gradually I am getting to understand *how much there is.* I cannot say it any other way, I mean how much there is in the world that I should find out about. I have given myself time. Perhaps I could not have grasped most of it earlier. But now I could begin as a respectful pupil. The things I find out become more and more important to me. I no longer try to respond with private and irrelevant gestures. All the things I find out remain in me for days and weeks, growing familiar with what they find in me already. But it is no longer crucial that these encounters occur in me; it is important that they occur at all.

This tenderness with which all *futility* fills one.

The whining resentment of everything one might have known and never did get to know.

The sorrow of the merchant: his wares become a sensitive part of his body.

He walks about in the street thoughtfully, seeking a life position at every step.

The trickster. The effect of a command and the effect of transformation meet within him, and the essence of freedom can be gleaned from him as from no other human figure that one knows. He begins as a chieftain, he gives orders and they are followed. But he drives his people's obedience ad absurdum, thereby getting rid of them.

He shakes everyone off, he destroys custom, obedience, his vehicle, his magic devices, finally his weapons, in order to be completely free of them, in order to be all alone. No sooner is he alone than he can talk to all creatures and things. He wants to isolate himself and is bent purely on *his* own transformations.

Freed of all those who belong to him, he starts out on his road. But he has no road. He wanders about aimlessly and has desires. He converses with parts of his body that lead a life of their own, his behind and his penis. He cuts into his own flesh. He eats from his own innards, not knowing where they come from, he finds them tasty. His right hand has a fight with his left hand.

He imitates everything badly, cannot orient himself anywhere, asks only false questions, for which he gets no answers or just misleading ones.

He adopts two tiny children, to nourish *himself*, not *them*, and takes such wrong care of them that they have to die. He makes himself into a woman, with false breasts and a false vagina, marries the son of a chieftain, and is pregnant several times. There is no inversion that he does not perform for people.

He tricks animals and people when he is hungry, but he is also tricked by them, he is nothing less than a hero and conqueror.

In his isolation, anything possible in life can happen to him. But because of this isolation, his life fails its purpose, seems absurd, and is thereby very instructive.

He is the forerunner of the fool, there is no period and no society that could not produce its fool, and he will always interest people. He entertains them by making everything clear through perverting it.

However, his experiences have to remain incoherent. Every inner sequence, every connection would make them meaningful and would rob them of their value, i.e., their freedom.

Sometimes one says one's best and most important things to *just anybody*. One need not be ashamed, for one does not always speak to ears. The words want to be said in order to exist.

I believe the effect of the new "moon" will be a good one. It will lead to a fully new kind of incentive in the rivalry between the technologically active powers: their competition is leaving the earth for the first time. War between them will become more and more impossible. It doesn't matter who is one step ahead of whom, the conflict would certainly spell a total annihilation of both parties. On the other hand, by shifting their ambition into outer space, they will gain a great deal of prestige from others, as the Russians have now managed to do. A rivalry will come out of it, both grand and childish at once: grand because of the vaster space in which it occurs, childish because every-thing aims so greatly at *emptiness,* while man himself is enormously *full,* and we still know *nothing* about him.

For only a tiny fragment of human memory is being called upon in conquering the moon and the planets. Everything else lies fallow next to it. Yet the simplicity of such goals makes them intelligible to all. A single two-crowd system could now grasp the entire earth, and all its tenants. Everything is so visible, as on a soccer field, but it is visible to *everyone.* The disquiet of those who have lost the first round could, in contrast, make them the first men on the moon. The pride of the others who have gotten a head start will make them secure enough not to stray into a war. It is conceivable that the explosive threats of the past few years will turn into nothing but a giant fireworks, a vastly vis-ible spectacle in the space around the earth, an entertainment for mankind and not yet a curse for the stars.

Every new person whose existence one recognizes will change one. Perhaps it is the inevitability of this change that one senses and shies away from, for it takes place before one *exhausts* what one was prior to that change.

Yesterday I read an old account on the calling of a man to become a magician among the Amazulus. It was more powerful, more convinc-ing, more original, more true than the noblest self-descriptions of *our* ascetics and ecstatics. These Negroes want the magician to find lost or stolen objects, and it is this faculty that is tested and taken seriously. The main thing would thus be the sense of a calling, while its *content* does not seem to matter.

It torments him that not everything he ever knew *flares up at the same time.*

1958

These Oxford philosphers scrape and scrape until nothing is left. I have learned a lot from them: I now know it's better not to start scraping at all.

One could, of course, think only about words instead of myths; and so long as one avoids defining them, one could get from them all the wisdom that has accumulated among men. Myths are *more fun,* however, because they are full of metamorphoses.

His heart is the lamp at night.

She now lives in his old room and loves it, as though he were dead. She is very annoyed when he comes in.

"A man's wealth is estimated according to the number of his books and the horses in his stable." (Timbuktu, c. 1500)

I sometimes feel as though everything I learn and read were invented. But the things I find myself seem as though they really always existed.

There is nothing more intricate than the paths of the mind. The way a person learns when he makes sure not to immediately use what he learns is more adventurous and more mysterious than any voyage of exploration. For in the mind, one cannot decide upon and calculate any roads. Certainly the mind has something like rough maps; but infinitely many more things lure one away on all sides, and what astonishment when finding oneself where one already was, a different person in the old place.

The more *definite* a mind is, the more it needs the *new.*

There is something similar about all stories, but I still don't know what it is.

To think that you still believe in a law, even though you know you will never find it, even though you know that nobody knows it.

I have always scarcely doubted; how young and energetic doubt still is for me.

A man who slowly turns into a bad conscience. Yet he feels so good all the while.

"Even now, men still rigorously make sure than an animal cannot be slaughtered until, having had the libation poured upon it, it indicates its agreement by nodding its head." (Plutarch, *Table Conversations*)

"In thirteenth-century Egypt, a mania for eating human flesh raged through all classes; physicians were the favorite prey. If a man was hungry, he pretended to be sick and sent for a doctor—not to consult him, but to devour him." (Humboldt) "People so greatly enjoyed this dreadful food that one even saw rich and very honorable men consuming it, making banquets of it, even storing it. Various ways were devised to prepare the flesh. . . . People used all possible tricks to waylay others or lure them into their homes on false pretenses. Three physicians who came to me met with this fate, and a bookdealer, who sold books to me, an old very fat man, fell into their snares and just barely escaped." (Abd-Allatif, a Baghdad physician, in his description of Egypt)

All events fear their words.

He is sorry about his lamenting pack. It got lost in England.

If it's a question of martyrs, then it ought to be all of them. Which martyr is worth more than the next?

There are too many roads in language, everything is already laid out.

The well-read man. B. doesn't care much for strenuous efforts. He doesn't like to work. He doesn't like to learn. He is curious and so he sometimes reads a book. But it has to be written very simply, in short, plain, direct sentences. It must contain no farfetched words and certainly no relative clauses. The reader should not have to stumble over anything and should be able to take in everything right away, without thinking. The best thing would be to be able to grasp an entire page at one view. Actually B. is looking for such pages. He opens up a volume at random, in back, in front, or in the middle, and his eye seizes one page. The page resists. It does not care to yield at one swoop. It wants the reader to spend twenty or thirty seconds with it. The page regards this as modesty; B. does not agree. Its resistance annoys him, he turns the page and, if he is not too angry as yet, he bites into the next one. He usually has the same experience here. This is too much for him; and in mounting indignation, he leaves this part of the book. He punishes it by opening to a completely different passage, a hundred pages further or earlier. Unimpressed by any page, he reads wherever he likes. In this way, he skips about through a book. Since he has *his own* way of doing it, it is no surprise that he feels like more of a connoisseur than all those decent plebeians who read in sequence. In this manner, he really acquires personal conceptions of a book. If it halfway appeals to him, he knows passages of ten or fifteen pages, strung together from the most disparate parts and always in an unusual sequence.

Sometimes he finds the courage to come out with his original conception and amaze people who do not know him. With somewhat more method, he could acquire the reputation of a highly individual mind. He would simply have to do it a bit more often, say, *one* book per month. That is naturally too much for him, and so he sticks to two or three books a year. But there is a further obstacle, that should not be hushed up. He lacks any special quality in the choice of books. He is interested only in those that everyone is talking about. First all the reputable critics of all reputable newspapers have to pass their unanimous verdict; first this verdict has to be such that everyone reaches for the book, and its qualities have to be shouted out from all the better rooftops; first he has to hear the author's name so often that it would be prestigious to make his acquaintance; then, but really only then, is he enticed to begin his leafing.

Yet he does not begin right off. He goes to his book-dealer, in the most elegant street in London, where duchesses do their shopping. He knows the book dealer well, he is one of his best clients. The man sometimes sends him, of his own accord, a book that might interest him; and even if he already owns a copy, he will never send it back. However, and especially since living in the world of the intellect, he prefers browsing himself. He has the book dealer show him this or that, rejects it in boredom without taking a look, and then, with a triumphant expression, he asks for the book that's been the talk of the town for two weeks. He approximates the title, he is not sure of the author's name; one should never pay too much respect to sudden fads that cannot look back upon generations of forebears. Usually, the book was among the ones that the dealer showed him and that he arrogantly pushed away. It takes tact not to let him sense this. For he knows what he wants, and he wants people to notice it.

So he casually takes the book under his arm and throws it on the upholstered seat of his Bentley. At home, in a gigantic, sumptuous room, with pictures of his ancestors hanging on the walls, he lays the book down flat on a large oval table, on which all the latest things are spread out, the books of the past few months that have found particular grace in the eyes of the critics. There it lies next to its own, and nothing else ever lies there. Everything is brand-new, and the new edition of an old work that may have wandered here thanks to the efforts of the Sunday papers might seem quite déplacé. Thus he has succeeded in shifting the fashionable bookshop amid his ancestors. *They* could not know what he has here; it is the only thing he has over them, and in proud moments, he lets them feel it.

Now, among the masterworks of modern life, he can make *his* selection. He is capable of enthusiasm, but he does not care to praise what he does not like; he too respects his own judgment. The moment comes when he decisively takes hold of the newly acquired book. He does this very quickly, like everything he does, with the bold movement of a bird of prey. Books containing relative clauses are excluded in advance. He has an eagle's eye for them and knows no mercy. But it also depends on the subject matter. Anything not pertaining to him strikes him as untrue. He wants truth; he quickly unmasks lying authors.

At times he stumbles upon writers who see through *him*. If they do it very nimbly, he is impressed. But ultimately, he seeks another page yielding itself at first glance. If *he* is the topic and if he can grasp at first sight the very first page he opens to, then he need not read on. He has discovered a masterpiece, his masterpiece, and from now on he tells it to everyone.

One always puts one's hopes in the wrong people, and if one knew it, one could not live another moment. Luckily, there are always others, to whom one was so innocent that one did not even place hope in them. Thus life goes on, along unexpected, surprising paths.

One cannot show any deeper respect for humanity than in the hunger for its myths; and when one has read more than the heart can endure, one may hope for the secret strength of this nourishment.

Hell is the most dreadful of inventions, and it is hard to understand how one can expect any good of people after this invention. Will they not *always* have to invent hells?

Everything is better than "I," but where do we put it?

His grief: that he has not always opened himself up to every least utterance of life. His grief: the decades of arrogance.

He considers himself better than himself, he finds it pleasant to have such a good and such a bad opinion of himself.

What does it mean: One should become better? More open, more yielding? Is that really better? Clearer? Yes. More unified? Not so much. Calmer? I don't know.

Sometimes I wished I could empty my head of everything that had settled in it, and thus begin thinking all over again as though there had never been anything there.
    I no longer wish for that. I recognize the population of my head and I try to get along with it.
    It is possible that I have become a provincial.

In an Italian paper, I read about a nun who has just died at the age of one hundred.
    She had already died once, as a seventeen-year-old girl, and the coffin was already nailed shut when her sister demanded that it be reopened. She came to and sat up. This miracle made her decide to become a nun and devote her life to God. Thus she lived another eighty-three years after her first death.

Man is very great; however much fear he is capable of, he can know it and hold it and live with it, and never forget it.

1959

On a Pacific atoll, people were eaten recently for the last time, in honor of an atomic explosion.

Everyone ought to watch himself eating.

As of a certain age, every man's word becomes heavy and counts. Absolve yourself of *this* gravity.

The precious sentences of fools.

The consumption by a work dragging on for years. The work can be right only if one draws away some of its life, so that it becomes hard and haggard. The more compulsive the work, the more comes out.

Whenever I hear the word "life's work," I think of an inhuman asceticism.

Another book, another great book? A thousand blown-up pages? In what row do you place yourself, and isn't everything already in existence better?

Pay no attention, everything has to be rethought.

The true feeling of strength, when no triumphs beckon.

All squandered veneration.

The hospital in which he lives, among nothing but entombed and seriously wounded books.

I like and dislike industriousness, according to the time of day or night. At night, I am passionately industrious, until dawn; during the day, I am just as passionately lazy.

One develops many qualities out of stubbornness. Then, when they bore one, one can no longer get rid of them.

Each man fully betrays himself in his divisions.

It is important to feel injured from time to time, namely, to see oneself as ignorant people see one.

I am sick and tired of hearing everyone accuse everyone else of his own shortcomings!

Sometimes it seems to me as if completion has become a sort of purpose in itself. I think of the goals I began with; of the confidence with which I wanted to do something real. While I worked on it, the world charged itself up with a thousand times more destruction. It is *restrained* destruction, but does that make a difference?

And what is this obsessiveness that drives me to oppose any destruction, as though I had named myself the protector of the world? What am I then myself—a helpless creature, seeing one close person after another dying, and not even able to keep his very own alive. Shipwreck on all sides and lamentable shrieks!

Whom do I help, whom do I serve with this unshakable defiance?

Nothing is left but this defiance. New people slide away, new words and conversations vanish; the past is still alive; when will chance attack it too? Nothing will remain, and I will still be standing here—a child standing on its own feet for the first time—and screaming "NO!" with all my strength.

One man says he can regret nothing. A god? A stone?

He dreams of detaching his heart from all who have sunk their teeth into it: suddenly he holds it intact in his hand.

Every word he writes down gives him strength. No matter what it may be; it may be nothing; but writing it down gives him strength.

Just why is it so good to speak to oneself? Because one wants nothing from oneself? Because one can go very far in hatred without bearing a grudge? Because one is a daredevil without endangering anyone? Because one finds out something about others whom one has hidden deep inside? Because one can get too close for comfort to one's arrogance, without making a cheap spectacle of it? Because one is earnest and pure in truth without preening onself with it? Because one neither asks nor pressures, and one is with an equal?

More and more faces recall other faces: overfilled life tries to disentangle itself.

The components of the world which one loves, and the whole thing, mis-composed, which one hates.

Nothing is more dismal than being the first, unless one really is the first and no one else has as yet been there.

Everything depends on the wrong model, human confusions occur because people happen to seize upon their models at some random moment and are never released from them again.

One thinks, one thinks, until everything thinks of its own accord, and then it means nothing more.

Do not always forge on to the very end. There are so many things in between.

Officials will make thunderstorms like Jupiter.

I feel at home when I write down German words with a pencil in my hand and everyone around me is speaking English.

Yesterday, the manuscript of *Crowds and Power* went off to Hamburg.
  In 1925, thirty-four years ago, I had my first thought about a book on the crowd. But the real seed for it came even earlier: a workers' demonstration in Frankfurt for the death of Rathenau; I was seventeen.
  However I look at it, my entire adult life was filled with this book; but since settling in England, that is, for the past twenty years, I have worked on scarcely anything else, albeit with tragic interruptions.
  Was it worth all this effort? Have I thereby lost many other works?

What can I say? I *had* to do what I have done. It was a compulsion that I will never understand.

I spoke about it before much more than the intention for the book existed. I announced it with the greatest claim in order to chain myself harder to it. While everyone who knew me kept driving me to complete it, I did not terminate it even one hour earlier than I thought proper. My best friends lost their faith in me during these years; it took too long, I couldn't blame them.

Now I tell myself that I have succeeded in grabbing this century by the throat.

The indifference about a decision once it's made—as though someone else had made it.

A man raises himself on the value of his time when it is suddenly limited—but only when it was his nature to leave himself a lot of time. The failure of his greatest wealth suddenly makes more of him—as though he actually had given everything away and were a beggar invited to feed on his own leftovers.

1960

You are so sure of your cause that one could despair of your right mind. But so long as the noise does not crash down upon you, this certainty need not be harmful. The most difficult thing is finding a hole through which you can slip out of your own work. You would like to be back in a free world without rules, which has not been violated by you. All order is tormenting, but one's own order is the most tormenting of all. You know that not all of it *can* be correct, but you will not let your composition be destroyed. You could try to undermine it, but then you yourself would still be in it. You want to be outside, free. You could, as someone else, write a dreadful attack against it. But you don't want to destroy it, after all. You merely want to change yourself.

The finest thing about Montaigne is that he never hurries. He is even slow in treating affects and thoughts that are full of impatience. His interest in himself is unshakable, he is never really ashamed of his own person, he is no Christian. Whatever he observes is important to him, but he is really inexhaustible only with himself. It gives him a kind of freedom to remain with himself. He is an object that can never be lost, he always has himself. This one life, which he never loses sight of, moves as slowly as his observation.

Montaigne's chapter on cannibals, which I read today, again greatly captivated me in his favor. He has that openness to every kind of humanity, an openness that is universal today and has even been raised to the level of a science. But he had it *back then,* in a fanatically self-righteous time. In this chapter, Montaigne praises the virtue of warlike courage, which cannot mean much to him for his own environment. By admiring the Brazilians for their courage, he seems to be asking: "Are *we* truly courageous? Just what is our courage anyway?" The Indian victim in the hands of his enemies bears the features of Cato for him. There is no one he venerates more: not as a model, but as the unattainable that shall ever be denied to him. For among the stars, there are such that we pull down; others are so high that we can never lay hands on them.

But Montaigne here also presents the picture of the good savage, that recurs almost two hundred years later in Rousseau. Only in the latter, it has become a sort of compulsion, as in the Sparta of Lycurgus.

The court jester, someone who possesses the very least, next to the all-possessor. As a kind of freedom, he always acts in front of his master, but then again is always at his mercy. The master *sees* the freedom of the unburdened fool, but since the fool belongs to him, he may think that the freedom belongs to him too.

Significant pains: every pain would have its graspable sense, it could only signify something precise, and the remedy would then be in the behavior of one's own mind. However, overcoming pain would then be difficult and always constitute an improvement of man. Instead of warning, pains would be inducements. The person with the most pains, if behaving correctly, would then get farthest: his treatment would be his own invention and accomplishment.

You only consist of structures. Were you born geometrically, or has time seized you and forced you into its hopeless straight forms? Do you no longer know the great secret? The secret of the *longest way?*

It would be blissful to take thoughts that have dominated one all one's life and let them sink so deep that they only surface in dreams.

The "dreadful" thinkers whom I admire include Hobbes and de Maistre. What I admire about such men is that they can *speak* the dreadful. However, the fear dominating them should not be the means of their self-aggrandizement. That is why I name these two, Hobbes and de Maistre: as different as they may be from one another, both of them did not always allow their thoughts to turn their heads; they remained plain in the utterances of their lives. In contrast to them, there is a different kind of thinker, who relishes turning terror against men, as though they could thereby draw some glory of their own. Terror becomes a whip for them to keep everything else at bay. They admire "greatness," but mean animal greatness. Nietzsche is such a thinker, his freedom is in painful contrast to his basic lust for power, to which he ultimately succumbed. Many of his sentences fill me with repugnance, like those of a vulgar despot. De Maistre articulated things that are more dreadful. But he says them because they exist in the world, he says them as their instrument and not out of lust. The thinkers who are filled with an honest fear of men are victims of this fear like all others, and do not secretly aspire to using it for their own purposes. They do not falsify the condition of the world, they remain in it, most exposed to the fear they feel. The resistance aroused by their thoughts is healthy and fruitful. Others pretend to be dangerous and splendid in order, as it were, to leap up from the world to themselves. Thus, what they say is falsified to the core and can be useful only to those employing it in order to rob mankind of its dignity and hope.

In his statements on war, de Maistre asked the right questions. That is something. He did not answer them with pious sentences. This is more. The answers he does find may be framed peculiarly; but they seem like pure mockery to a man of our time, who has learned a thing or two. It is hard to find any inducement *against* war that could be more effective than these very lines of de Maistre's.

It is a wonderful feeling to find quiet for thinking amid very many people. For one thing, one has to put some effort into the specific measure of isolation one aims at; one is not easily alone, and it has more weight if one ultimately appears that way to oneself. One can then not help feeling an animosity towards others who hem one in on all sides. It is no serious animosity, however, for one imagines one is thinking along for all of them, and the responsibility one feels for them warms the animosity into love.

The paranoid as Buddhist: Schopenhauer's uniqueness.

Burckhardt as Atlas: a Basel citizen who contains and holds up the world.

One needs infinitely distant sentences that one barely understands, as a mainstay over the millennia.

To invent a faith, introduce it, get others to accept it, and then abolish it, until it has totally vanished from among men.

But not even the man who succeeds in this knows what faith is.

The atoms in Democrites have the character of a crowd conception. It is remarkable that the Greek theory of nature, which has proved to be the most fruitful, owes its origin to an obsession with an invisible crowd consisting of the smallest units.

I feel close to Democrites in many respects; some of his sentences seem to be speaking out of my very heart. It is unfortunate that Aristotle's complete works instead of his have come down to us. How inimical I find Aristotle's mind! How it goes against my grain to read him! Democrites was no less many-sided, no less curious than Aristotle. But the latter is a collector and respects power; even Socrates' hairsplitting has gone into him. Democrites lived away from Athens; that was good for him. Perhaps he set too much store by the righteousness of the man who lives alone. A plain self-complacence holds him together, but it tinges none of his grand ideas, in which he sees something for the first time. There is a private statement of his, for which I would give all of Aristotle: Democrites says he would rather find a single explanation than gain possession of the Persian Empire.

Academies whose task would be to abolish certain words from time to time.

For him, all windows seem to be leading to infinity. But if he looks through some window from the outside, he feels as if he were settling into life from infinity.

I am interested in living people and I am interested in literary characters. I despise any cross between them.

The leap into the universal is so dangerous that one has to keep practicing it, and always in the same spot.

Without books, joys turn rotten.

It is good to think of certain words and to keep saying them to oneself. It is not good that only words like "God" have achieved this highest intensity of repetition. The Allah-sayers in Marrakesh reminded me of this, and I would now like to serve many splendors of language in the very same way.

One can now keep wanting more and more in any direction. All goals have virtually shifted to infinity, yet they nevertheless seem attainable.

One can gain anything with the mind, and with the mind alone. But mind refers only to an isolated form of activity, which needs less and less material substrata. It is enough to think in a certain way and in a certain direction. The ascetic nature of this thinking includes its unerringness. The power it grants is comparable to the one held by religious advisors in religiously uniform states. It is a decisive power, but it likes to keep hidden, and it requires no immediate personal splendor.

The splendor is reserved for the moment of annihilation.

I think I have found a key to *Metamorphoses* and inserted it in the lock, but I have not turned the key. The door is shut, one cannot enter. We will have a lot more trouble with it.

Ordering thought around four or five words might still make sense, it leaves some space. How dreadful are the mystics of *one* word.

The subtlety of a literary figure, even when I admire it, as a product of this time, provokes contradiction in me: it strikes me as too self-complaisant. For the writer to give it the kick it deserves, it must somewhere be capable of feeling it.

Even after the first war, some writers were still able to content themselves with deep breathing and crystal polishing. But today, after the second war, after gas chambers and atomic bombs, being human requires more in its utmost imperilment and degradation. One must turn to brutality as it always was, and coarsen one's hands and mind on it. One must grab man as he is, hard and unredeemed. But one must not permit him to lay his hands on hope. Hope can flow only from darkest knowledge, otherwise it will become a derisive superstition and speed up the destruction that looms more and more ominously.

More and more delicate the watches, more and more dangerous time.

The most difficult thing is to reduce oneself after fulfilling oneself. The fulfilled man's presumption of his special importance is as wrong as the self-satisfaction of the ever-empty man. A man who was preoccupied with either the worst or the best has to become simple again as at the beginning. The insights he has gained must not be employed for his own private use, he must leave them to other people and release himself from them.

Estrangement from a work without actual dislike. One reads it without noting what one reads. A coolness emanates from it as from a sun that has set.

The towns one has lived in become neighborhoods in the town one dies in.

Now he submerges once again into the sea of the unread and then surfaces puffing and rejuvenated, as proud as if he had stolen Poseidon's trident.

Galileo's recantation in Brecht's play reminded me of Fifty's recantation in my play *The Numbered.* It is a recantation to gain time, but not changing anything whatsoever in the true opinion of the threatened man. Fifty is conceived more severely and he also goes further: for he has to witness what he has caused with his passion for truth. Brecht's Galileo, conceived earlier, can still nonchalantly eat his roast goose. He lacks an entire dimension, the one that has become most important for us today. What right do I have to an explosive truth, which I alone know, and must I not try to make it harmless at any price? It is in me, its sole bearer still, that the process of rendering it harmless and dissolving it must commence.

Truth thus has its twofold gravity. Discovery and acceptance are merely the *one* aspect of this gravity; infinitely more serious is the second aspect, that of responsibility.

Otherwise, circuitously, one restores to the inquisitors the right that they had already half lost. Galileo is not lamentable for recanting, for he then wrote the *Discorsi.* He is lamentable for managing to eat his goose so *unsuspectingly:* the future has gone blind for him.

All at once, the end had come for all faith. A feeling of infinite happiness spread out among men. Everyone danced by himself until he collapsed. Everyone then got up again at some distance from the others. The sun shone stronger. But the air was thin. The ocean became incomprehensible.

The lament for the dead aims at reanimation, *that* is its passion. The lament is to last until it succeeds. But it stops too soon: not enough passion.

It might be that the man who refuses to kill will ultimately not be allowed any free decision. Yet even were he to be totally paralyzed: he shall not kill.

How he fears his own words! The things he says have such power over him that they never let go of him again. After the first acute stages of pain that they cause him, they lie down and wait. Then they leap up again, they most certainly leap up again, and pounce upon him as though they had just been said anew. His own words achieve their power only when he has *heard* them. They come out of him, and yet they come as if from some alien place. He confronts them head-on, escape would be impossible, nor does he want to escape. Often he plunges into their midst, they pelt down upon him from right and left, he prefers more than anything to yield to them in cloudbursts. It is not a chaos that they arouse in him, but it *is* strong and clear pains. Whatever they say, he understands, even when it is quite obscure; where they come from is an enigma to him.

A man flatters until one finally replies amicably in order to get rid of him. He builds his reputation on these replies.

By its very nature, all fame is deception. Sometimes it does turn out that there is something behind it. What a surprise!

In every life, you may find the dead on which a man has been feeding. In tender, decent, brutal, wicked people—everywhere, there are misused dead. How can a man who knows this about himself still endure living? By lending his own life to his dead, never losing it and making them eternal.

I am not a poet: I cannot keep silent. But many people are silent within me, people I do not know. Their outbursts sometimes make me a poet.

Every believer I encounter, as long as he truly *is* a believer, makes me feel friendly. The simple utterance of his faith moves me, and if it seems so absurd that one would have to laugh, it then moves me most deeply.

However, he must not belong to a faith to which the world now belongs. No sooner do I feel the power of a victorious church behind it, no sooner do I realize that the believer is trying to cover himself with this power, use it for threat and terror, than I am seized with disgust and horror.

Is it faith that moves me, or merely an underdog faith?

In grief, something is always preparing itself, yet it doesn't help to point this out to oneself.

My grief has nothing liberating about it. For I always know too well that I have not succeeded in doing anything against death.

Ataraxia? Acquiring indifference? Where one is most vulnerable? That is the very place where one should never acquire it!

I can endure dreams only when they are intact and whole, as a mystery. They are so alien that one is only very slow to grasp them. As for other people's dreams, I can comprehend them only one at a time. One takes them up, carefully and reluctantly. Woe to the fool who interprets them immediately, he loses them and never holds them again, they wither before they could turn green for him.

Likewise, one should not pile dreams up together if they never belonged to one another. They get their blood by emanating into reality. The materialization of a dream is everything, but it comes in a different way than the normal interpreters imagine. A dream has to animate reality by penetrating it, in all possible ways, from every direction whatsoever, and especially from where one least suspected. As a flock of birds, a dream perches here and there, it rises and returns, it flees and no sooner has it fled than it darkens the light of the sun. The ungraspable in the dream is its most graspable aspect; and yet it does have its shape, but it has to gain its shape itself, by slipping into the shapes of reality, and one must not give it that shape from the outside.

How vast is the damage caused by interpreted dreams. Their disruption remains concealed, but how sensitive is a dream! There is no blood on the axes of the slaughterers when they strike the cobwebs; but what destruction they have wrought! And never again will the same thing be spun. The uniqueness of every dream is sensed by very few people; how else could they then expose it to any commonplace?

Perhaps, of all people, only Klee treated dreams with the proper awe, as the most inviolable thing to occur in a human being.

It is hard to find one's way back to the paces and sounds of innocent people after being preoccupied with the ruthless hunt after the wielders of power. How one hated them, and how one grew accustomed to this hatred! And how simple should one become again, how gentle and how pleasant? It is as though one had put oneself into retirement and were cultivating flowers after a lifelong hunt for dangerous monsters.

However, the hunter will never forget what he was, and he will hunt himself in his dreams at least.

Every word should recall the fact that it was once palpable: the roundness of words: they lay in the hand.

A life that develops no plays or parts out of itself is inconceivable. Even an idiot has his coquetry, and a saint also who does not go among men is sought out by them.

A woman who has to smile at everyone, who smiles herself into the greatest confusion, who cannot give up her smile in misery, who smiles upon her deathbed and dies with a smile, in order to be liked by anyone who might see her corpse. She smiles in the coffin and under the earth.

It is not enough to think, one also has to breathe. Dangerous are the thinkers who have not breathed enough.

The man who really knew what ties people together would be able to save them from death. The enigma of life is a social enigma. No one is on its track.

Mysticism: seeing-through has already occurred once and for all. It is the same seeing-through. It is uneventful. It cannot be taken back.

The man who wants to find something truly new must, above all, guard against any method of investigation. Later on, after finding something, he may feel an urge to define his method of investigation after the fact. But that is a tactical question, especially when he has to gain recognition for his findings during his lifetime. The original process itself is characterized by absolute freedom and uncertainty; and the man moving in this way for the first time cannot have the least inkling as to the direction of his movement.

The responsibility lies in the entire man and not in this special undertaking.

I can make friends only with minds that know death. Of course, it makes me happy when they succeed in holding their tongues about death: for *I* cannot.

An insight having nothing of its occasion adhering to it is worthless. The occasion of the thinker lives again in the occasion of the reader. An old experience is suddenly young again after centuries. The same star shines again and encounters the same eye.

The darkness sinks into his letters, and they get a different meaning. They look as if they had existed for a much longer time, fuller, stronger, filled with the same night since time immemorial. They come apart and join together again, secure and loving, by a clear, but inexhaustible law. Their fear has vanished, and they have nothing to be ashamed of. It may be that some *day* they will feel like that too, but that day is far.

A pub in which all have gone mute. The patrons sit mutely, alone or in groups, and down their drinks. The waitress mutely hands you a menu, you point to a spot, she nods, brings you what you want, and puts it mutely on the table. Everyone looks wordlessly at everyone else. The air halts in this room where there is no speaking. Everything seems made of glass. The people seem more fragile than the objects. It turns out that words give movements their fluidity; without words, everything is rigid. Gazes are eery and unintelligible. It is possible that nothing is thought but hatred. Someone stands up. What is he going to do? Everyone is scared. A child, like a painting, opens its mouth wide, but no shriek sounds out. The parents say nothing and close his mouth.

The light goes out, one hears a smashing. The light goes on again, but no one is shattered. Payment is by coins, which are as familiar as small animals. A cat leaps on the table and dominates the place. The cat has never gone mute, for it was always silent.

Now the place is livened up with dead people.

1961

One would have to say it in as few sentences as Lao-tse or Heraclites; and so long as one cannot do that, one really has nothing to say.

Knowledge crosses its arms and faces the fight. Humble knowledge disgusts him, he vomits it up. But how attracted he is to knowledge as a foe!

The worst people: those who know everything and believe they do.

Could a man who has lived hundreds of years still know, in all his entanglements, just who he is?
Would he know it *again?*

Is the dramatic character of a *sage* possible, and what would it have to be like? Dramatically speaking, the wise man would be the only one who recognizes the others; who never speaks about himself; who has nothing to say about himself; who lives in hearing, in listening, who becomes wise from the things heard and who knows nothing before hearing; who can make a clean slate of himself for every man, but preserves in himself all the other full slates without thinking of them.

The drama plays transformations and unmaskings back and forth, and their alternation produces what we call suspense.
The masks have to provoke terror, but they also have to be taken off. Without masks that are taken quite seriously, there is no drama. However, a drama that remains stuck in the masks is boring.

A city with secret street-names; policemen tell you where you are if they trust you.

One takes in more than one realizes. But how does one administer it?

Ten heavens surmounting one another, and the angels more *eloquent* in each.

An act of violence for the ritual commemoration of the abolition of all violence.

The translator penetrates a familiar sphere. Everything around him is well-cultivated, and he is never lonely. He moves about as in a park landscape or among clearly bordered fields. Words address him like people and bid him good-day. The path is shown to him, and he can scarcely go astray. He has to accept as true whatever is said to him, and he cannot doubt it. The power of seeing through something is denied to the translator. He would be a fool if he lost his confidence here. The terrain has always been precisely marked out.

The thinker, in contrast, has emptiness around him. He pushes everything away until there is enough emptiness around him, and then starts leaping from this to that. In his leaps, he creates his road. The ground is sure only because he steps on it; everything in between is doubt.

The translation into another language of thoughts one has been concerned with for more than twenty years. Their discontent, because they were not born in this language. Their boldness dies, they refuse to shine. They tow along things that do not belong and drop important things on the way. They pale, they change color. They feel cowardly and cautious; the angle under which they originally came is lost to them. They once flew like birds of prey, now they flutter like bats. They ran like cheetahs, now they creep along like blindworms.

Humiliating to think that they will meet with more sympathy in this reduction, this constraint and emasculation!

In order to escape the *gravity* of reading (as though everything had to be employed exactly as it is read), a man should occasionally plunge into a chaos of books, the kind he despises because he no longer knows them, and the kind he despises because he never knew them. If his biases get confused, there is hope for him, he shall finally make an easy time of it.

All people experience the same thing: but no one is allowed to realize this. Identity of secrets. Destinies are iridescent in changing light. But in the dark, it's all the same again.

He owns up to being innocent or guilty, all according to the date.

In every generation, only one person will die—as an intimidation.

He went mute out of distrust against adjectives.

The hottest man may indulge in the coldness of description.

The earth a light blue, the sky black, reversal of the familiar condition: for the earth was threatened for us by darkness, we put our trust in the blue sky. But once a man is outside, the earth becomes bright for him and the sky black.

Blind men under the table, deaf-mutes in the corners, and he, as a lame giant, choking in the elevator. A woman turns the key in the ceiling and pelts him with chickenfeed instead of words. He gasps for air, and his mouth is full of grains. The blind scream, the deaf-mutes start hitting away at one another. He smashes the elevator and finds himself in a tangle of people in the room. People who can see and speak praise him as cured. He awakens in an anthill.

Dream in the noonday sun on a slope over Delphi.

Indestructible, the loveliest, most meaningful place in the world: A servant with a straw broom sweeps the Castalian fount. A professor with his students tests the acoustics of the theater in French. A nymph, leaning on a column of the Apollo Temple, leafs about in a guide and asks in American: "Where is Delphi?"

Catunia: Early morning, the English penitent meditating by the Euripus. Dark and gaunt, like a bearded saint in an icon, he greets the stroller with "good morning," and converses with him about Oxford and the merits of the Greek church.

Lord Byron in the taverna, six resin gatherers around him, two Greek Orthodox priests at the next table, Lord Byron stutters and pays for everyone.

St. John's Day in the seaside chapel. Small cubes of bread are handed around. A dolphin bounds up not far from the faithful, who kiss one another. In the distance, Mount Parnassus looms over the Euripus.

Christianity seems most intimate where it misjudges the sleeping gods. The figtree in Catunia speaks Greek.

The way each faith blindly contains the previous one, never referring to it at all and thus better protecting it, as though it were openly in the eye of the new faith.

A heart that has rolled through all centuries chewed up.

A hell of flatterer-devils.

The belated reactions: A man always speaks to the wrong person because he speaks to an earlier one who is no longer here. He cannot say it at the right moment because he notices only too late what he has grasped. The character of the *Dislocated Man* and the things he causes.

Sometimes when he can't see anything at all, he is saved by an hour in *fog*.

Everything he experienced was futile: the karma of the spendthrift.

He seeks the best, since he seeks it for himself. Others may be content with less. He feels like an overseer and justifies his privilege with rejection and severity. The effort that others expend on their performance is expended by him on testing. Anything he has not tested himself is worthless. Only the things on which his eye has fallen can be precious. He leaves most things aside; let them dissolve, since he didn't notice them.

He stands up high in the costume of an examiner and gives warning whistles. One has to see him sucking in chosen air and expelling it again in the guise of high tones!

To see each person in such a way as though one had already seen him a hundred times and were seeing him for the first time.

The victim who in death turns into his own killer and calls for help in his voice. (Ramayana)

The ear, not the brain, as the seat of the mind. (Mesopotamia)

Illuminating and *ordering* minds. Heraclites and Aristotle as extreme cases.

The illuminating mind is like lightning, it flashes rapidly over the greatest distances. It leaves everything aside and shoots for one thing, which it does not know before illuminating it. Its effectivity begins when it strikes. Without some minimum of destruction, without terror, it never takes shape for human beings. Illumination per se is too boundless and too shapeless. The fate of the new knowledge depends on the place of the striking. For this lightning, man is largely virgin soil.

The illuminated thing is left to the orderers. Their operations are as slow as those of the others are fast; they are the cartographers of the striking, which they mistrust; and with the things they do, they strive to prevent further lightning from striking.

A city in which the classes use different streets. The upper and the lower classes never bump into one another. Necessary communications go by wires. Embarrassing work is done invisibly. One class looks at the ground, the other sideways. The upper class dresses in ears, the lower in hands. A hander who goes astray is horrified to come among ears; while these listen away, he carries out the penalty for his aberration and strangles himself. The ears open to his final sigh and praise his class consciousness. Renegade ears starve to death among hands and lie rotten in the streets of the lower class.

Even their dogs are separated and never dare mix.

The self-dissolution of history in its acts of revenge.

1962

The anecdotes of the Chinese with their one-syllable names: everything reduced to formulas that we cannot imitate. Even the most ambivalent thing is correct; every word, in its precise shape, is like a musical note, and when it sounds together with other notes, they have a unique and solid stamp. Something of this emanates into the rest of the world: the world is safer, but not locked. Filled with solid points, it is animated. It performs orders and yet remains free. All individual stamps remain independent of one another.

A nice trick: throwing something into the world without being pulled in by it.

A man for whom everything he has learned is transformed into objects, and they plunge in on him from all sides and kill him.

Do you really want to be one of those for whom things get better and better?

In order to take himself seriously, he acts bitter.

He lays sentences like eggs, but he forgets to brood them.

What have you awaited these forty years? Lack of time, or experience?

". . . And once again he puts off the end with that enigmatic faith in an endless lifetime." (Schönberg)

Wherever I reach, I find hair to grab and use it to pull forth people. Some are whole, others half, these I can recognize. Others are in pieces, and I quickly throw them back. If I had the heart to keep looking at them, they would join together with others and stand up around me as a new population. But I have become unsure, alien things push in among them and knock and demand admission; promises have been given, and there is still room. I cannot deny anyone entrance because I feel guilty.

There is no order to be gained in the human remnants that one keeps locked up in oneself; only memory or falsification.

When taking leave, everyone there jumps up on the table and keeps silent.

His justification: having a response for nothing.

"L'homme est périssable. Il se peut; mais périssons en résistant et, si le néant nous est reservé, ne faisons que ce soit une justice."
["Man is perishable. That may be; but let us die in resistance, and, if nothingness lies ahead, let us not act as if it were just."] (Sénancour, *Obermann*)

He plays too many instruments at once. But thinking is *not* composing. In thinking, something is ruthlessly driven to extremes. The process of knowledge consists above all in throwing everything overboard in order to more rapidly and more easily reach a goal that one senses. A. cannot throw anything overboard. He always drags himself along whole. He never gets anywhere.

Everything he knows is always present to him. He knocks on all doors and enters nowhere. Having knocked, he thinks he has been there.

His well-papered mind.

His thoughts in clouds, they yield everywhere; suddenly, you can't see; you know you are in one of his thoughts.

Dignity of the match.

She kept on her final piece of clothing, the lip curled in scorn.

Unsatisfied noses in one row.

Nakedness without applause is true nakedness.

A mountain opens; out come eighty giant earthworms with wings and saddles; on each one rides a famous poet.

How can a man remain behind without his work? Others touch it, it is no longer his work, it changes under their eyes and fingers. The released work is fair game. The former keeper, anemic and poor, can only perform reduced, senseless movements. He, who once breathed for the earth, now breathes clandestinely for himself. He, who felt borne by all people, now walks on wretched feet. He had continent-boots, now he creeps along inch by inch. He was as generous as a god, now he trembles over ciphers. He drove everything up with him, now he is a shriveled balloon. He had the whole world tenderly in himself, now it spits him out like a cherrystone.

They write as if the war had been a dream, a dream by others.

The dread of the year 1000. An error, it should have been 2000—if we get that far.

All days referring to days that will never come.

The joy of the weaker: to give something to the stronger.

Napoleon dying, dreadfully, as though he had never known anything of death, as though he were experiencing it for the first time.

The declamatory griper. He bickers thoroughly in well-reflected periods, censors interjections, and illuminates the night for himself.
　　He sleeps by day to avoid meeting any foe. Question marks animate, and cast doubt on, his sleep. Upon awakening, he is already in the next period, nit-picking the same thing in a different sequence.
　　He has no lack of sentences, just reasons for complaining.

Laments that precede misfortune and make it denser, thunder-laments.
　　Laments that emasculate misfortune, blade-laments.
　　Laments that hangs on to misfortune, guilt-and-token-laments.

People stood humbly before the thrones of the animals, awaiting their judgment.

Voices that bewilder heaven.

Snakes as road signs.

He comforts himself with purity for his lack of success.

The chatterer as a legacy.

There the dead live on in clouds and, as rain, they inseminate women.

There the gods remain small, while people grow. When they have grown so tall that they no longer see the gods, they have to strangle each other.

There they keep serpents as forebears and die of their bites.

The barking of dogs serves as their oracle. When the dogs stop barking, their tribe dies out.

There they speak a mangled language in the marketplace and are paralyzed at home.

There everyone is ruled by an innate worm and takes care of him and is obedient.

There they act only in groups of one hundred; the individual, who has never heard himself named, knows nothing about himself and oozes away.

There they whisper to one another and punish a loud word with exile.

There the living fast and feed the dead.

There they settle in giant trees, which they never leave. Far away on the horizon, other trees appear, unattainable and evil.

An English professor of classics, twenty-five years old, like Nietzsche, but in Australia, studies German in order to read Nietzsche, learns him by heart. Back in England, he elevates himself to fox-hunting. From Dante, whom he recites in Italian, he learns how greatly parties ought to hate one another. He has been elected to Parliament and is as hard-working as a German, which surprises his colleagues. What will become of all this?

The Moorish king was officially removed from all crèches.

A rare bird: a refugee who is ashamed of his earlier prosperity.

He plants sugarcane on his bitterness and sells the dubious harvest at maximum prices.

The family stood around her as dense as a lamenting pack, crowded in on her, until she gave up the ghost and sang her last words.

John Aubrey, who, in the seventeenth century, saw people the way the most cunning writer does today. He recorded them in terse sentences, omitting nothing, adding nothing. He recorded everyone he knew something about. He did not take it upon himself to find them good or bad, he didn't much care for preachers anyway. For one man, he only writes a single sentence; for Hobbes, his friend, he leaves twenty pages, the most intimate portrait of a philosopher to be found in world literature.

In his difficult script, everything remained in disorder; and when it was finally deciphered and published after centuries, it was still ahead of its time; the people, such as he saw them, are only alive today.

1963

I call him P., the practical peacock, and for a while, I would like to see everything with *his* eyes.

P. wants to level all graveyards, they take away too much space.

P. wants to destroy all registers, so that no one knows who lived before.

P. abolishes history in schools.

P. can't decide what should be done with family names, they keep alive the memory of fathers, grandfathers, and similar dead men.

P. has nothing against inheritances, he's in favor of useful things, but they should not be tied to the names of earlier owners.

P. goes even further than the Chinese philosopher Mo-tzu: he is against burials per se and not just the expense of funerals.

P. wants the earth for the living, away with the dead, even the bare moon is too good for them, though it might be used as a transition instead of a cemetery. Anything dead is shot to the moon from time to time. The moon as a trash heap and graveyard. Monuments? Why? They block up squares and streets. P. hates the dead, the space they take up, they are spreading everywhere.

P. has only young mistresses. At the first sign of slackness, he sends them away.

P. says: "Loyalty? Loyalty is dangerous, it ends with the dead."

P. precedes, where he can, with a good example and invents hair-raising impieties.

P. censors a newspaper: *This* is how it ought to be. No death announcements. No obituaries.

P., who is very rich, buys up all mummies and destroys them publicly and personally.

P., however, does not favor killing, only the killing of the dead.

P. rewrites the Bible for his modern purposes. He is also interested in other sacred books and purges them all in his terms.

P. dresses in such a way that he never reminds anyone of the dead.

P. permits no objects in his home that are known to come from the dead.

P. destroys all letters and pictures of people who have died, destroys them the moment they die.

P. invents an effective art of forgetting.

P. visits sick people only when they are well again. For dying people, there are secret places nobody knows, or people assigned to deal with them.

P. thinks that we treat animals properly. He rejects only the fuss over dead pets and fights against it.

P. demands a retraining of doctors.

P.'s special prayer. There are features in God that he approves of. He regards Christ as an imposter.

P. *walks* differently, as though he didn't know any dead people.

P. is convinced that we are infested forever by the sight of a corpse and shall never recover.

P. claims he will never grow old because he takes no notice of the dead.

The prestabilized harmony of annihilation.

After each round, the nations exchanged their names.

It was not possible to keep pace with the changes. Somebody certainly always won, but nobody knew who it was.

He would have been doomed had he not read Swift before Schiller.

The gods who still harass us from within glass cases.

When the Bakairi are dissatisfied with their chieftain, they leave the village and ask him to rule alone. (Von den Steinen)

One wants to become better, one says; one wishes only to have an easier time of it.

Many lamentable emotions: don't take them too seriously, they change; the good ones, however, are the same.

The most unbearable god would be he who is exactly as one wishes him.

The most difficult thing: to remove oneself from a life which one has entered fully. To writhe out of the many names that do not concern one at all. To exhale the stolen air, since it has gone stale. To finally open one's hands, which held the wrong things.

How much can one love wash away from the others? The deception of faithfulness.

Prohibitions, his inspirations.

A man finds another, whom he never knew, after thirty years of seeking. He recognizes him immediately. Likewise the sought man recognizes the seeker. The fury of recognition forces them to kill one another.

Whenever he goes too far, he has not gone far enough.

The most difficult thing of all, however, is to spare others what one criticizes in oneself.

A saint is a person who has succeeded in turning all moral torment against himself.

A sage, however, should be a man who does not torment himself anymore either. He knows there is no such thing as perfection, and the passion for it has left him.

The year in which the lake froze over, the year in which death got even with him.

When the beaten man twists on the ground, knows nothing, and wants only one thing: the return of this dead, when he is ready to give all living persons for this one thing; then, only then, does he grasp that death has annihilated him, and it would be better had he never been born.

Say it often, say it to yourself again, it is the only thing that holds you. This repetition, this rabid, unremitting reiteration is the homage that grief pays to life. It always sneaks in to the repetition of the lament. The silent endure too much—or do they go mute before they can assess what they endure?

It is no game, for it leaves nothing outside. It is a game, for it splits you in order to say itself.

It makes you no better, for you seek the fault in yourself, yet you accuse everyone else.

Black cloud, do not leave me now. Remain over me so that my old age does not go stale, remain inside me, poison of grief, so that I shall not forget the dying.

The unbroken, how do they do it? The unshaken, what are they made of? When it is past, what do they breathe? When it is still, what do they hear? When the felled one does not stand up again, how do they walk? Where do they find a word? What wind blows over their eyelashes? Who opens the dead ear for them? Who breathes the frozen name? When the sun of eyes goes out, where do they find the light?

One knows the person who has died; one mistakes all the living.

His black eye, nourished by death.

Now, everything is dark; but memory steams.

The knots of existence are where one brings back a dead man from the eyes of the living. But one wants the latter to *know* this, one does not spare them. One is unspeakably chary with the dead.

It might be that only the unhappiest man is truly capable of some happiness, and this could almost seem like justice—but then there are the dead, and they seem to be silent about that.

1964

Societies

A society in which people can be old or young at will and keep alternating.

A society in which all people sleep standing, in the middle of the street, with nothing disturbing them.

A society in which there is only one eye, it keeps making the rounds incessantly. All people want to see the same thing; they see it.

A society in which people weep only once in a lifetime. They do it very sparingly; and once it is past, they have nothing to look forward to and have become old and tired.

A society in which every man is painted and prays to his picture.

A society in which people suddenly vanish, but no one knows they are dead, there is no death, there is no word for it, they are content with that.

A society in which people laugh instead of eating.

A society in which never more than two people stand together, anything else is unthinkable and unbearable. When a third party approaches, the two of them, shaken with disgust, quickly separate.

A society in which one trains an animal to speak; it then speaks for him, while he goes mute.

A society consisting only of old people who blindly keep procreating even older ones.

A society in which there are no excrements, everything dissolves in the body. There are people without guilt feelings, smiling and eating.

A society in which the good stink, and everyone avoids them. However, they are admired from afar.

A society in which no one dies alone. A thousand people get together of their own accord and are publicly executed; their festival.

A society in which everyone speaks openly just to the other sex, men to women, women to men; but no man to another man, no woman to another woman, or just quite secretly.

A society in which children serve as executioners so that no adult smears his hand with blood.

A society in which people breathe only once a year.

What if *everyone* believed the wrong thing? Or if *everyone* achieved the opposite of what he believes?

Just look at them, the fierce fanatics who could believe so strongly that they have infected thousands upon thousands! The Christian faith of love and the inquisition! The founder of Germany's thousand-year Reich: its shattering and bewilderment. The white savior of the Aztecs in the guise of the Spaniards, who wipes them out. The distinction of the Jews as the chosen people and the end of their distinction in the gas-chambers. The belief in progress: its ultimate perfection in the atomic bomb.

It is as though each faith were its own curse. Would we have to start from there in order to solve the riddle of faith?

He cannot admire what calms him. Since everything remains in disquiet, how shall *he* find refuge in calm?

Oh, good man, whom else do you want to stick in your beggar's pouch?

He feels calibrated, but he doesn't know the measure.

It seems that some people can love only with a strong feeling of guilt. Their passion ignites on whatever they are ashamed of; it becomes their haven, like God for believers after they have sinned. Their love is repeatedly their purging; but everything in them is frightened of a permanent state of purgedness. They want to be afraid and they love a person only if their fear of him never dies. When he stops reproaching them and does not punish them for anything, when they have won him over to such an extent that he is satisfied with them, their love dies and everything ends.

To devise a man who is so good that God would have to envy him.

Love has the least amount of pity. It is part of love that the tiniest thing counts and nothing is forgotten: this thoroughness and precision constitutes love. When one says: I want *everything,* one *means* everything. Perhaps only a cannibal would be consistent here. But spiritual cannibalism is more complicated. Furthermore, there are *two* cannibals here eating one another at the same time.

One articulates some things merely so as not to believe them too much anymore.

In purgatory, people speak a lot. In hell, they hold their tongues.

He seeks me in order to tell me that his wickedness has remained alive, and he thinks he is entertaining me with this news. I seek him in order to tell him that his wickedness does not entertain me, I have enough of a job fighting against my own.

The wretch whom people admire because he never forgets himself.

The trick is not to fool oneself about certain things: small rocky islands in the sea of self-deception. Clutching them and not drowning is the utmost that a human being achieves.

Buddhism does not satisfy me because it gives up too much. It offers no answer to death, it sidesteps it. Christianity has at least put dying at its center: what else is the cross? There is no Indian teaching that really deals with death, for none has opposed it absolutely: the worthlessness of life has exonerated death.

We would still have to see what kind of faith arises in the man who sees and acknowledges the *enormity* of death and denies it any positive meaning. The incorruptibility premised by such an attitude towards death has never existed: man is too weak and gives up the struggle before he even resolves to begin it.

All the things one has forgotten scream for help in dreams.

Of the many who have known him, some will bear witness. Will there be a single recognizable testimony among them?

The illusory reparation of the dead: one cannot improve anything, they know of nothing. Thus everyone lives on with incalculable debts, and their burden grows and grows until one suffocates. Perhaps one dies because of one's growing debts to the dead.

There is no stronger relationship than that of two people who meet under the torment of such debts. One can carry the debt of the other for a while, unburden him, exculpate him, for just a short time; but even these short moments of reburdening can save his life.

I knew him when he walked down the street with hateful fingers and snarled. He was still young, and he thought he needed no one. The distaste he felt towards aging passers-by influenced his motion, he walked along in kicks as it were. He noticed everyone, because he disliked everyone. As for friends, he knew—and he was fortunate— that he had no friends. It rained on everyone, and it humiliated him that the others felt the very same drops on their skin as he did. At street corners, he was hungry. He sought the best-fed victim, and as soon as he was sure of his choice, he scornfully let him go. For there was one thing he could not do: dirty his fingers by touching another person. In his mind's eye, however, he kept wiping his hands, to which passers-by some distance away struck him as suitable. I saw him at various times of the day, he never changed, he was impervious to influences and moods. He became a sort of snarling ornament; whenever he was absent, the streets seemed chaotic.

1965

He would like to start from scratch. Where is scratch?

The man who imagines everything so that it won't happen.

Man's integrity consists in his being able at any time to tell himself what he thinks.

His insights always struck him as suspicious whenever he managed to defend them convincingly.

The question is: how capable a man is if he is not prepared to immediately risk it for something better.

He speaks in *prices*. There's always something to say in that regard. They go up, down, there are prices in other countries. He travels a great deal and reports faithfully about prices. In foreign lands, he can report about the prices here. He always finds people who are interested in his conversations; and if he doesn't know the language, he helps himself out with his fingers. He points to an object, makes an impressive pause, and then performs the homeland price on his hands.

An inexhaustible man. His silence is dreadful. But one can be sure that he is memorizing a pricelist even then.

I knew him when he was a little boy and went to steal prices. He dashed off very quickly, and no one could catch him. He was a smart boy and wormed his way into all prices. He played hookey, otherwise nothing would have become of him. For a while, he toyed with the idea of moving to America. But then it hit him that Europe had more currencies and more prices. He remained and never regretted it. Inflations came to his aid, he became a great man. Every day, he takes his little constitutional through the neighborhood, quietly whistling prices to himself.

One would like to say a thing in such a way that it is said once and for all, even if one would subsequently have to say the opposite.

One squeezes against the person one loves as though he or she were the center of the world.

One gets over nothing and loves all the more.

The hardest things to forgive are *infringements*. They leap over the holiest thing that is also the most sensitive: nearness.

How greatly one needs declarations in love, and how greatly one fears them, as though they *used up* something that would otherwise survive longer.

This enigmatic addiction to beauty, even in very coarse people—what else is it but the remnant of ancient polytheism. Yet it is still peculiar that the ugliest, the lowliest dare to approach the most beautiful, as though this were their due, as though it were promised.

Probably, thanks to the mixing of all cultures, there are more beautiful people today than ever before. They are the vestiges of the vanished gods. All approaches to these gods, usually unsuccessful, are preserved in beautiful people.

With kitsch, he thinks he can protect himself against his future. There is fortunate and unfortunate kitsch. He relies on the unfortunate kind.

It seems that one cannot be *severe* all of a lifetime. It seems that something takes vengeance in one, and one becomes like everyone else. But precisely because one becomes like everyone else, the arrogance of love comes into being.

She likes meat so much that when she dies, she would like to be torn to pieces by birds of prey.

The story of a man who keeps the death of his near and dear a secret from the world.

Is he ashamed of her death? And how does he succeed in keeping it from everyone else? Does he regain her life from all those who know nothing of her death? Where is she? Is she with him? In what form? He takes care of her, clothes her, feeds her. But she can never leave the place, and he never travels, never goes away for more than a few short hours.

He receives no visitors. She supposedly doesn't want to see anyone. She supposedly has become peculiar and can't stand anyone. But sometimes, he speaks like her on the telphone and also writes all her letters.

Thus he lives for both of them, he *becomes* both. He tells her everything, he reads to her. As earlier, he discusses with her what he should do, and sometimes he is annoyed at her obduracy. But ultimately, he always manages to get her to answer.

She is very sad because she sees no one, and he has to comfort her and cheer her up.

He, with such a secret, becomes the strangest man in the world, he has to understand all people so that they will not understand him.

Burn the justifications when they have done their duty? And what if you burn up with them?

How lovely magnanimity would be, if only it had a different name!

One never suddenly gets rid of a word that has become dangerous. One first has to go to a great deal of bother to use it in the wrong sense.

The most embarrassing illusion of psychoanalytical treatment is listening eternally to the patient. He spends hours upon hours speaking, but he is not really listened to, only that is heard which is already known before he even opens his mouth. He could just as well sit mutely through every session. If that were not so, the entire theory of psychoanalysis would long ago have dissolved into nothing. For a single person whom one really listens to brings one to completely new thoughts. Thus the achievement of the psychoanalyst consists in resisting his patient, who can say whatever he likes, but the result is already known and anticipated as though by some unshakable decree of fate. The pose of listening is arrogance, nothing more. The changes and schisms in the doctrine are due to the few moments in which someone forgets himself enough to listen. Those things are varied, according to the extent of this "error" and the nature of the person who "erred."

Freud himself must have listened a great deal, otherwise he could not have erred and changed so much.

Disgust at the "divine wars"—*Les Guerres divines*—of de Maistre. His usefulness consists in this disgust he arouses: things one believed and wanted for so long that they seem stale become important again through the conviction with which he advocates the opposite.

He is one of the unintentional satirists, like Aristotle with his slavery or Nietzsche with his superman. He has the advantage of a charged and yet plain language. One understands what he advocates, as precisely as thought he meant to kill and destroy it. Just what makes up the "charged" quality of his language? For one thing, the concentrated sureness of his belief, he *knows* what he considers bad, there is not even the shadow of a doubt, he is one of those who have God on their side dead-sure, his opinion always has the ardor of faith; and though he argues and operates with reasons, they are superfluous for him. He never writes like a theologian and therefore he seems modern, he always reads as though he were speaking from worldly experience. He takes off from the wickedness of man, it is his unshakable conviction. Yet he concedes everything to the power that ought to tame that wickedness, he makes the hangman a kind of priest.

All thinkers who begin with human wickedness are characterized by an enormous persuasiveness. They sound experienced, courageous, and truthful. They look at reality point-blank and never fear calling it by its name. One does not notice until later that it is never total reality. And it would be more courageous to see the germ of another reality in that one without falsifying or beautifying it. But the man who admits that would have to know wickedness better, have it in himself, seek it in himself, find it in himself, a poet.

The split of the lamenting pack in *The Persians* of Aeschylus: a split into those who are strong enough to bring back the dead man and into those who uselessly lament with the survivor.

The actual drama begins with Atossa, the king's widow: *her* dream is the first harbinger of disaster; and until the actual messenger comes, that dream is everything. Then the messenger, in his tale, brings the true figure of disaster. The chorus, thereby aroused, becomes a lamenting pack and evokes the highest dead man in the presence of his widow. His verdict of guilt precedes the apparition of the guilty man, and it is as though the dead man had brought the living man, the father the son, the founder the destroyer.

Thus *The Persians* consists of three successive conjurations; dream or vision elicits reality. Atossa's dream brings the messenger; the visionary report of the messenger (through the lamenting pack that he arouses) brings the most venerable dead man; and finally, his verdict brings the beaten son.

Ten or twelve very young people around me, in a very small room, at various small tables, in groups that are quite dissimilar. Threatened by them, I stubbornly keep writing. I can oppose their cold, scornful looks only with the warmth and curiosity of my age. They want my table, they gradually occupy it, they bang on it rhythmically, perhaps not even to disturb my writing, but merely to feel their rhythm in every object, confer it on everything, the table is such an object and perhaps so am I. They talk past me, they soar into my ears. I hold out against them and try not to show them my annoyance.

They are amazed at my patience, for which they have nothing but scorn. The rigidity of a human body in which only a pencil moves is beyond their grasp. I could try to sing, but it would never be their song. I could try to speak, but my words would be Greek to them. Under no circumstances could I mean anything to them. My curiosity, which they may sense, arouses their loathing. They would love to spit in my face; if one of them did, the others would do the same.

I hold out against them only because I eavesdrop on them. They have no inkling that there are individual things to eavesdrop on, they feel like something universal here. Their girls are devoted to them. Does one of the girls attract me? I don't know, I know nothing. I experience what I devised as a pack.

1966

Predator of grief, man.

The hallucinations vanish, and truth, more dreadful, takes their place.

To light up the hours of night, he goes among men during the day. He asks them for nothing. They ask him for a great deal. He is tormented by their faces. There are people among them who love having killed him. But that doesn't bother him. He knows he will escape them at night. When they sleep, he will be able to breathe by the lamp, free of them.

Say: it was all for nothing. But it was not for nothing so long as I do not say so.

Attack the successful? No need. They have success as putrefaction in their bodies.

One can peer head-on at the most dreadful thoughts, and yet one cannot be consoled about some that are far less dreadful.

To hate a man on and on, until one loves him.

There ought to be a court of appeals that absolves you of death if you answer all its questions honestly.

The fascination of snakes. Because they are deaf? Because they bear their poison openly, namely in *one* spot? But even the non-poisonous ones are fascinating. Because they eat so seldom? Because they too love each other?
   The story of the snake that lost its entire skin when caught by thorns: that twisted, rosy and naked, among laughing aborigines; and

the embarrassment of the catcher, who could not bear its degradation and hid it away.

Animals are stranger than we if for no other reason than because they experience so much but cannot articulate it. A talking animal would be no more than a human being.

Reindeer shoots man. "A reindeer named Rudolf, drawing a sleigh with three hunters in it, shot one of them in the leg. Rudolf's antlers got caught in a rifle, and he pulled the hammer."
    When will all animals learn how to shoot? When will it become dangerous for every hunter to shoot? When will animals, like rebels, steal rifles, stash them away, and practice marksmanship? Horned animals would be especially well off; but they could also shoot hunters with toes and teeth. And if innocent people were hurt? But how many innocent animals. . . !

The new, the actual discoveries about animals are possible only because our pride as God's highest creature is a thing of the past. It turns out that we are really God's lowest creature, that is to say, God's executioner in his world.

Legislators who have to set an example in everything precisely.

"The Oriental church fathers claimed that Christ was uglier than any man who ever lived. For in order to redeem mankind, he had to take upon himself all of Adam's sins and even his physical blemishes."

Hearts as beakers from which one drinks. One can take them from the chest and offer them to others. One can pawn one's heart with someone else by implanting it in him. Anyone who loves, runs about with someone else's heart. Anyone who dies, takes someone else's heart along into the grave, and his own heart lives on in that person.

One and the same person serves many as someone who is survived.

He likes the few and always declaims about the many.

Don't say: I was there. Always say: I was never there.

I have not come into being. So many words, so much noise, and I still have not come into being.

There are ludicrous chatterers. There are also ludicrous silent people.

The *uncounted* days are the fortune of life, and the counted years its rationality.

Would this be the actual effect of pity: that it turns the guilt of the pitied man into error?

A useful profession alone, like a physician's, is not enough to protect a writer against arrogance. The disgust at experience, initially fruitful, nourishes, as a contrast to itself, a sort of highness of the person, which manages to overcome the disgust. The writer who has resisted the disgust becomes his own self-purpose.

There are only chosen peoples: all who still exist.

Mountains as a blue skyline in the distance. Tender, untouchable pride.

They sang so loud, one could hear them from afar. They had formed a circle; where the traffic was heaviest, twenty of them stood in a large circle and sang as though with one voice. Some were in uniform, others in work smocks or street clothes. The women among them looked like men, though they wore no trousers. Their voices blared like trumpets. Every song has several stanzas, and when one was over, another began immediately without their first discussing it. All of them had very red faces. "That's caused by the strain, or are they that healthy?" The passers-by squeezed past, most of them were in a hurry and didn't want to disturb them. But a few halted and admired them. Their lips twitched and they would have liked to sing. "Why don't we join in? Why don't we sing along? We simply can't sing that beautifully?" The cars passing by very closely made sure not to honk. A policeman, directing traffic just a few yards away, moved to another point and managed to direct the traffic from there. His uniform was not theirs and he was alone. He wouldn't have minded joining them. Two dogs on leashes howled away and pushed into the circle of singers. A master, a mistress strenuously held them back and forbade them to howl.

Each of the singers had a white stick, and when the jubilation of singing became overpowering, he would hold it aloft ecstatically. He waved it in the air and stretched out high and enthusiastically and struck the other sticks. It wasn't as regulated as the singing, it went in all directions and hobbled awkwardly against a heavenly sidewalk. Then the jubilation waned, the sticks dropped and stood modestly on the ground. Between one song and the next, one could hear the quick barking of the insatiable dogs. A honking, that had forgotten itself, broke off hurriedly when the new singing began. The words were so strong that one could hardly understand them, and only one word, which kept recurring, was immediately intelligible. It came back in every stanza and referred to the highest being. Gradually, the other words also became clear. They linked to that one word, which was at the crux, and they draped it in loud colors.

Some of the singers had closed their eyes and didn't open them even when the strain was greatest. Others, who kept their eyes wide open, stared blankly in the same direction all the time. But none of them used his eyes as singers are wont to do. They sang so stormily because they could see nothing. They never stopped because they didn't wish to go anywhere. All of them were blind and thanked God and sang about their sins.

Among the annoying words of propitiation in English life, there is "Relax!" I try to imagine someone saying to Shakespeare, "Relax!"

It is a writer's drive to deceive the people he loves—deceive them of what they would get from everyone else. What *he* gives them should only be what *he* can give them. They, however, even if they don't realize it, long for the nourishment of the most ordinary life, and ultimately they have to hate him bitterly for its withdrawal. He cannot stop trying desperately to persuade them that something else is at stake; and so long as *he* determines what it should be, he is satisfied.

He does nothing himself. He imagines what others do, and then he has them report to him.

Asceticism without a stench, what kind of asceticism is that?

The wonder of human survival: even more of a wonder since the snoring of these wretched creatures gives them away at night to predators. The only wild animals that snore like us are anthropoid apes.

May a man who learns nothing more still feel responsibility?

Circe, who transforms all men into newspapers.

Man, the animal that notes what it murders.

Once every month, supposedly, a demon appeared to them from the sea, from the people of spirits, and it looked like *a ship full of lamps.* When I peered out, I saw, to my great amazement, something like a big ship that seemed to be full of lamps and torches. And they said: "That is the demon . . ." (Ibn Battuta on the Maldives)

He escaped the platitudinous present by fleeing into any old lie.

A man who grows older because of certain *words.*

To find the basic relationships *today,* like those five in Confucius.

He constructs thoughts like a carpenter. They have to have corners.

A character who keeps speaking until he dreams.

Theophrastes: Thus everything already existed among the Greeks, even the characters of later bad comedies.

The woman who gathers gazes: she makes sure that not a single gaze aimed at her escapes her, and she says thank you for each one. She gets very many and administers them over weeks and years. She invests them as small, separate funds, never mixes them, always knows where new ones are sure to be found, and pays interest on them in her way. Her enterprises gradually expand over many countries, there are gazes she travels to.

She refuses to employ an administrator and does everything herself.

An invented youth that comes true in old age.

A flatterer who, to his dismay, sees all people becoming what he pretends to them.

Leap-money, like fleas.

A woman who does not succeed in making the man she loves jealous. The more she tries to confuse him, the more surely he believes in her. She tries everything to denigrate her image in him; but it shines all the more purely for him. She hires people to tell him the worst things about her. He hears and laughs. He isn't even indignant. He listens as though they were talking about someone else.

His unshakability torments her more and more, and she begins doing things that repel her, in order to ravage her image. She confers with his best enemy, who suggests where her lover might be most vulnerable. The outcome is that he has a reconciliation with his enemy. Everything that comes near her is lovely and precious to him.

There is no telling how the thing will end.

Ears for listening away, ears for flying, ears for obeying.

Dwarf helicopters that land on bald heads.

The judge sits on the floor, all the others stand around him, the defendants hang from the ceiling. The verdict is whispered. If declared innocent, the defendant is let down from the ceiling and taken in among the standing people. A condemned man, however, is placed next to the judge and rubs his cheek against his. Then the judge kisses him on his eyes, which he is never allowed to open again: his punishment.

To bring back the profound emotion from names.

Why the ineffable sacrifices, the blood of animals, the torment and guilt—so that we too should die!

Wretched the man who knows. How wretched God must be, all-knowing.

Not even Goethe was spared the final agony. But one adds a few peaceful hours to it, so that it may seem more beautiful and more appropriate to his habits.

A last wish, circling around the earth and not changing for millennia.

Clouds instead of thoughts, they form at the heads of thinkers, the wind drives them away, and they gush out in countries poor in thought.

Streets that feel pain. One learns to spare their feelings.

Books that can select their readers and close off to most of them.

A family in which no one knows anyone else's name, a discreet family.

The poetess says: I have borrowed every line. All debtors love me. I have become famous. It was quite easy. One should merely never say anything aside from borrowed lines. Silence is mighty. How the lines flatter the debtors! They never find me boring. They lend me their meaning. The man who knows the magnanimity of vanity will never go wrong.

I was in a few places too. They were exquisite places, like the people I borrowed from. All these places are my biography. There can't be too many of them. They are famous places, anyone can easily retain them. Their renown has entered my name.

A *thinker*. It begins with his pushing everything aside. Whatever is said to him is incorrect.

Someone introduces himself and gives his name. "What did you say?"—"So-and-so."—"What is that?"—"That's my name."—"But what does it mean?"

Someone tells where he comes from. "That doesn't mean anything."—"I was born there."—"How do you know?"—"I've always known."—"Were you present?"—"I must have been present!"—"Do you remember it?"—"No.—"Then how do you know it's true?"

Someone mentions his father. "Where does he live?"—"He's dead."—"Then he no longer exists."—"But he was my father."—"The dead don't exist; so your father doesn't exist; so he's not your father."

Someone talks about where he was the day before. "How do you know that?"—"I was there."—"When?"—"Yesterday."—"Yesterday no longer exists. There is no such thing as yesterday. Hence, you were nowhere."

1967

More than ever before, there are things in the world that would like to be said.

The man who starts at the beginning is considered a proud spirit. He is only more distrustful.

Too many people, say those who don't know a single person; too few, says the man who starts getting to know them.

The tormenting thing about Indian philosophy is the arrogance of redemption. How can a man who knows about others dare to think about redemption for himself? Even if it were possible to achieve redemption, he would lose the others, who would be the only true redemption.

These people who, with a smile, make use of a death drive in defense of death. What else are they saying than that the resistance against him is too small in any event?

Omitting human beings altogether: mathematics. The consequences.

A heaven alive with cosmic idiots. The yawning of the stars.

They appear like new gods, the people who succeed in leaving the earth. The new gods ought to be those who cannot die.

Ears already reach to the antipodes. When fingers get that far then no one will know whom he's crazy about.

The one ambition that is always legitimate, keeping people alive longer, has been specialized into a profession that feeds people: medicine. Doctors see most deaths and grow more accustomed to them than other people do. Their ambition gets stale, however, in regard to their professional accidents. These people, who have always done the most against the religious devotion to death, ultimately take death for granted. One would wish for physicians who draw a new attitude from their activity: an unshakable defiance of death, which they loathe deeper and deeper the more they witness it. Their defeats would be the nourishment of a new faith.

A pain so great that one no longer refers it to oneself.

Pascal reaches to my very marrow. Mathematics in a state of innocence. And already it's doing penance.

Every old person sees himself as a sum total of successful tricks. Every young person feels himself to be the source of the world.

To dissect a river into its brooks. To understand a human being.

In every family that is not one's own, one suffocates. One also suffocates in one's own, but one doesn't realize it.

What will these many people be like, how much air will be left for each one, will they learn to get along without food? Will they populate the atmosphere and the inside of the earth in many storeys? Will they forgo movement and simply meditate? No longer smell? Whisper? Shine?

An unknown God, concealed on Mars, sleeplessly waits for us until he can finally go to sleep after our landing.

Robert Walser's special characteristic as a writer is that he never formulates his motives. He is the most camouflaged of all writers. He is always well off, he is always delighted by everything. But his enthusiasm is cold, since it leaves out one part of himself, and that is why it is sinister. For him, everything is *external* nature, and the essential thing about it, its innermost being, fear, was something he denied all his life.

It was only later that the voices crystallized, getting back at him for all the concealment.

His writings are an unflagging attempt at hushing his fear. He escapes everywhere before too much fear gathers in him (his wandering life), and, to save himself, he often changes into something subservient and small. His deep and instinctive distaste for everything "lofty," for everything that has rank and privilege, makes him an essential writer of our time, which is choking on power. One hesitates calling him a "great" writer according to the normal usage, nothing is so repugnant to him as "greatness." It is only the *brilliance* of greatness to which he submits, and not its demand. His pleasure is to contemplate the brilliance without taking part in it. One cannot read him without being ashamed of everything that was important to one in external life, and thus he is a peculiar saint, not one according to outmoded and deflated prescriptions.

His experience with the "struggle for existence" takes him into the only sphere where that struggle no longer exists, the madhouse, the monastery of modern times.

Every writer who has made a name for himself and asserts that name knows quite well that for this reason he is no longer a writer, for he administers positions like any burgher. But he has known people who were so utterly and purely writers that they simply couldn't succeed at this. They wound up extinguished and suffocated, and they have the choice of burdening others as beggars or living in a madhouse. The writer who asserts himself, who knows that they were purer than he, can't endure having them around for long, but he is quite prepared to venerate them in the asylum. They are his split-off wounds and keep vegetating as such. It is exalting to contemplate and know the wounds so long as one does not feel them in oneself anymore.

The torment of success: it is always taken away from others, and only the unsuspecting, the limited, who do not tell themselves that there were better people than they among the robbed—they are able to enjoy success.

The prestige that writers draw from their martyrs: from Hölderlin, Kleist, Walser. Thus with all their claim to freedom, vastness, and inventiveness, they merely form a sect.

I am tired of riding the high horse of this pretense. I am not yet even a human being.

"I can breathe only in the lower regions." This statement by Robert Walser would be the slogan of writers. But the courtiers do not speak it, and those who have won fame no longer dare to even think it. "Couldn't you forget a little about being famous?" he said to Hofmannsthal, and no one more forcefully characterized the embarrassing thing about the people above.

I wonder whether among those who build their leisurely, secure, linear academic lives on the lives of writers who lived in poverty and despair—I wonder whether even *one* of those people is ashamed.

Every writer would like to push the next writer into the past and feel sorry for him there.

A man who knows people down to their very future and therefore fears no one.

One is bored to death by people who are right and know it. The truly intelligent man conceals being right.

The dancing legacy. The burning bush, à la Bengal.

High stairway-personalities, praying out of windows.

He recognized me from far away. I hadn't seen him for a long time. He said: "You haven't changed." I said: "No one would recognize you." He envied me. I envied him. "Why don't we change roles?" we both said at the same time. Now I recognize him from far away, and he hasn't seen me for a long time.

The incomprehensible, that everyone accepts as though it might contain a secret justification.

He let his heirs take anything they wished, and he remained alive.

She married him to have him around always. He married her to forget her.

He doesn't want to weep for anyone. But how much he wants to be wept for!

I want to die, she said, and gulped down ten men.

The widow dressed in dark weeds here in order to show herself in bright, transparent veils in Spain. Six months there and she returns here to her dark clothes. Six months here and she goes to Spain to undress into her veils. She needs both, she says, she can't have one without the other. Her husband was always so good to her and poisoned himself for her veil period.

He prides himself on being concerned for *all* people, not just for those in a few countries, since death makes no distinction between people, he too makes none.

He does wonder, how he would feel if the earth were suddenly faced with an alien invasion. Would he hate the aliens he does not know as bitterly as the old nations hated one another in that antediluvian age before the atom bomb? Would he say: "Destroy them no matter what they're like, all means are fine, *we* are the best in any event"?

Any expansion one exults in already contains the new narrowness that will make others suffocate.

We carry some names about for a long time, imbedding them in veneration. It may take twenty years until what actually belongs to them, their substance, the work, is seriously imparted to us. It then happens in a kind of intimacy because the name was in us for so long, one understands very suddenly, and everything belongs to us, there is no resistance as there usually is against every major experience. Probably, the first thing that happens to us is always the name; but those among them that can be preserved for a long time seem quite different, they concentrate us *from the inside,* we crystallize around them, they give us hardness and transparency.

The best thoughts that come to one are initially alien and eery, and one first has to forget them before one can even start to understand them.

Part of thinking is its cruelty, aside from its contents. It is the process itself that is cruel, the process of detachment from everything else, the ripping, the wrenching, the sharpness of cutting.

Some people achieve their greatest wickedness in silence.

One never takes raging people seriously enough. It is only when thousands copy their raging that one respectfully perks up one ears; but it is precisely at this point that one should maintain an icy coldness.

He says nothing, but how he explains it!

A panopticon of couples.

To write letters for after death, for years from now, addressed to all the people one has loved or hated.
Or: a kind of confession for after death, an admission in gradual stages over many years.

The end, no matter how one glosses over it, is so senseless that no attempt at explaining Creation will mean anything, not even the concept of God as a playing child: the child would have lost interest long ago.

In these new towns, one can find the old houses only in people.

Stupidity has become less interesting, it spreads in the twinkling of an eye and is always the same in everyone.

He wants to become better and practices every day before breakfast.

The fly he couldn't harm has died.

I am. I am not. Mankind's new counting game.

Instinctively, I feel *affection* for all experiments and the people doing them. Why? Because they are defiant enough to start at a beginning as though nothing had ever happened before. Because they are carried by the attitude that what one does oneself is important. Because all at once, the individual man counts, anyone who presumes, but also takes something upon himself. Because they demand stubbornness and two traits that are the most important in their combination: resistance and patience.
Instinctively, I feel *distrust* towards all experimenters. Why? Because

they are after success and want to make it. It often turns out that the ballast they threw away was totally unknown to them, they want to reach the top with less baggage, that is to say, more *easily*. They accept any ally, they show understanding for the power structure of the world such as they find it, and they promiscuously use everything not reaching into the very narrow sphere of their experiment for its propagation. Anything they have omitted in order to gain their new things is suddenly here again, as their weapon. They often live in cliques, form coteries, think, calculate, administer. The contrast between their real aim and their behavior among others is horrendous. They stress this contrast, they have to stress it, for any balancing compromise between the two aspects of their existence would cancel out their experiment as such.

But what should they do? What can be expected in this world? Their experiment wants to live; shall they starve? Very few of them are meant to be martyrs. They practice their resistance on a very delimited terrain, and it is quite likely that the rest of their personalities is not touched by that in any way. When they join together with others, it is because they think that these others understand them and are after the same thing; they are also imitated by them, and their resistance is nourished by that.

The thing that one *expects* of them corresponds to an ascetic postulate and often has absolutely nothing to do with their efforts towards the new. At bottom, one wishes that they may become fools through their experiments and ultimately fail. Later, when they are crazy or dead, that is, out of the way, others may then hit upon what they have done and they can utilize it. One need not think anything special of these imitators, they are utilizers of other people's inventions, but so is everyone else, after all.

One thus wishes the purity of experiment, its separation and severity. One believes it only then, one wants it without its history. Inventors and saints are melted into one figure.

Structures everywhere, the anti-dream to destruction.

I have not sought destruction in Rimbaud; it struck me as ludicrous to cultivate destruction as a literary tradition, I found it in my own time, in my own life, I felt it, regarded it, weighed it, rejected it. What do I care about the vanity of a sixteen-year-old if the earth is bursting into pieces and my people dying?

By the time Nietzsche was feeding his European mind on Taine in the *Revue des Deux Mondes,* Rimbaud was already running guns in Harrar.

The German word *Dichter* (poet, writer) no longer attracts me, I shy away from using it.

Because I no longer am a *Dichter?* I don't really think so. Because it no longer contains everything I demand of myself? Probably.

Gulliver the giant becomes Gulliver the dwarf: reversal as a device of satire.

The satirist changes the nature of punishment. He appoints himself as judge, but he has no standard. His law is arbitrariness and exaggeration. His whip is endless, reaching into the most far-flung mouseholes. He hauls out anything that doesn't concern him, and he whips it as though he had to wreak vengeance for his own injury. His effectiveness is in his lack of qualms. He never tests *himself.* The moment he tests *himself,* he's done for, his arms grow weak, the whip falls.

It would be quite wrong to seek justice in the satirist. He knows very well what justice is, but he never finds it in others, and, not finding it, he usurps it and manipulates its devices. He is always a tyrant, he has to be, otherwise he degrades himself to a courtier and toady. As a tyrant, he is starved for affection and gets it secretly (*Diary to Stella*).

The true satirist remains dreadful throughout the centuries. Aristophanes, Juvenal, Quevedo, Swift. His function is to keep indicating the limits of what is human by ruthlessly crossing them. The terror he strikes throws men back to their limits.

The satirist lays hands on gods. When it is too dangerous for him to attack the god of his own society, he gets other gods, older ones, for this very purpose. He smashes in on them publicly, but everyone senses whom he really means.

What terror is it that drives the satirist? Does he fear the people he wants to improve? Yet he doesn't believe he can improve them, and even if he talks himself into it, he doesn't wish it, for he does not care to live without his whip.

It is said the satirist hates himself, but that is a misleading opinion. Crucial for him is that he doesn't look upon himself, and that may be easier for him with a bodily deformity. His gaze is concentrated on others, his activity is the very thing he needs. It betrays love rather than hatred for himself: the vehement need to ignore one's own defects, to conceal them more effectively behind the enormities of others.

It is a dreadful thought that perhaps no one is better than anyone else, and any claim to that is deception.

The foe says "Good." And one has just said "Bad." Great confusion. Damage. Shame.

A writer who knows, from other people's sentences alone. His pride is the sum of the prides of those he robbed. His strength is that nothing is by him. His fall, that he suddenly relies upon himself after finding nothing more in others.

The wooer speaks a great deal and is despised for that. The witnesses forget that Homer and Dante also made propaganda for themselves, and who were the witnesses to measure the specific weight of the propagator?

To begin with the unusual; never to exhaust it; breathe in it until the usual has itself become unusual: everything unusual.

The things that were not stored for long in the mind, that grazed it only quickly and vehemently, hold out best against time.

Yet it has to be a mind that has known effort, otherwise nothing can graze it vehemently.

The rich in words grow obsolete first. First the adjectives wither, then the verbs.

A writer may take care of his injustices. If he keeps retesting everything that was repugnant to him, and if he corrects his distastes, then nothing will be left of him.

His "morality" is what he rejects. But everything may spur him on so long as his "morality" is intact.

The thing that often seems boring in Goethe: the fact that he is always there *complete*. The older he gets, the more and more he distrusts passionate onesidednesses. But he is naturally so much, that he needs a different balance from other people. It is not stilts that he walks on, he always rests roundly upon himself as a gigantic world-globe of the mind; and in order to understand him, one has to orbit him like a small moon, a humiliating role, but the only suitable one in his case.

He gives one the strength not of boldness but of persistence, and I do not know of another great writer in whose proximity death is concealed for so long.

To find new, unfulfilled wishes until very old age.

Everywhere, two paces from your daily paths, there is a different air skeptically waiting for you.

A writer would have to endlessly invent his life, and he would thus be the only one to *know* where he is.

There is a wailing wall of humanity, and that is where I stand.

My respect for Buddha is based exclusively on the fact that his doctrine was triggered by the sight of a dead man.

The greatest strain in life is not getting accustomed to death.

A philosopher ought to be someone for whom people remain as important as ideas.

All the books showing only how we reached our modern-day opinions on animals, man, nature, the world make me uneasy. How far *have* we reached? In the works of past thinkers, people seek out sentences that gradually led to our view of the world. The larger and erroneous portion of their opinions is regretted. What can be more sterile than this kind of reading? It is precisely the "erroneous" opinions of earlier thinkers that interest me most about them. They might contain the germs of things that we desperately need, that could lead us out of the dreadful cul-de-sac of our modern-day view of the world.

People regarded as thinkers because they pride themselves on our wickedness.

Excluding the world, so important from time to time, is permissible only if it floods back in with even greater force.

At least twice in the history of philosophy, crowd ideas were crucial for a new conception of the world. The first time in Democrites: the multiplicity of atoms; the second time in Giordano Bruno: the multiplicity of worlds.

Thoughts like detritus. Thoughts like lava. Thoughts like rain.

Now that it can be achieved through explosions, nothingness has lost its brilliance and its beauty.

It seems as if people feel guiltier about earthquakes than about wars, which they start themselves.

The store of faces that a man has in himself after living a while.

How great is this store and as of when does it no longer increase? A man operates with, let's say, five hundred faces, which are live for him, and he sees all others in their terms. His knowledge of human beings would thus be ordered, but limited. "I know him," he says to himself upon seeing an unfamiliar person, and he puts him aside with a familiar person. The new person may be different in every way, aside from the type of his features; but for the man who knows men, he is the same.

This would thus be the deepest root of all false evaluations. The store of faces varies in size from one person to the next. The man who has appropriated very many seems like a man of the world and is regarded as such. However, he is distinguished only by a memory for faces and, for that very reason, he can become especially stupid.

My own experience is that for some ten years now I have been tending more and more to see new faces in terms of earlier ones. There seldom used to be likenesses that struck me suddenly and unexpectedly. I never sought them, they sought me. Now I look for them myself and force them to come, though I may not always be fully convinced. It could be that I am no longer capable of fully grasping new faces as such.

Two reasons for this reaction could be possible. A man is no longer vehement enough to seize the new—the animal strength of the senses has waned; or else one is already over-populated, and the inner city or hell—whatever one cares to call what one carries inside oneself—has no more room for new tenants.

A third possibility, however, cannot be fully excluded; one no longer so easily *fears* new "animals," one has become slyer, one relies on established defense reactions without closer scrutiny.

If the "animals" were really new, one would fear them enough to grasp them.

A very old man who takes no nourishment. He lives on his years.

So long as one says "tomorrow," one means "always"; that's why one loves saying "tomorrow."

This warmth! says everyone whom he flees.

Every opinion, if it is to be something that moves others, is like a book that one keeps working on incessantly and that never ends.

A man says about himself: throughout my life, not a single person has ever died.

This man, this man alone, is the man that I envy of all people.

Oh, that collections are so costly! Thus, no one will upset them.

One could at least throw them into confusion, put them together, mix them up, exchange them, take them apart. One could find rules for them and various games.

There is too much self-conplaisance in the collections and confidence of the keepers. Incomprehensible that more isn't stolen from them for this very reason: merely to change them. There ought to be special devils working against their confidence day and night. Who falsify paintings until they are considered inauthentic. Who reduce astronomical prices to almost nothing over night. Who successfully exchange names and periods.

I went down many steps in a dream, I came out on the peak of Mont Ventoux.

He preaches in his sleep. When awake, he remembers nothing.

We will some day find out so much about sleep that people will no longer care to stay awake.

Aristophanes is full of packs, and the seductive thing about them is that they tend to come as animals. They are animals and men at once, wasps, birds, they *appear* as these and speak like human beings. Thus they present the oldest metamorphoses, metamorphosis per se. Comedy is not yet reduced to its pure human dimensions, the age of its boredom and uninventiveness has not yet begun.

A postage stamp for every word. They learned to converse in silence.

He no longer can endure music, he is so full of unexploited noises.

We would have to observe how much fear touches in one, where it creeps off to after the first attack has been beaten off.

It seems that fear likes to find the old channels.

Distrust itself is a defense against fear. It forestalls the worst, as though it would shame fear. It postulates a threat which far exceeds the threat of fear. It thereby gives one courage to look things straight in the eyes, more than fear would have dared. Thus, distrust could make one strong, if it remained simple, virtually stuck to the subject. But it won't, it takes in more and more, and ultimately turns into an automatic creator of fear.

For, cold and hard as it may act, it is nourished by the same hostile power which it wants to protect us against. The fear that attacks openly and head-on is joined by the secret fear that sneaks into distrust. The body of distrust has its special arteries, the blood flowing in them is fear.

All the functions of a life that have stopped, and how they avenge themselves. The man who was never a father raises false sons. The man who was never after business, advises others in their speculations. The man who never wrote his books invents them for strangers. The man who was never a priest constructs new religions. That pride of self-denial may have been great, but all denial wreaks vengeance. Is there no such things as a true renunciation?

A good man could only be the person who is never regarded as such anywhere. Thus a man cannot really become good, if, as a child, he always wanted to hear that he was good.

There is no disguise for goodness, and it endures no applause.

1968

Lichtenberg

His curiosity is not bound by anything, it jumps from everywhere, on everything.

His lucidity: even the darkest things turn light when he thinks them. He sheds light, he wants to strike but not kill, his mind is not murderous. Nor does anything become part of his body, he has no fat or swelling.

He is not dissatisfied with himself because he has too many ideas. A teeming mind, but there is always room in the teeming. The fact that he won't round anything off, that he finishes nothing is his and our good fortune: he thereby wrote the richest book in world literature. One would like to keep hugging him for this abstinence.

There is no one I would more gladly have spoken with, but it's not necessary.

He does not evade theories, but every theory spurs his ideas. He can play with systems but not get entangled in them. He can flick the most difficult things away like a speck of dust from his jacket. In his movement, one grows light oneself. One takes everything seriously with him, but not overly. An erudition as easy as light.

He is too unique to be envied. The ponderousness of even the greatest minds is so blatantly lacking in him that one might almost not regard him as a human being.

It is true that he seduces one into taking leaps. But who is capable of them? Lichtenberg is a flea with a human mind. He has that incomparable strength to leap away from himself—where will he leap to next?

His whim finds all books that inspire him to leap. When others become devils due to the weight of books, he nourishes his sharpest tenderness on them.

How much reading one could spare oneself if one knew the writers earlier. *All* reading?

There are no *new* stories. Since there are infinitely many new things, there are no new stories.

The sequence in which one learns things is what ultimately makes up a man's individuality.

To find an old man who has forgotten how to count.

Who will bring me news when I no longer exist, who will report to me?

At last Cardano's autobiography has come into my hands.

It is badly written, divided into individual topics à la Suetonius and thus consisting solely of lists of similar things. It is interesting all the same, at least for its dreams, which are often filled with crowds. It moves one because it is carried by an enormous pain: Cardano witnessed the execution of his son for killing his own wife. With a lot of money that he did not possess, he could have ransomed him from his accusers. He is convinced that they sentenced his son to death in order to get at him, the father, and so he feels a guilt from which there is no release.

He counts up his faults as well as his merits, but though undertaking not to conceal anything, he can tire one like an empty braggart. One senses how dangerous it is when a man takes himself seriously in everything, even in the things he chides himself for. He is too solemn, he lacks humor. His playful tendencies, which he does not lack, are absorbed in chess and in games of chance. Not even the ancient models do him any good. He is too blatantly after immortality, that is to say, without realizing that one has to *take along* everything and everybody around one, it is the only thing justifying that dubious passion. No one can live on by himself, a name per se, anything a man has accomplished is dreary, and even if one succeeds in this sort of immortality, it will always retain something repulsive and artificial. A systematic list of all personal peculiarities is basically monstrous, unless serving, to deter as in Suetonius' biographies of emperors. In Plutarch, who wants to set up models, the selection of traits is masterful and superior, he never sticks to details for their own sake.

And perhaps it is impossible to write an autobiography only at the end of a long life. There is too much there, and one must content oneself chiefly with unilluminated lists.

Perhaps Kafka has ruined one for all open or concealed boasting. When the "beautiful" people of the past (and I am not thinking of Cardano) depict their lives, as though it befitted them, without doubts, without qualms, without self-consciousness about their influence (or about the state of the world), one feels impatience and disbelief, as though reading about the inhabitants of some other star, about whom one *cannot* know anything worth taking seriously.

With Kafka, something new came into the world, a more precise feeling for its dubiousness, a feeling, however, that is coupled not with hatred, but with respect for life. The combination of these two emotional stances—respect and dubiousness—is unique, and once one has experienced it, one cannot miss it anymore.

You can't do anything with your distrust. It's too familiar. You've thought about it too much, written about it too much. It has become fruitless, you are the official of this distrust and can at best advance within it.

People who fall in love with others only while driving past, from car to car.

To vanish now and then, never for good.

Don't embrace me, I'm made of grains and I'll scatter.

I respect the weakness that is not an end in itself, that makes everything transparent, that surrenders no one, that encounters power tenaciously.

To write without teeth. Just try!

What are you so ashamed of when you read Kafka? You're ashamed of your strength.

242

The young Greek asks me what being old means. It means, I tell him, that I have an overview of the lives of many people I have known. It means that I wish them and myself a life of three hundred years so that I can see even more, for every further inch that one knows makes life more astonishing, more dubious, more hopeful, more perceptive, and more inexplicable.

He sees many beautiful people. He is happy because others will enjoy them. He will not live to see them destroyed. He will not destroy them himself.

Most important of all is talking to unknown people. But it has to be done in such a way that *they* do the talking, and the only thing one does oneself is to get *them* to talk.

When that is no longer possible for a man, then death has begun.

Too brief, too brief, too little time for the people in the world. If he had known all of them, it would not be enough, and he would have wanted to know more.

It is easy to convince oneself that human will is aimed at stupid and disgusting things. It is more important to see what *else* they want.

He feeds rosebuds to his does and whispers Rilke.

There is nothing that men and animals have more in common than love.

Death in human beings has become something different. Man has gotten such power through death that he now carries it for all creatures.

The connection of death and love is an aesthetic one. The fact that it has led to a higher evaluation of death is its sin, one of the gravest sins, it cannot be atoned for by anything.

The true temptation of the thinking man is to fall silent. A thought achieves its highest dignity in silence: it has no further aim. It explains nothing, it does not expand. The thought that silences itself forgoes contact.

Perhaps even this thought can kill. But it doesn't know that. It did not wish that. It does not insist on surviving.

So long as one remains in self-observation, one has to hate oneself, at least for the sake of the disproportion: there would be so many other people to contemplate, *better* ones, whom one neglects.

Can one turn calm through precision? Isn't precision the supreme restlessness?

He read so much about himself that he no longer knew who he was and he didn't recognize his own name.

Great names, once achieved, ought to be smashed by their own bearers.

He laughs like a thousand small flashes of lightning, all the people who hear this laughter turn hot and bright.

He sliced the desk in half and sat down to write twofold.

The concept that life is a present *given* to one strikes me as monstrous.

The biggest thing is that which has gotten so small that it makes all bigness superfluous.

I read *The Plowman of Bohemia* in school, and I have to read it again today. I want to find out whether the hatred and defiance of death, which fill this dialogue, are real or simply rhetorical. How little genuine hatred of death there is in the literature handed down to us! But this little bit must be found, gathered, and concentrated. Such a Bible against death could supply many people with strength when they are on the point of slackening. It would also remove some of the arrogance from one's own defiance, for how could one possibly be alone in seeing through death? I am not seeking allies, I am seeking other witnesses. For would it not be dreadful if my own hard, unshakable stance against death could be psychologically "explained away," as though it came solely from the special conditions of my own life and were therefore valid solely for myself? Wherever that stance is to be found among others, it belongs to a *different* life, and there would be a greater likelihood of its having to belong to *every* life.

Not to wait until ideas become laments.

1968

At the wishes of many people, he decided to write the same thing yet again.

I don't think much of the effect of one's own thoughts on other people, or, more precisely, I don't know what sort of effect that might be. Usually, one has put new phrases into the world, but that is not the real effect; everything, no matter what, ultimately becomes a phrase, and something that has become conspicuously easy does not necessarily have to be bad.

The real effect consists of sudden thrusts that others receive; for inexplicable reasons, a sentence, a word becomes a source of energy. By striking someone else, it releases a rockfall that one could never have predicted oneself, if only because one does not really know another person's terrain. These rockfalls may be good or bad; if they are very violent, they are then mostly destructive. But all this has absolutely nothing to do with what one actually thought and aimed for; and thus any effect is blind. If one didn't know how greatly one required such effects oneself before being able to think something for oneself, one might despair and fall silent altogether.

It still is something to have lived, thought, and fought with oneself, even if no one else ever finds out about it.

The hopeful things in every system: whatever is left out of it.

A machine invents a world language. Since no one can understand it, it is accepted by all.

The ambivalence of all social phenomena is such that one can interpret them at will. But the most contestable thing of all is the attempt at defining and draining them as functions.

It could be conceivable that society is *not* an organism, that it has *no* structure, that it functions only temporarily or seemingly. The most obvious analogies are *not* the best.

My self-confidence halts in front of a few, very few figures of intellect. It is by no means those who have accomplished the most; these, on the contrary, merely goad one on. It is really those who saw something more important beyond their achievement, something unattainable, so that their achievement seemed to shrink until it disappeared.

One such figure is Kafka, and he has affected me more profoundly than Proust, who achieved incomparably more.

One keeps saying the same thing, but the fact that one *has* to say it is eery.

When he ate slowly, he considered himself better as though feeling sadness and melancholy over the fate of what was eaten.

An elegant young man with a tiny mouth. In order to eat, he has to hold his mouth open with two fingers in the corners.

"A worm living exclusively under the eyelids of a hippopotamus and feeding on its tears."

He needs God in order to pat him on the back and tell him how he should have done it.

If one had to answer for all the noble sentences one has ever uttered! If one had to answer for even *one* of them!

The gesture of knowledge: one pulls out a book, opens up quickly to several different places, and has something to say about each of them. The other person, who cannot follow the leaps, is amazed and envious.

Superlatives fighting it out with sabers.

Malraux, fed by Nietzsche, adds up his "dangers." All excitement, adventure, courage, and then becoming minister.

He has sucked out the sky, and now he despises the void.

Great words ought to suddenly begin whistling, like a tea-kettle in which water is being heated: as a warning.

I like reading Hsün-Tse, he does not fool himself about man, and yet he hopes. But I cannot deny that I also like reading Mencius because he does fool himself about man.
   I will never get away from the Chinese "mentors." I have dealt only

with the pre-Socratics as long as with them: my entire life. I can never grow weary of either. Together, but only together, they contain everything a thinking man needs as a goad—or else not quite everything, something decisive remains, which ought to be added, it concerns death, and I would like to add it.

The Chinese knew more about goodness than the Greeks. That wonderful vanity of the Greeks, to which we owe so much, deprived them of the simplicity for goodness.

Likewise, the traditions of the Chinese were determined quite early by man's existence in crowds. Even the developed Greek polis, which knows the crowd quite well, occurs among the thinkers basically only in terms of its rejection.

Of these thinkers, Empedocles is most like a Chinese sage. The atoms of Democrites may be uncountable, but they act through each other, not as a real crowd.

Perhaps it was the existence of slaves that prevented the Greeks from reaching an extreme concept of the crowd.

Of all thinkers, only the ancient Chinese have an endurable dignity. Would one still feel this way if they *spoke* to us rather than our *reading* their very rare utterances?

There is so little by them, and that alone is dignity.

In Buddha, for instance, I am disturbed that he said everything so often and so fully (the chief drawback of the Indians).

The litanies of the ancient Chinese are in their behavior, not in their statements.

This combination of the patriarchal and the fraternal, which exists only among the Chinese.

No one is backward if he is eaten up by the concern for human destiny. The backward man is the one consoling himself with putrescent phrases.

1969

The sciences bite off pieces of life, and life shrouds itself in pain and grief.

In history, there seems to be only a negative learning. One notes what one has done to others in order to hold it against them.

His eyes bleed, but never his heart.

Fullness becomes banal, but terseness is irresponsible. It is hard to settle into the right point between them.

The humiliating thing about life: ultimately, one accepts everything that one has loathed with strength and pride. One thereby returns to the point at which one started when young, into the same environment as back then, transformed into it. Yet where is one now? One is in the hardness with which one sees and records it.

Two kinds of mind: those that settle in wounds and those that settle in houses.

Not even Pascal was serious enough.

No religion has subjugated me, but how they all happened to me!

Would people made of glass be better? Would they have to be more careful with others? Man is not fragile enough. His mortality does not settle the issue. He would have to be very fragile.

He baked a fragrant prophet of bread, and when it was old and stony, they all broke their teeth on it.

To know one man, just one single man, who will come into the world *after me!* It is bothersome to consider technological details of the future if one doesn't know a single person from then.

A man who *eats* more after every announcement of a death.

Words, sucked full, like bedbugs.

He sweats peace out of every pore. But his mouth is teeming with war.

August Pfizmaier, the Viennese scholar, absorbed in his translation of the *Manyoshu,* knew nothing about the Franco-Prussian War of 1870–71 until a year after it broke out. He finally learned about it from a Japanese newspaper that reached him very belatedly in Vienna.

He can never tire of reality unless it is art.

He left everything he possessed to the oldest man in Europe.

Not to write about anyone that he is marked by death. Even writing that down is a sin.

The breathing man says: I still have everything to breathe. The unhappy man says: I still have room for other people's misfortunes. The dead man says: I don't know anything as yet, how can I be dead?

If there were an afterlife, he would not like to take anything of his along. He would like everything to remain here.

A Buddha today—unthinkable, even a Christ. All that's possible is a Mohammed.

The book about the "harmless people," the Bushmen. For them, the sun is a piece of meat, and without melons they would have to die of thirst in the desert.

What a strange thing meat is in the history of mankind. The leap from the flesh of prey to one's own flesh is the enigma of all enigmas. Compassion begins with it, arising from a feeling for one's own flesh. Today, the butchers' shops futilely recall one's own flesh.

It's useful to have stories about cannibals. The plaintiveness they arouse turns into compassion.

In one hour, more people passed on the street than a Bushman sees in his entire life.
The many things he sees are animals, and these he must kill.

To question oneself totally and catch oneself abroad.

A language in which a certain consonant is said to be lethal. Whoever pronounces it, drops dead. Whoever hears it, goes deaf.

All attempts at explaining are irresistible for man. The sequence of his explanation attempts has become his destiny. If only someone could understand this sequence, if only someone knew more about it. The chronological exchange of two explanations would have changed the course of history.
   Would there by anything to exchange now? Is everything determined now? And if so, when did the determination begin, at what exact point?

The worst notion of the future for him would be the abolition of the wind.

Nature has grown small, measured by our megalomaniacal behavior, a *Biedermeier* nature among monsters, which take all liberties with it.

Lovers already feel spied upon from the moon.

The disappointing thing about the moon is that everything is correct. Everything we calculated—distance, size, weight—turns out to be right. Everything is real.

Settlement of the moon by air-continents. Wars over air.

The moon is leprous ever since we touched it. The hand-felt moon: with every picture of human traces on it, we feel more and more as though we had to justify some offense.

1969

When I think of the moon, all people suddenly appear to me under *one* color.

Only people attract me, that explains my distaste for the empty moon. Even in the deserts of the earth, I am most fascinated by the thought of the few people finding one another there.

The courage of the moon travelers is great: it is not greater than that of a Bushman hunting alone in the Kalahari Desert or, together with a few comrades, driving lions from his prey. But one dreadful thing is new: everything happens by way of radioed commands, and nothing is spontaneous.

Musical instruments in the crust of the moon, put there for spreading tremors.

The lack of any other creature there. Robinson Crusoe among minerals, as a robot, taking no step without an order from afar. Functioning remote orders, a dreadful vision of the future. Do this, do that; and in between, silly jokes for the audience on earth.

Strange that I feel no pity for the moon travelers, as though they were really robots.

The return from the moon has made any other return hotter.

Moon hermits as earth worshipers.

Secrets deposited on the moon.

When the sun comes out, he says to himself scornfully, We'll soon have the sun too on our leash.

The difference today is that everything gets photographed. There is no misery left that can be kept secret. All misery has gone public.
    But this merely signifies that everyone can more easily grow used to it.
    In the past, a man could pretend to know nothing. Today he can pretend to be helpless, for he knows *too much.*

All conversations, even among friends, have become more hypocritical. Indignation can spread over too much. Every day, every person has heard about several things that are terrible.

But even the man who concludes that nothing concerns him, precisely because there is so much, does *know* what is happening; not even a deaf-mute, not even a blind man could possibly close himself off to it: and even a moron would have to be frightened, at least for himself.

Thus, every instant of apparent quiet is abysmal hypocrisy.

Hide, otherwise you won't find out anything.

The necessity of individual sentences: they occur to one from a steeper angle; they strike and lodge more deeply; but not without first glowing and lighting up an entire countryside, which was never encompassed in this way and will never again fully darken.

The instant of receptivity for such a sentence cannot be determined in advance. It emerges and it happens.

Language, grasped as a system, goes dumb.

Writers in a free-for-all for their place in the shade. Squabbling bull's-eyes.

This hasty respect for people who are always attached to the *same* persons. As though they were better for being easier to read! Indolence of the viewer, who would like to have an easier time with his knowledge of human beings.

He tied her story around his neck and carried it through the streets with a wink.

Yesterday, in Italy, a man died at ninety-three; he had been living in railroads for twenty years. He kept transferring from one train to the next and had no other home. As a former member of Parliament, he had a free railroad pass; his great fortune had melted, all he had left was the pass. He died in the main terminal of Turin while changing trains.

Whatever their activity, the active consider themselves better.

To regard every topic as a glove. Turn it inside-out.

He talks away at her so that she won't bitch; she doesn't listen. She bitches so that he won't talk: he doesn't listen.

A man who guesses other people's every thought without knowing his own.

The prisoners admire their persecutors in order to remain alive. The more gratefully and respectfully they talk about them, the more hope they have of escaping them.

"You're terrific! Let me go!" said the mouse to the cat and licked her claws.

How one resents adulators when they demand the return of their adulation!

A fame as vast as the sun; people with a sweet tooth nibble on it, burning their lips and tongue.

Shift hunger to the head.

It is very hard not to say more than one wants to.

Those statements one makes unconsciously during a lifetime! One may just as well have said the opposite. All the real things occur later when one fills them with meaning. At first, they are like empty programs. Then comes the music. How wonderful the music sometimes is that one devises for the most mindless programs!

Balance every observation of oneself with a hundred observations of others. There is something satisfied and tender even in the harshest observation of one's own person.

If we investigate the essence of Musil, then hygiene has to be a central notion.

It is not, as in Kafka, the hygiene of a threatened man, a sectarian. The *truest* milieu he lived in was, for Kafka, Jungbrunn; nothing but his own kind, nothing but sectarians of hygiene.

Musil's hygiene is that of a man who loves his body, is satisfied with it, and finds it beautiful.

Through his own body, he understands women, who are mainly occupied with their bodies.

He treats his mind like a body, on which he can rely in the last analysis.

The terrible thing about guilt feelings: not even *they* are right.

F., the perfect hypocrite, profusely apologizes for every bad emotion of his, in order to make them seem rare. Thus he can totally conceal the worst among them, his honesty covers all traces.

The man taking note of all his habits would no longer know who he is.

To find a stronger word for love, a word that would be like wind, but from under the earth, a word that doesn't need mountains, but enormous caves in which it houses, from which it plunges over valleys and plains, like waters that are not water, like fire that doesn't burn, but shines thoroughly, like crystal, but doesn't cut, it is transparent, and it is all form, a word like the voices of animals, but they understand one another, a word like the dead, but they are all back here again.

Joys that better represent us to pain.

It's all in the newspapers. One merely has to read them with enough hatred.

You mountains, you mountains, you see it all and yet you still haven't fallen on us.

A single ugly young woman, in her futile hope, renders love, which has become cheap, precious again.

On January 17, 1776, a pair of twins was hanged together in Tyburn. "When the cart was pulled away from under their feet, their hands intertwined. Thus they swung side by side for nearly a minute. Then, when they lost consciousness, their hands slowly came undone from each other."

254

Goodness, he says. But what does he mean? Couldn't he say it somewhat more accurately? He means a wakefulness that won't be fooled and doesn't fool itself. He means a very acute distrust of any use of people for purposes that are supposedly "higher" but are merely other people's purposes. He means openness and spontaneity, a never-tiring curiosity for people, which takes them in and understands them. He means gratitude for those people who haven't done anything for one, but who come towards one, they see one and they have words. He means memory that omits nothing and releases nothing. He means hope in spite of, but not concealing, despair. He also means animals, even though we eat them. He especially means everything that is more stupid than oneself. He means powerlessness and never power. The man who is good to power, yielding to it or flattering it for his own protection—that man is bad. He means passions that also let those of others live. He means amazement. But he also means concern. He does not mean loftiness, arrogance, being above it all, self-deification, harshness, and order, through which one keeps others down. The goodness he means is mentally in motion and doubts everything. He does not mean the goodness that "makes it," but the kind that suddenly stands there empty-handed. He means being affected, even at a very advanced age, by anger and accusation; but only if they do not bring power to the angry or accusing man. He also means speech, he certainly does not mean silence. He means knowledge, but no office, no position, no payment. He means concern for people *here,* no petitioning for their souls.

1970

All responsibility is concealed. In its concealment, it is indestructible.

He is not a nation, he is all nations.

Dialectics, a kind of false teeth.

"For not even one of the creatures may be wiped out from the world."

"When one feels very humbled, only one thing is left: to comfort and raise up another humbled man."

"He does not join any school, and yet he does not reject a thought simply because it comes from someone else." Chuang-tzu

The reality of the fantastic in Chuang-tzu. It is never reduced to anything ideal. The untouchable is reality itself, and not something behind it.

The thing that always attracted me about Taoism is that it knows and approves of metamorphosis without reaching the position of Indian or European idealism.

Taoism sets very great store in longevity and immortality in *this* life, and the many different shames it helps one to are down here. It is the religion of poets, even if they do not realize it.

The tension between three chief doctrines of China, between Mencius, Mo-tzu, and Chuang-tzu, strikes me as topical; nor can the tension in modern man be grasped any more precisely. The traditional European tension between "worldly" and "otherworldly" strikes me as untrue and artificial.

Today, man can read nothing that concerns him more directly than the early Chinese philosophers. All inessentials vanish here. As far as possible, one is spared being deformed by the conceptual here. Definition is not an end in itself. It is always a matter of the possible attitudes towards *life* and not the attitudes towards *concepts*.

Proof destroys. It even destroys the truest things.

To find sentences so simple that they are no longer one's own.

To lose recognizability; that is the hardest thing.

To find a remark again after a hundred years: now it is unforgettable.

He does not close himself off to experience, but he can not keep pace with it. Even in the smallest splinters of what has been destroyed he keeps searching for some meaning.

Words are not too old, only people are too old if they use the same words too frequently.

He wants to keep going on, to where he has never been, he wants to change the ground beneath him, which has become safe under his steps, he wants to slip into the unsafe, find refuge where he has never connected anything, so that he may connect other things, force other things together, have an intuition of other things.

Even if someone could be found to sense more in an hour than others in a lifetime, he should not be satisfied with that. He ought to learn how to reject his inklings, even the ones he loves most, and to find unheard-of inklings that will *threaten* him.

Your asceticism would be even more than silence: to live without admiration.

A day in a different sequence, a happy day.
It depends on what one *gets rid of;* not so much what one does, but what one *removes* from oneself.

Can one resent a language? Perhaps, but only in that language itself. Any resentment of a language expressed in another language is suspicious.

He frolicked like a daredevil on the catastrophe, while his brother lay dreaming on the beach, sunning himself.

An Aztec as a cook in Hampstead. "Quetzalcoatl," I say to him; he doesn't understand me. "Steak au poivre," I say, and his face is wreathed in a grin.

For an hour, I observed his thoughts, they were playing between his nose and moustache like pride and surrender.

It tempts me not to find an audience.

Writers recognize one another by generous speeches. My new friend, the dark sage from Agra, carries on about misers in his broken English just as I would: his visiting card.

Svevo's belated renown: a gift from Joyce. The paid teacher, who felt humiliated, showers the "burgher" with his sudden wealth: fame.

Some figures in novels are so strong that they imprison their author and strangle him.

The dissolution of the character in recent literature: the figures that our time would need are so monstrous that no one is daredevil enough to invent them.

To take off one's old clothes. To remember, yes. But not in the old clothes.

Céline in *Castle to Castle* depicts himself with amazing veracity: his conformity to the powerful in Sigmaringen; his paranoid situation, which he is always aware of, he was truly in great danger. (The war is ending. The Pétain government and its leading figures are in Sigmaringen, on the run.)

While writing this book about events that were a good twelve years old, a new hatred formed in him against the people getting him to write, his publishers; Achille is Gaston Gallimard.

His function as a doctor in Sigmaringen brings him together with all the people there. The German staff physician in uniform, whose prostate he examines. The hotel proprietress, whom he gives an injection and who, naked, asks him for his wife, a Parisian, to make love. The SS-Kommandant, from a family of junkers, whom he treats with particular caution. He is sought out as a doctor by all, he is sent everywhere, they respect him only when it turns out that he has cyanide.

Everything happening in Céline is turned by him into something crowded with people. In this, he is very imprecise, like all paranoiacs; yet one does get the sense of a dangerously teeming life, that is also repugnant. He is not so lavish with "Juifs" in this book as earlier. But every German is a "Boche," and the word contains all the loathing he is capable of.

The book is a detailed recollection by a man who usually, indeed always feels persecuted. This is also the secret of its readability, he is always in danger, and that feeling is transferred to the reader. Céline is as readable as a detective story for most people. He never avoids any embarrassing terms, this creates an impression of continuous truth.

He has seen a great deal, already as a doctor, and then through his adventurous destiny. One is surprised that not all physicians feel life as he does. He has not developed a thick skin like the other doctors. Perhaps that's also connected to his remaining a doctor for the poor. The sense of his importance as a writer, which he certainly has, appears differently in him than in other writers. It gives him the right to attack anything. But he has no arrogance as the others do; because all phenomena of life, even his own, are much too dubious for him.

He falsifies terribly, as in the very crowdedness of nearly all the scenes he remembers. Yet he has comic accounts of great power, which have something of Rabelais. Accounts of conversations with individual people: the scene with Laval and Brisselonne, or the other one with Abetz and Chateaubriand. He is a story-teller of the oldest school; that could fill one with hope for the narrative. He incessantly disrupts his tale with divagations, which remove its triviality. His conception of sexual processes is that of a doctor and thoroughly convincing. He hates women almost more than men. The silly self-glorification of sex, which makes Miller and his imitators unbearable, is as foreign to him as to a medieval theologian.

He almost always felt bad; that reconciles one a bit to his hatefulness, which is promiscuous and monstrous. He does not pounce upon the people who are taboo in present-day France: when he defends himself through his manner of presentation, he also defends them. He has much noblesse, astonishing in his medium. He hates all power and all worship.

Memory wants to come undisturbed and in its own time, and nobody who was present *back then* should interfere with it.

How little you have read, how little you know; but your random reading determines what you are.

A character who manages to destroy everything through endurance.

Myth? Do you mean something so old that it is *no longer* boring?

Instead of a literary history of influences, a literary history of counter-influences; it would be more informative. Counter-images, not always obvious, are often more important than model-images.

To base the biography of a man on everything that repulsed him. It penetrates in a very different way, it remains under the skin, lost but awake. Once rejected, it can forget itself, yet this forgetting is only a semblance, and the repulsed as the rejected can be *used* without fear.

A seemingly fat person, consisting of twelve well-packed thin people, who all squeak at once.

The praise-gatherer is annoyed at the silence of the streets. He walks them tirelessly in order to force them to praise, and he is vexed at their resistance. The newspapers are too daily for him. People throw them away together with his picture. Would it be enough for him if the newspapers ran something new about him every day? No! He does need the papers, he kept reading them until he appeared in them; but he wants a lot more.

He wants to block the events of the world. He wants people to think about him, not about earthquakes and wars. He finds the preoccupation with the moon quite absurd. He resents the moon for being talked about so much.

The praise-gatherer fills a house with his name. The smallest, but also every large piece of paper bearing his name is saved.

Sometimes he reads through the entire house, always the same thing, even though it's old. But he prefers new things.

He awaits new phrases, new sentences, such as he has never heard before, a whole language of praise, invented for him alone. Dead men may sometimes also be praised, he gets hold of their blessings.

The praise-gatherer would be willing to impose capital punishment for any vilification or even mere criticism. He is not inhuman, he does not regret its abolition; it ought to be reintroduced only for such special cases, namely in regard to him.

The praise-gatherer never overlooks any praise, he has room even for things that have been said twice, thrice, four times. He grows fatter and fatter, but he likes his fat. He always finds women who love him for it. They lick his praise and hope to get some of it.

Reversals

At the funeral, the coffin went astray. The mourners were hastily shoveled into the grave. The corpse suddenly emerged from ambush and threw a handful of earth after everyone into his grave.

The lights went out, the town was sheathed in darkness. The criminals got scared and let the policemen go.

The dog took off his master's muzzle but kept him on the leash.

In a neon advertising sign, the letters changed places and warned against the lauded commodity.

The cat draped the mouse in its claws and released it into life.

God put the rib back into Adam's side, blew out his breath, and deformed him back into clay.

1971

An annual murder festival in Sarajevo. The population is dressed in the animal hides of Franz Ferdinand's victims. The successor to the throne drives from city hall to the murder museum, shooting all the way. Thousands of victims fall dead into the small river. Is there again, is there still, war?

On the corner, the man playing Princip leaps out and shoots the mass murderer in the heart.

He sank into the arms of the ghost of mankind.

Tolstoy's disguise as a bug at a ball. Would Kafka, who admired Tolstoy, have cared to read about that after writing *Metamorphosis?*

The reader who cannot stop, who keeps on and on, reading more and more, always more old things, has become a respected figure, a kind of confidant for others, who rely on him: if only he doesn't stop, he will be sure—so they think—to find what's crucial.

The Cynics as a mass movement of our time. A giant barrel of Diogenes, in which a hundred thousand people get together.

In a real writer, the thing I treasure most is what he conceals out of pride.

I am not interested in grasping precisely a man I know. I am interested only in exaggerating him precisely.

One wonders what God would have said, had he watched Tolstoy. Enough praying was done, but that can hardly interest God.

The events ought to have caught God's eye. Perhaps Tolstoy would have aroused his jealousy. Perhaps he would have accepted him as a brother.

I cannot forget his picture, it hovers before me like an ancestor. What strength must ancestor worship have given men. What do we honor? What can we honor?

One ought to mention that Tolstoy lived to be eighty-two and Dostoievsky only fifty-nine. Twenty-three years are a very long time. Would Tolstoy really exist if he had died in 1887?

It is quite impossible to get over the injustice as to lengths of lives.

I like God best of all as Tolstoy.

To become better can only mean that one *knows* better. It must, however, be a knowledge that gives one no peace, a driving knowledge. A knowledge that relaxes is deadly.

It is very important to reject certain knowledge. One has to be able to await the moment in which knowledge becomes a goad: every inkling its own pain.

How lamentable to have only *one* specific age! One would like to have two ages at once and know it. "How old are you?"—"Twenty-seven and sixty-five."—"And you?"—"Forty-one and twelve."

From these double ages, one could derive new and enticing forms of life.

The insolence of the rich man who *counsels* the poor.

I know quite well what "bourgeois" is. As soon as someone pronounces the word, I no longer know.

One never knows what will happen if things are suddenly changed. But do we know what will happen if they are *not* changed?

"I climb over two very small boys lying on the floor and clutching one another like monkeys. Refugees say that their village was burned down about a week ago, and everyone in it was killed except for these two. 'We've had them here for three days,' says the doctor, 'and no one knows who they are. They are so horrified over what happened that they are incapable of speaking. They just lie there, clutching one another. It's almost impossible to separate them, even long enough to feed them. It is hard to say when they'll be able to speak again.' "

The written acount has a threefold horror. Some people can't read it. Nevertheless, it can fade from memory.

Could it be possible that the sensitivity of those who have not hardened because they did not see it—could it be possible that their sensitivity affects those who *were* present?

Is that the function of horror, that could not resign itself because it did not have to resign itself?

If that were so, then it would be meaningful that people were never killers. But their number is small and the number of killers or witnesses too big.

Perhaps not a single person is *worthy* to have a child.

Were the transgressions of hell less serious when people still believed in them? Were our infernal natures more bearable when they knew where they would wind up?

We, proud of abolishing hell, are now spreading it everywhere.

The last people will not weep.

The enemy of my enemy is *not* my friend.

I too am one of the "mild" people, who try to explain crimes, thereby excusing them half and half. I hate the penalty meted out by people who are certain. I loathe force. But I also accurately know the abysmal wickedness of man. I know it in myself.

Is it then indulgence towards myself that I obtain through these explanations?

No, I am very harsh when settling accounts with myself.

Yet I have sidestepped crimes and hence any public punishment. How can I desire penalties for others, if these penalties will never strike me? Must one commit crimes in order to recognize punishments? No, that would be malice and hypocrisy.

What way is there to make penalties fair without making things easy for oneself?

A country in which the judges also punish themselves. No justice that does not cut into their own flesh. No punishment that is not meted out to them too. No acquittal that doesn't benefit them, only an acquittal costs them nothing.

Self-accusations do not make anything better. The deeper they reach, the more surely they end in self-complaisance: "What a great guy I am! I can even say that with impunity!"

Certain words, one feels, are too terrible for everyone but onself.

All the pessimists in world history together are nothing against reality. None of the old religions can suffice, they all come from idyllic periods.

To find the path through the labyrinth of one's own time without giving in to one's own time, and without jumping out.

He would have had more self-confidence if he had never heard anything about himself.

What if it should turn out that we, the everlasting penitents for the future, had lived in the best of all possible times!
    If we were envied for the millions of starving Bengals?
    If our discontent and our miserable consciences were ridiculed as delightful Biedermeier airs!
    If people were to keep trying, even a thousand times, to examine how we managed to have so much freedom, so much air, so many ideas!
    If our unsuspectingness were declared the pinnacle of humanity and our distaste for death were recognized as a *harmless* murderousness!

The blind, those know-it-alls.

The acumen in all areas of life, always driving them apart, and no acumen for bridging the chasms between them.

So many men in one's mind and what they said! And yet one has to find it oneself and say it oneself.

In the vanity of his dialectics, he puts off any decision until he is capable of none; and he regards that as thinking.

He wields his saw alternately from either side. What he saws up exists no more.

His sawdust is occasionally witty.

Many worm-thoughts: cut in two, they continue to grow.

This whole immense life, multiplying endlessly—for us? Only God can believe that.

Every day, he thought of a hundred structures, he couldn't sleep because of structures, he spoke and ate and swallowed, he emptied himself of structures. When I met him, he sang new structures to me; when I left, he said goodbye with structures.

When the interlocutors reach a certain age, every articulated conversation becomes bottomless and diabolical, as though each man wanted to don a scalp of words and scurry off.

Yet nothing is windier than a scalp of words. Words remain heard only if they are sent back to their opener. Their return is supposed to arouse disturbed dreams, which, by way of gratitude, entrust themselves to the honest finder.

A dream springing back and forth is the utmost that people can get from one another.

The time at which something interests him is his own. Freedom from other people's schedules.

But also freedom from one's own: exchange the consequences, prefer them, put them back, recall them, forget them.

Do not overestimate the unusual. Provide the usual with barbs.

Thanks to his forgetfulness, something finally became of him.

To be free today, he serves all masters of the past and the future.

The Russian astronauts were dead when they landed on the earth. They landed successfully and died of their landing with no external injuries. If their hearts failed, then it was all three hearts at once. An end that is more touching than a disappearance in space. Thus they were found, a warning. It would be best if no reason for their death were ever discovered.

But we still have to seriously consider the collective mourning of the Russians for their three dead. If such tasks could assume the function of wars, as a collective participation in a mortally dangerous enterprise, then the space journeys would have a meaning withal.

It is necessary that people try to reflect on everything that exists *aside from technology*. How else can we come upon the forces that will set us free from the domination of technology?

He would be happy if, for inexplicable reasons, a completely different starry sky were suddenly overhead.

He leaned towards the religions in which the gods elude one another and human beings through transformations.

I am nourished by myths. I sometimes try to escape them. I do not wish to violate them.

"The silkworm from a worm of patient Job."

With the gods of the ancients, so much has gotten lost that one could fear that something would be lost with our own, simpler God.

Yet I cannot find my way back to the one who brought death into the world. I see a god of life nowhere, just blind men decorating their misdeeds with God.

Are my expectations childlike when I notice a crack in a man's shell and I suddenly feel: All is not lost; with a little help, a faltering heart can be made to beat again.

I always know better, I have a terribly accurate knowledge of people; yet this knowledge does not interest me, anyone who has lived a while could have it. I am interested in what refutes this knowledge, what annuls it. I would like to turn a usurer into a benefactor, a bookkeeper into a poet. I am interested in the leap, the surprising metamorphosis.

I have never given up hope, I often try to punish myself for it and mock it cruelly. But it lives on in me, intact.

It may be as ridiculous as that other, far greater, that gigantic hope that a dead man could suddenly be standing before me and it would not be a dream.

The man who is understood is misunderstood. Everything only keeps operating in misunderstandings. It is nevertheless crucial that one lives to be truly understood.

A first conversation with people whom he has known by sight for ten years, whom he has looked at questioningly every day and they at him.

One should have many such people and then, after years, address them.

The man from Asia, having settled in Africa, been driven to England, not arrived here.

How many faces can a man register? Is there an upper limit? And is that limit reached only by people like Napoleon, who register people so that they may die for them?

He likes sentences individually, single sentences, one can turn them over in one's hand, one can bolt them, one can choke them.

Chinese names have something of the ultimate language, in which all human languages will end.

Will the unread books take vengeance? Will they, neglected, refuse to follow him to the graveside? Will they pounce upon the sated, much-read books and tear them to shreds?

I admire Musil at least for never abandoning the things even if he saw through them. He remained in them for forty years and died while still caught in them.

I am reading Ovid's *Metamorphoses* as though for the first time. It is not the speeches and feelings of the characters that impress me: they are too artistic, their rhetoric passed into European literature from the beginning and was purified into a better truth by later writers. But the inspiration of the poem, its subject matter, is metamorphosis, and Ovid thereby anticipated something that has profoundly interested writers until the present day. He is not content with *naming* metamorphoses, he tracks them down, he describes them, they become graphic processes. He thus detaches the very essence of myth from its usual context and gives it a conspicuousness that it never loses again. He is concerned with *all* metamorphoses, not just this one or that one, he gathers them, he lines them up, each single one of them is investigated in all its ramifications, and even where they still bear common traits by their very nature, they nevertheless seem like fresh, believably seized miracles.

Often it is the metamorphoses of flight, but they are unique; often it is those of pain. Their definitive character is what constitutes their earnestness. If there are rescues, they are dearly purchased; the freedom of the transformed being is lost forever. But the wealth and variation of the series of metamorphoses helps to maintain the mythic fluidity as a whole.

What he has thereby salvaged for the Christian world is invaluable: the very thing that was most lost to its consciousness. Into its hierarchically paralyzed doctrine, its cumbersome system of virtues and vices, he breathed the older, more liberating breath of metamorphosis. He is the father of a modernism that always existed; its traces could still be readily demonstrated today.

One has to stop before one has said everything. Some people have said everything before they begin.

There is nothing more to be found, no unknown species of man. Now is the time for entangling all that we know.

He has plucked out all the myths like blades of grass.

Eyes that see only the inner body, but bloodily and accurately. One eye towards the inside, one eye towards the outside. If afflicted with this twofold gaze—what would people be like?

One does not view most mystics as poets, but one does view the Persian mystics as poets.

They talk more about animals and also about boys. Their writing is more entangled, their elan more earthly, their similes have something hot like the breath of love and yet something delimited like everyday life.

They lack the lamblike quality of monastic living. One feels they have wandered and often been silent and have suddenly spoken with passion after a long silence.

They are wise, but their diction is vehement. They babble and speak wondrously. They have something of acrobats about them.

He hunts for the one sentence. He conceives a hundred thousand sentences in order to find the only one.

In what language could the one sentence be found? Are the words of the one sentence heavenly bodies? Hearts? Deaths? Animals?

The one sentence is the sentence that he himself never repeats, no one repeats it.

The smashers of language are looking for a new justice among words. It does not exist. Words are unequal and unjust.

Ariosto's liveliness passed into Stendhal, the swiftness, the love of metamorphosis, and the arbitrariness.

Stendhal got a great deal more from Ariosto than from Shakespeare.

Stendhal's measured attitude towards death, despite the early loss of his mother and his disgust at God, "from whom it came," can be explained only by the French Revolution: his happiness at the execution of the king. A death which deeply disturbed his father, whom he hated, appeared to him as a good fortune, and put him in debt to death.

Three people Stendhal looked up to in his childhood: the skeptical grandfather, who always *thought* something; the proud aunt with her Spanish nobility; the hedonist Romain Gagnon, his uncle, a womanizer and man of the moment. But even stronger are the *anti-models* of his youth: the calculating father, the other aunt, who squabbled and persecuted him with hatred, and his teacher, the Jesuit Raillane. This split into love and hatred, into models and anti-models, is depicted more clearly and more excitedly than in any other autobiography.

Henri Brulard's theoretical value, for me, is particularly there. But almost nothing in him is not immensely valuable. There are all early experiences of death, so true and powerful as to haunt the reader. There is the stubborn sense of places, formed only sometimes, but always recorded precisely. There is a moral candor that conceals no baseness and yet always momentarily sides with generosity. There is his curiosity about every person and the continuous sensitivity to the charm of women. His later sensibility for paintings cannot be otherwise understood.

I owe Stendhal the conviction that every person—were he to succeed in getting himself fully down on paper—would be exciting and amazing and also irreplaceable.

It is the spontaneity of his thinking and feeling that I love in him, the openness and happy testiness of his nature, the quickness that, however, never forgets, the incessant movement that never loses itself, the nobility that never brags, the gratitude that knows exactly what it is grateful for, the lack of embellishment (except in regard to paintings), the filled chasm in which there is always light. There is light in him everywhere, his very thinking is light. But it is no religious or mystical light—that was always suspicious to him; it is the light of the life processes themselves, reflecting themselves in every concrete detail.

It is hard to maintain the cruelty that is indispensable for unerring observation. The warmth of memory spreads everywhere, and some day, when one has become pure memory, one will no longer be able to see anybody with the harsh eyes of reality.

What man is permitted to go his way, what man is not incessantly buffeted back and forth, out into the desert, where he finds nothing of himself and has to wither away, stuttering for help, sinking into salt, without leaves or blossoms, scorched, accursed?

No man knows the full bitterness awaiting him, and if it should suddenly appear like a dream, he would contest it and avert his eyes from it.

That's hope.

There is no pain that cannot be surpassed, the only infinity is pain.

The philosophers who would like to give death along to one, as though it were inside one from the very start.

They cannot endure seeing it only at the end, they prefer prolonging it back to the beginning, they make it the most intimate escort of a whole lifetime, and thus, in this adulteration and familiarity, it becomes bearable for them.

They fail to understand that they have thereby given it more power

than is its due. "It does not matter that you die," they seem to be saying, "you have been dying all your life anyway." They do not sense
that they are guilty of a vile and cowardly trick, for they thus bind the
strength of those who might fight against death. They prevent the one
struggle worth waging. They declare surrender to be wisdom. They
talk everyone into their own cowardice.

Those among them who consider themselves Christians are poisoning
the very core of their faith, which drew its strength from overcoming death. If they had their way, every resurrection that Christ successfully performed in the gospels would be meaningless.

"Death, where is thy sting?" It is no sting, they say, for it is always
there, ingrown in life, its Siamese twin.

They abandon man to death as to an invisible blood that pulses
through his veins incessantly; let it be called the blood of capitulation,
the secret shadow of the true blood that renews itself unendingly in
order to live.

Freud's death drive is a scion of old, dark philosophical teachings, but
more dangerous than they because it is garbed in biological terminol-
ogy that has a semblance of modernity.

This psychology, which is no philosophy, lives from philosophy's
worst legacy.

The language philosophers, who omit death as though it were something "metaphysical." But the shift of death into metaphysics changes
nothing in its being the oldest fact, older and more penetrating than
any language.

The Stoics overcome death by death. The death one commits on oneself
doesn't harm one any more, so one need not fear it.

The man who has cut off his own head feels no pains.

One knows nothing immediately; whatever one thinks one knows immediately was found out long before.

All that counts is the knowledge that has been hidden in one for a
long time.

The vain man does not want to ask God for assistance prematurely. He
first mirrors himself in the strength he doesn't have, watches the disap-

pearance of things he falsely claimed, enjoys his weakness, and suddenly says in stupendous insolence: God. As though God had always secretly been there for him.

A tongue that reaches to hell.

Everyone stood as monuments and waited motionless. Until the next fad, then they began twitching and writhing.

Pause until the rediscovery of eternity.

A world that does not arouse the passion of the man in whom it is absorbed is no world at all. Mere seeping is not enough. Man, who is like a Karst landscape, has to form his underground rivers, and they must come to light enormous and unexpected.

A thunderstorm lasting a whole week. Darkness everywhere. Reading only when there is lightning. To remember and connect what one reads during the flashes.

How much flattery does a man need to become better? One tells him how he supposedly is, and he likes himself.

There is no mind that would not be interesting. One merely has to put oneself into it.

I wonder whether it is unforgivable to deliberately sum up in old age. For it might be conceivable that one closes oneself off towards the outside under the pressure of the things one hauls up, unwilling to absorb anything and absorbing nothing more.

Perhaps the value of the things we receive late in life is dubious. It does not penetrate everywhere, it trickles away on the surface, one wears an impermeable coat against new things.

The openness towards the *inside,* on the contrary, grows so greatly that one *must* give in to it when the profit even half justifies it. The difficulty is that a glow adheres to all earlier things merely because they were earlier; in particular, it is a glow from the dead. One is not meant to distrust this glow, for it contains the gratitude for past life. It *can* only be one's past life, one's very own; and the guilt one occasionally may feel because it is not the past lives of all others, because it virtually excludes them, is a presumptuous guilt, for how could one have lived the lives of all people?

Memory is good because it increases the measure of the knowable. But we especially have to make sure that it never excludes the dreadful.

Memory may grasp it otherwise than as it appeared in its terrible presence, otherwise but no less cruel, no more endurable, no less absurd, cutting, bitter, and not content because it is past, nothing is ever past.

The actual value of memory lies in this insight that nothing is past.

One cannot see oneself severely enough. But it has to be a *thorough* severity; as soon as it is simplified, it becomes the worthless pose of condemnation, which wrongly gives pleasure.

To give a sigh of relief, standing among animals: they don't realize what's in store for them.

Long before the creation of the world, there were philosophers. They were lying in ambush in order to be able to say that everything is good. For hadn't they thought of it? And how could something they had thought of fail to be good?

As their thought, they brought forth the dubious formation, and they giggled over the correctness of their prophesy.

Guilt as karma—unspeakable hubris of man: in the animals in which it takes up its dwelling, the baseness of his soul is said to be punished.

How can he dare to punish animals with his soul? Did they invite it? Can they wish to be degraded by it? They do not want the soul of man, they loathe it, it is too puffed up, too ugly for them. They prefer their graceful poverty, and they would much rather be devoured by animals than people.

274

1972

Tasso, fearing persecution, offers himself to it. He forestalls it, he demands its severity. It doesn't want him, he runs towards it. He begs it to notice him, it eludes him. He accuses it, it propitiates him. I don't want you, it says; he throws himself at its feet.

He wavers back and forth between the great of this world and spiritual persecution. When fleeing the great, he takes refuge in persecution. But it is only the church's persecution that he recognizes; he contests that of the great, and when they get too close for comfort, he escapes to the church's persecution.

No one measures the extent of the poet's humiliation among the great. He seeks the forces that are stronger than they and offers himself to them as a prey. The poet, aware of his own greatness, must go insane among the great of the world. If he lived among them since his youth, there is only one salvation for him: they have to recognize him as one of their kind.

Tasso's money problems recall Baudelaire's. Baudelaire's satanism was also in Tasso. But Tasso witnessed the church persecution in France; not long before the Night of St. Bartholomew, in the immediately foregoing atmosphere, he was in Paris and learned about massacres in other cities. Thus his fear of this persecution grew, and that which was a semi-frivolous game for a nineteenth-century man was deadly serious for Tasso. He once again believed in hell, which he had sometimes doubted, and he felt it as an acute danger. The punishment of the church would save him from that as from persecution by the powerful.

In all the Renaissance, there was probably no man who was as "modern" as Tasso. Because for us the collective powers are urgently back again, it is inconceivable that an intellectual man does not think about his relationship to them. No matter how hard he may strain to elude their power, something in him acknowledges them. He feels guilty about his resistance, as guilty as a faithful son of the church back then.

For those writers whose fear is never dormant, who remain themselves, there is no salvation. For a while, they can yield to one of the great collective units, but they cannot keep yielding without suffering if they live in their precinct.

Every cowardice, every restraint is a sin for the writer. His boldness lies in utterance. *Though* he bears responsibility for it, he has to say it.

Even if there were only one single uncontested world religion, he would have the right to ignore it and not say anything about it. But he would have this right only if he had something urgent to say, which only he can say.

But what is urgent? What he feels and recognizes in others and what they cannot say. He must first have felt and recognized it and then found it again in others. The congruence creates the urgency. He has to be capable of two things: to feel strongly and to think; and to *hear* the others and take them seriously in a never-ending passion. The impression of congruence must be sincere, undimmed by any vanity.

But he must also be able to say it: if said insufficiently, it loses its urgency, and he is guilty of squandering the congruence. It is the most precious but also the most terrifying thing that a man can experience. He must be able to keep it upright when it threatens to crumble, he has to nourish it incessantly through new experience and effort.

He tries not to lose too many biases at once. Caution, go slowly; otherwise, nothing will be left of him.

The name "moralist" sounds like a perversion, one wouldn't be surprised at finding it suddenly in Krafft-Ebing.

He pictures throwing morality off like the lid of a coffin. What an utterly lively corpse would make an appearance!

He shook hands with all dead people and joined them as the last one.

He's bothered by his hated and concealed characters.

He infected all with his gloominess and escaped them.

276

1972

The bitter man must sparkle; when dried out, he is useless. His sparks have to contain hope, which he himself no longer tolerates.

There is something like a physical disgust at every person that one is not oneself.

How much consciousness of one's own person is part of that? Would one feel this disgust if one came upon oneself in disguise and not immediately recognizable?

To be hung with refusals and go outside and spread nothing but no-no-no all around.

The self-hater loves himself *more*. He reels before death and says: "That is the best thing we have."

It's long, long past that he lived under cover of hatred.

He was dispossessed of old age.

Everything the seventy-five-year-old mouse remembers is wrong. But no one talks to her when she doesn't remember. So she talks and claims, and if only just a few names are correct, one allows her to grow older and to know less and less and less.

Finally, she is too small for even the last hole and she evaporates.

The philosophers gather to demonstrate their number, which is not to be despised. They order themselves into schools wearing special uniforms.

Deserters throw off their uniforms and run naked and trembling to the others. There they are greeted jubilantly and put in uniforms.

Some schools shrink down to a single follower. He is never permitted to leave his place, otherwise the school will be done for. Sometimes, a whole, very large school is carried off by an epidemic, to which all others are immune.

New schools also form suddenly, out of thin air, with names that make others perk up their ears. They are proclaimed by heralds, who are not philosophers and are not supposed to understand what they say.

Very handsome heralds are allowed to proclaim several new schools in a row. But hunchbacked or crippled heralds are also popular. They get a fixing wine to drink, it establishes their shape forever, the most persistent thing in the fleetingness of the philosophers.

Not be more rational than one is. Not over anything with reason. Not run ahead with reason. Use reason against one's innate wickedness, but not for disguising knowledge.

There are sentences that mean something only in another language. They wait for their translator as for a midwife.

A man sends for poor people and gives them rich ones.

The beggar gave him back the gold piece, shook his head, and said, "Copper!"

One group sleeps while the other stays awake and labors. Only when the latter goes to sleep does the former wake up. Now they walk about through their daily schedule. They ignore the sleepers, at most they curve around them so as not to disturb them. Then they go back to sleep, and it is the turn of the others.

Thus the two groups never speak to one another, they never know one another when awake.

But in secret, they cudgel their brains about the sleepers, whom they are not supposed to speak about, it is in bad taste. The groups know one another by their works, but are never present when those works are done.

Unhappy love focuses on sleepers. An afterlife, a distant world, is superfluous, one always sees it in the sleepers. The Beyond is always there, asleep. What would happen if it awoke? This core thought is the substance of their metaphysics. They encounter one another in dreams. But they live unknown in the same place.

Horses needing no fodder: they feed on their hoofbeats.

Trout hunting swallows.

The swaying of the peacocks, their screeches: screaming ballerinas.

Men are slaves there. Orders come only from women. Wars too are fought by slaves, while women sit aloft, watching and yawning.

No woman has ever killed, her sense of station is based on that. Men are slaves there because they soil one another through killing.

How can a man feel, coming home from prison, and for him, for him alone, a million people have been killed?

He survived it, but just barely. Is it more endurable to be a survivor if one has survived just barely?

Revenge? Revenge? Everything comes back by itself, very precisely; and revenge confuses it.

Bad books in their hell are served by witty devils.

Now the writers will once again have to forget what is naked.

It is important what a man still plans at the end. It shows the measure of injustice in his death.

Lenz, freezing to death on a Moscow street, sends Goethe his last dream.

The man drunk with age.

It became so dangerous that no living creature dared to show itself on the entire surface of the earth. Below, things were still very lively. The crust was as deserted as the moon's. Even little clouds of smoke were dangerous. The terror when people, deep below, bumped into one another somewhere. All mankind a nation of miners, shafts upon shafts, and precise knowledge of dangerous gases. The most powerful in the depths with their hoards of air. Towards the surface, half-asphyxiated riffraff, constantly building dams towards the top. What a Great Wall of China! The whole surface a well-cemented protection rind, always being repaired, fixed, patched up, revamped. The slaves bent. The powerful on thrones of compressed air, never standing up, never leaving their treasures for even an instant.

The "deepest," it was the most cowardly. The wall we run up against should not be thought away.

To take the unbearable weight upon oneself. Not deny anything. Not caper away.

Not loneliness, not frailties, not the lament of the old—nothing is able to convert you. Your attitude is as quiet and inescapable as a tiger. Is this self-complaisance? Can you say yes to the tiniest piece of history? Yet it should not end.

How can things be different after this history? Can it be hidden, denied, changed? Do you have a recipe for it?

It is possible, however, that we are seeing a *false* history. Perhaps the correct one can be revealed only when death is beaten.

The efforts of individuals to ward off death gave rise to the monstrous structure of power.

Countless deaths were demanded for the survival of one individual. The resulting confusion is known as history.

The true enlightenment ought to begin here, basing the right of *every* individual on survival.

When one knows how false everything is, when one is capable of measuring the extent of falseness, then and only then is stubbornness the best thing: endless striding of the tiger along the bars of the cage so as not to miss the single tiny instant of salvation.

What one thinks daily may not always be important. But what one has not thought daily is tremendously important.

There, all people are obliged to meet again after fifty years. A great deal of effort is devoted to their finding each other again. The process of rediscovery becomes the substance of a new life. They have to seek, meet, and listen to each other. They have to compare the worst exemplars with themselves; but they bump into better ones than they themselves were and settle accounts silently. They are entitled to neither reproach nor disgust. The person one sees again must never find out what one thinks of him. The crux is insight, knowledge, and shame. The crux is the multiplicity of paths that were not one's own.

The least person has a claim to being found again and listened to.

The happiest has to face the unhappiest. The time for such confrontations is viewed as more important than any vocational or familial demands.

Even the man who has emigrated and lost his first language is required to make a serious and strenuous effort at communicating.

Very heavy penalties are applied for the use of proxies. One can apply for permission to commence the process of rediscovery even before the fifty years are up.